Online Resource Guide

for

Law Enforcement

Tim Dees

Prentice
Hall

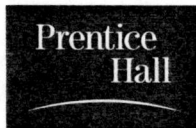

Upper Saddle River, New Jersey 07458

Library of Congress Cataloging-in-Publication Data

Dees, Timothy M.
  Online resource guide for law enforcement / Timothy M. Dees.
    p. cm.
  Includes index.
  ISBN 0-13-018685-6
  1. Law enforcement—Computer network resources.   2. Internet.   I. Title.

HV7921 .D395 2001
025.061'3632—dc21   2001021687

Publisher: Jeff Johnston
Senior Acquisitions Editor: Kim Davies
Production Editor: Jennifer Murtoff
Production Liaison: Barbara Marttine Cappuccio
Director of Production and Manufacturing: Bruce Johnson
Managing Editor: Mary Carnis
Manufacturing Manager: Cathleen Petersen
Cover Design Coordinator: Miguel Ortiz
Cover Designer: Marianne Frasco
Cover Image: Tracey L. Williams/Courtesy of the Bernards
  Township Police Department, Basking Ridge, N.J., Chief Thomas Kelly
Marketing Manager: Ramona Sherman
Editorial Assistant: Sarah Holle
Interior Design and Composition: Lithokraft II
Printing and Binding: Von Hoffmann Press, Inc.

Prentice-Hall International (UK) Limited, *London*
Prentice-Hall of Australia Pty. Limited, *Sydney*
Prentice-Hall Canada Inc., *Toronto*
Prentice-Hall Hispanoamericana, S.A., *Mexico*
Prentice-Hall of India Private Limited, *New Delhi*
Prentice-Hall of Japan, Inc., *Tokyo*
Prentice-Hall Singapore Pte. Ltd.
Editora Prentice-Hall do Brasil, Ltda., *Rio de Janeiro*

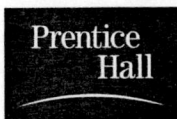

Prentice
Hall

10 9 8 7 6 5 4 3 2 1
ISBN 0-13-018685-6

This book is for Teresa,
who is the only reason that I do anything.

Contents

Preface

The Internet has become intertwined with nearly every aspect of our lives. Life online has gone from the domain of technically oriented "geeks" who hung out at Radio Shack to an integral and vital component for most every organization. Individuals and businesses have been mapping out their Internet strategies for years, but the law enforcement community is still coming up to speed on this phenomenon. The *Online Resource Guide for Law Enforcement* is intended to serve as a reference for police agencies and agents to use in developing an online presence and taking advantage of the resources available via the Internet.

There are many "how to" books for novices to the Internet, but until now none were directed specifically at the law enforcement audience. Law enforcement officers have many of the same needs and concerns as anyone else that is looking to get online. What kind of hardware do I need? How do I set up the software? Which company do I use for Internet access? All of these questions, much the same as anyone else would have, are addressed in detail here. However, this information is presented from the perspective of a former law enforcement officer who understands the special needs of the police community. Protection of one's personal privacy, the methods that one may use to access the Internet anonymously, and the ability to gather investigative and criminal intelligence information are addressed throughout the book.

Technical jargon intimidates many new Internet users, and police officers can be especially reluctant to ask for advice from individuals whom they do not know and trust. The author explains technical terms as they are introduced but also provides a glossary of terms and definitions for easy access to readers. Technical specifications of equipment and software are presented in a user-friendly style, as are some of the lesser-known online resources, such as chat rooms, Usenet newsgroups, and restricted mailing lists.

This book is intended mainly for law enforcement officers and those of a similar mindset who have no background in computers but want to see what the online world is about. Even so, many experienced computer users may find information new to them here, whether it involves configuring an e-mail program or web browser or subscribing to a special interest newsgroup.

viii

Author's Note

One of the most discouraging aspects of writing about technology is that the information frequently becomes obsolete before the book can get to press, and the situation just gets worse from there. The latest-and-greatest new gadgets are blasé in six months, web sites are abandoned or vanish altogether, and technologies that have not even been thought of as this is written will be ripe for marketing by the time that the first copy is sold. This will be a limitation as long as people are dependent on paper-based references (also known as the "dead tree" version) for information—but this also provides a market for technology writers, who create new works to replace the obsolete ones. I have no way of knowing how much of the information in this book may no longer be applicable by the time it is in your hands. Someone may find a way to stream broadband over electrical lines, and you might be able to plug into the Internet anyplace that there is a wall socket. I don't think that this is going to happen anytime soon, but then I never thought that I would pay $1.50 for a bottle of drinking water in my hometown, either. Some things you just don't see coming.

So, if in reading this you see something that you discover is no longer true, I'm sorry, but it was inevitable. We'll try to make it right in the next book, and I'll be making the same apology then.

The book has also been written with the PC user (as opposed to those who use Macintosh, or Mac, computers) in mind. Many, if not most, of the techniques described in these pages are not applicable to Mac computers. PCs are far more common in the business and law enforcement environments, and to address the same techniques for Macs would mean almost doubling the size of the book to accommodate a very small audience.

About the Author

Tim Dees is a former law enforcement officer with fifteen years experience. He followed that career by teaching criminal justice for six years at four different colleges across the United States. He now consults to law enforcement organizations on how to make better use of technology in their operations and writes columns and feature articles on police technology issues for *Law and Order Magazine*. Dees earned a master's degree in criminal justice from The University of Alabama and also holds the Certified Protection Professional credential from the American Society for Industrial Security. He is an active member of the American Society for Law Enforcement Training (ASLET). He resides in Kennewick, Washington with his wife, Teresa, and Qantas, the world's best dog.

THE INTERNET

No one saw the **Internet** coming, not even its creators, but it has revolutionized communications to a greater degree than any other development in technology, except for possibly the printing press and the telephone. The telephone provided a means of instant communication that allowed the speaker to include emotional content, add multiple voices, and supplement the communication with extraneous sounds, all increasing the impact of basic message. There are few of us who cannot remember a time when just about anyone could not be reached by dialing a telephone, but this was truly amazing technology when it was first introduced. It was also expensive. In 1927 a five-minute transatlantic telephone call by two-way radio (there were no undersea cables yet) cost $75.00[1]—which is $734.48 in year-2000 dollars.[2] Telephone rates have fallen drastically since then, and we may see the day when all worldwide telephone communications will be billed as a local call.

As people become busier and business spans many time zones, telephone calls as a primary form of communication are less than ideal. A person in

---

[1] American Telephone and Telegraph Corporation. *A Brief History of AT&T*, n.d. <http://www.att.com/history/history2.html> (June 26, 2000).

[2] American Institute of Economic Research. *Cost of Living Calculator*, n.d. <http://www.aier.org/colcalc.html> (June 26, 2000).

California must place a business call to New Jersey before 2 pm, because the two states are separated by three time zones; 2 pm in California is 5 pm in New Jersey. Acquaintances from different countries likewise must take care to avoid calling each other in the middle of the night.

For these reasons, the concept of asynchronous communication has become widely valued. A telephone call is a synchronous communication; the two parties involved communicate simultaneously. E-mail, web pages, and faxes are asynchronous; once sent, they wait to be read by the addressee or consumer at his or her convenience. This medium also allows the attachment of sound/voice files, images, or documents, giving them as much or more impact than a simple voice call. Factor in the aspect that this form of communication is available in unlimited form for less than the price of local phone access, and it is not difficult to see why the Internet has become so important.

History of the Internet

What is now known as the Internet was first developed by the Department of Defense's Advanced Research Projects Agency, or ARPA, which was comprised largely of university-based scientists who were working on various defense projects. These researchers needed a method whereby they could rapidly communicate and share data among themselves. Telephones, TWX, and similar methods were available, but they were less than ideal because of reduced security and the time zone problem discussed above. In 1969 ARPA introduced **ARPANET** (**Advanced Research Projects Agency NETwork**), which connected Stanford Research Institute, UCLA, UC Santa Barbara, and the University of Utah. By 1971 there were twenty-three university research centers connected by ARPANET, and by 1973 international links in England and Norway were established. ARPANET gradually metamorphosed into what we now know as the Internet between 1982 and 1987, when it started to become available to establishments outside of the academic and defense communities.[3]

Largely due to its defense roots, ARPANET was developed as a decentralized network. In a traditional, centralized network, such as the telephone system, all telephone lines run to a central office, on a kind of hub-and-spoke arrangement. The hub is the central switching office, and the spokes are the lines running to each user. Hubs are typically connected to other hubs. The weakness of

---

[3] Public Broadcasting System Online. *Life on the Internet: Net Timeline,* n.d. <http://www.pbs.org/internet/timeline/timeline-txt.html> (June 26, 2000).

this system is that if a hub is taken out, most of the connections to that hub stop working. In the early ARPANET days, there was no central **server** or hub. The various points on the network were connected in a web-like architecture, arranged so that the shutdown of one nexus would not affect the others. Although ARPANET was not intended to be bomb- or war-proof, it was fabricated at a time when there was a strong antimilitary sentiment in the United States, especially on college campuses. Sabotage of defense-related offices on college campuses was relatively commonplace. If one node on the ARPANET system were taken out, it would not destroy the entire network.

The modern Internet is still a distributed system, but it tends to be more of a hub-and-spoke arrangement on the local level because of the use of telephone and other local communications lines. A troublemaker could destroy the servers at an **Internet Service Provider** (**ISP**) and cut off Internet access to the community served by that node, but the system would find alternate paths to other servers downstream of the outage, and service would continue for users not served directly by that ISP.

In the early 1980s, corporate organizations, especially those with defense contracts, and universities continued to join the Internet, which was still called ARPANET at that point, because of the easy access it provided to electronic messaging, which was fairly primitive by today's standards. This was largely because universities and corporations were the most likely places to find people with regular access to computers. The only private individuals with computers were hobbyists with electronics backgrounds who built their machines from kits. The capacity of these machines was less than what is in a $10 digital watch today, but they were *computers*, something that had previously been available only to large corporations. Their "displays" were a couple of rows of lights on the front panel, and programming was accomplished by flipping switches on and off to indicate the ones and zeros that make up **binary** code.

The first home computer capable of any Internet-type communication was the Apple, and a few years later, in 1981, the IBM PC. There still was not any easy way for them to connect to the Internet, though, because these connections were still based at corporations and universities. A few people, usually employees of these organizations, could dial in to their employers from their home computers and read their electronic mail interactively while connected to the few dial-up lines that were available. Most online activities were relegated to electronic bulletin board services and commercial online services, which became increasingly difficult to distinguish as the industry developed.

Electronic **Bulletin Board Services**, or **BBS**es, flourished rapidly, mainly because anyone with a computer and a phone line available to dedicate could set one up. A BBS was a service where users could post messages and files for other users. Most BBSes had a theme or function; there were BBSes for political parties, stamp collectors, and ham radio operators, as well as for pedophiles, hatemongers, and anarchists. Users could communicate and conspire with other users of that BBS, although communication among BBSes was extremely limited. There was a network of BBSes called FIDONet, which enabled messages posted on one FIDONet-member BBS to be passed on to others, but the system was not terribly reliable or consistent. Most BBSes gradually fell into obsolescence, although a few persisted and eventually moved onto the **World Wide Web (WWW)**. The WELL, a BBS started by Stewart Brand and Larry Brilliant, eventually became its own online service, now located at http://www.thewell.com. *WELL* stands for Whole Earth 'Lectronic Link,[4] an homage to Stewart Brand's magnum opus, *The Whole Earth Catalog*, a very popular book in the sixties and seventies.

Some BBS operators charged a subscription for their services, but some did it for their own personal amusement. Running a BBS afforded an individual a lot of controlling power; the system operator, or **sysop**, could grant or deny access to users, look into any of their files or communications, and generally be king of an online world. The smallest BBSes had only a single phone line for access, and in many cases, the sysops, some of whom were barely teenagers, shared the line with conventional users in the household. The larger ones had hundreds of phone lines, some in locations many miles from the BBS itself, and thus could be reached by a local call.

At the same time, some universities and local governments were setting up freenets, which were not unlike BBS servers, but generally larger and with more access lines. Freenet users usually had to have some connection with the host provider to get a subscription, but the connection did not have to be a particularly strong one. Being an alumnus, living in the community, or even having a library card was usually enough to get a user account and communicate with the others on that freenet.

The other venue for early online activities were the commercial online services, such as The Source, GEnie, CompuServe, Prodigy, and an upstart that no one took too seriously, called America Online. These services were generally built on the backbones of existing telephone networks already used by corporate clients for their daily operations. GEnie, for example, was an offering of General

---

[4] The WELL, LLC. *About The WELL*, n.d <http://www.thewell.com/aboutwell.html> (June 29, 2000).

Electric, which used the same network for their corporate communications. These services had the benefit of offering local telephone access numbers nationwide, all connecting to a central server where messages and files were stored. Within these online services, special interest groups, called forums or roundtables, developed for subscribers who wanted to communicate with others of similar interests. One of the earliest and most active online conferences of law enforcement officers gathered on a CompuServe forum called Safetynet, which was also shared with fire, EMS, and occupational safety professionals. This same forum is still in operation on CompuServe, now owned by America Online, although it has gone through several major changes since inception.

The online services offered several ways of communicating. The most basic method was **electronic mail** (**e-mail**), where one user would send a message to another. The message would sit in the addressee's mailbox until the recipient logged onto the service to read and respond to the message. It was also possible to attach separate files to the message, so that a user who wanted a policy on off-duty employment, for example, could get the policy in electronic form from another user who had already written one. The effect was not unlike sharing experiences and advice with colleagues at a training seminar but did not incur the expenses of travel or even a long distance phone call. Files of interest to many users could be posted in forum libraries, where they could be downloaded at any time by anyone who belonged to that forum.

Forum messages, unless they were marked as private, were seen by everyone on the forum, which led to some very prolonged discussions in some cases. When the infamous Rodney King incident hit the press, the discussion on Safetynet went on for weeks and generated thousands of messages. Computer forums are one of the last truly democratic venues left; everyone has an equal voice. It is not possible to shout down or drown out the words of someone else; all messages have the same impact. Forum sysops usually have the power to delete messages that are offensive or otherwise inappropriate for the forum, but this power is used sparingly, because if it is overused, members leave the forum, resentful of the censorship.

The problem with the online services is that they did not usually interact with one another. A subscriber to CompuServe could not send a message to someone on GEnie, because the networks were separate. An apt analogy might be the pneumatic tube system used in some retail stores. The system at Sears allows a message to be sent up to someone in accounting, but it is useless to try to communicate with an employee at J.C. Penney. The same problem existed for the commercial online services as well as for BBSes. Subscriptions usually ran around $20–$25 per month, so few users subscribed to more than one service.

This led to shakeouts among the major online services, with some being purchased by others, but it did not resolve the problem entirely.

The Internet, which was still known interchangeably at that time as ARPANET, was growing exponentially, with schools of all levels, government entities, and government contractors all signing on as hosts. The speed, reliability, and economy of this method of communication were too much to pass up. In 1990 ARPANET was decommissioned, and control passed over to the National Science Foundation, which had already assumed responsibility for the Internet **backbone**, or infrastructure, that is used to transmit the traffic on the Internet. Purely profit-driven traffic, such as that from the commercial online services, was still banned; the Internet was supposed to be an egalitarian venture, unpolluted with crass commercialism. To no one's great surprise, this restriction was lifted in 1991, and the Internet backbone was made available for commercial traffic.

In short order, the commercial online services attached themselves to this network of networks, and the user IDs of the online services were converted into Internet-friendly formats. Some of these names were still a little unwieldy, though. The author's old CompuServe ID of 73240,1237 remained just as clumsy—73240.1237@compuserve.com—and other online services did not do much better. Later on, the services developed the capability to assign **aliases** to user accounts, so that messages addressed to dees@compuserve.com would arrive in the same mailbox as the ones designated for the longer, numerical address.

This also opened the door to the registration of **domain names**, the part of an e-mail address that comes after the "@." Domain name registration was free for several years, and a few prescient entrepreneurs saw the value of registering generic domain names, like Internet.com and sex.com, as well as some more specific choices, like burgerking.com. This led to some nasty infighting over trademark infringement, most of which were settled by the payment of a settlement fee to the person who registered the name, that usually being less expensive than a prolonged legal battle. The cost of domain name registration was eventually set at $70 for two years and $35 per year thereafter to keep the use of the domain name. At the time this was written, most of the short, easily remembered domain names had already been registered,[5] and domain names are a brisk sale item on online auction sites like eBay. Most common last names

---

[5] Open Veld, Inc. *Statistics of Registered Domain Names,* n.d. <http://veld.com/domains/statistics.html> (June 29, 2000).

have been registered, although it is still often possible to get a domain name that is a combination of a relatively uncommon first and last name.

The opening of the Internet to commercialization led to the establishment of new ways to access the network. Commercial online services, like America Online, flourished, but the door also opened for the small businessman to make some money. As individuals sought to get online, they flocked to small Internet service providers, many of which were little more than operations conducted from a spare room. These were close to being an ideal home business. They conducted almost all of their business over the Internet or by mail and telephone, had little inventory to store, and did not require much in the way of power or other utilities. If the ISP was close enough to a telephone company central station to tap into a T1 line, all they had to do was buy a server for a few thousand dollars and a rack of modems, and they were on their way. There are still quite a number of small town ISPs in business, mostly in small communities that have to dial a long distance number to reach one of the major ISPs. However, these are slowly being bought by the larger companies that are looking to expand their customer database.

However, the most sweeping revolution for the Internet, and the component that piqued the interest of most, was the advent the World Wide Web. A group of researchers, including Marc Andreesen, at the National Center for Supercomputing Applications on the campus of University of Illinois at Urbana-Champaign developed a piece of software called a **browser**. Browsers allowed users on the Internet to translate a new computer code called **HyperText Markup Language** (**HTML**) into easy-to-read graphics and text and allowed for hypertext, which creates a link between two related pages. HTML was simple and straightforward enough that nonprogrammers could create their own **web pages**, and for those who did not want to bother, HTML editors capable of creating the code soon became available.

This technology had more of an impact on the ability of the individual to communicate ideas than anything since the advent of the printing press. Even in its early days, a printing press was expensive, and publication of a book or circular required an investment in paper, ink, and the printer's time. Even then, the publication had to be distributed, which cost more money, and a significant portion of the population was illiterate anyway. The Web, however, allows everyone to become a publisher. For those who do not have computers, there are **Internet cafes**, kiosks available for rent at copy centers such as Kinko's, and terminals in libraries. Sites hungry to sell advertising give away space on their servers for free, so long as the user does not mind an ad or two popping up over the page. Pages ranging from absurd to very important are equally accessible.

Consider how commonplace the Internet has become in everyday life and communications. In the middle of the 1990s, most people would have had no idea of the significance of the term *dot com* or what a line beginning with www... at the end of a movie ad referred to. Few people used electronic mail for anything other than business communications. Even fewer had their own web pages. Now, however, instant messaging, Napster, online trading, and streaming video are part of our daily lives. The Internet is not just here; it has burrowed its way into every portion of our lives, and the world will never again be the same.

WHY USE THE INTERNET?

Although the online community is a far more efficient method of communication than has previously been available, it is nothing more than an alternative method of networking. To most the idea of networking is a familiar concept; informal contacts with people of similar interests are used for mutual gain. This is the essence of the online community. It is normally necessary to attend professional meetings or make a lot of telephone calls to network with other criminal justice professionals. However, the online phenomenon this to be done continuously, at low cost, and on a scale that rivals anything previously possible.

This is possibly best illustrated by example. A small police department in the Midwest starts having difficulty with the brake system on their fleet of patrol cars. Officers are complaining of a rapid brake fade, and repairs are required frequently at a substantial cost. A lieutenant from that department posts the information in a message on CompuServe's Safetynet, which has over 1,000 subscribers with a personal or professional interest in public safety.[1] Within a day, his message generates replies from officers with similar problems in other parts of the country, from a writer who specializes in police vehicles, and from a

---

[1] CompuServe has made these forums available via the World Wide Web, even to nonsubscribers of CompuServe (although nonsubscribers do not have full privileges on the forum). The Law Enforcement Forum can be reached at <http://forums.compuserve.com/vlforums/default.asp?SRV=LawEnforcement>.

vendor of the vehicles. He learns that the police package was found to be inadequate in many instances and that the manufacturer will perform repairs and upgrades at no cost—although this was not known to the local dealer who had the contract to service the department's patrol cars. The lieutenant then reports to his chief with a cost-saving solution to the vehicle problem.[2]

Another example from the real world involved a rapist in Las Vegas, Nevada, who had struck repeatedly, been arrested, and was released on bail. He fled from the court's jurisdiction, and an FBI agent in Las Vegas got word that he had surfaced in Scotland. Dennis Cobb, a former lieutenant (now a captain) with the Las Vegas Metropolitan Police Department, got this information from the FBI agent and contacted Jim McNulty, a detective with the Strathclyde Police in Scotland. Both Cobb and McNulty were regulars on the Safetynet Forum on CompuServe. McNulty was able to locate the fugitive within a few days so that an informed decision could be made about extradition. Not long afterward, McNulty and Cobb again combined forces to start a program which distributed retired but serviceable body armor to officers in the United Kingdom, where the items are both expensive and difficult to obtain. They handled the coordination of this program mainly via CompuServe, which is both economical and quick. It costs no more to send a message from the United States to Scotland than it costs to send one a few miles away, and the information arrives almost instantaneously.[3]

The lieutenant with the vehicle problem might not have had any idea where to go to solve his specific dilemma, but he knew the advantages of being online. By posting his message online, he took advantage of the universe of experience that is available from people who log on and download the most recent messages and reply to those that interest them. Sometimes the users **lurk,** or simply read the message traffic passively, and in other cases they take an active role. There are similar success stories from users who have found training providers, prewritten policies, legal assistance, career placement advice, and other kinds of advice and assistance, all for the price of a few minutes of connect time.

The reference sources available online, many of them free, can make research in almost any area of law enforcement easier, cheaper, and often more thorough. A response might be "We don't do all that much research," but most criminal justice agencies do lots of it; they just do not call it research. For example:

---

[2] Timothy M. Dees. "Online Services for Law Enforcement," *Law Enforcement Bulletin* (October 1996): 1–7.
[3] Ibid.

♦ An officer needs to find a supplier for a certain type of equipment or is trying to locate all of the businesses where a suspect in a crime might have worked. Accessing several of the telephone directories that are online can do this easily and quickly.

♦ A D.A.R.E. officer has an upcoming class and wants to know how many people in the United States smoke regularly. The web page of the U.S. Bureau of the Census provides this information in the statistical abstract of the United States.

♦ A police chief wants to apply for a grant for a special project but is not sure where to start. Web pages are full of grant referrals, including some from the U.S. Department of Justice.

♦ A new Supreme Court case could impact departmental policies. Recent Supreme Court cases are posted online as soon as they are released.

♦ The FBI *Law Enforcement Bulletin* had an article a few months ago that a lieutenant wants to read, but she cannot find her copy. All FBI *LEB* articles are posted online in full text.

♦ Sometimes high-tech equipment fails to work and the tech support line is busy. Almost all of the high-tech companies maintain web pages and online technical assistance.

♦ Notices of an upcoming training program must be sent to other law enforcement officials, but a mass mailing would be expensive. A mass e-mail mailing costs almost nothing, and it arrives almost immediately. E-mail addresses can be collected from listservs such as POLICE-L, from various agencies' home pages, and from other bulletin boards, forums, and mailing lists.

The online community also provides text files of every description, from humor to essays. These are posted by anyone with the rights to the material (and unfortunately, by some people that do not have those rights) who feel that someone else might be interested in seeing it. Anyone looking for this information can download any of these files into their computers and either read them on the screen or print them out as needed. In some cases, these files are imported in whole or part to word processing documents under construction in the user's machine. The online network is full of software and other computer-related products. Some of these are free and some of these are a try-before-you-buy product called **shareware**. In either case, there is often a very specific solution to the problem is as close as a telephone and modem.

The Internet is also an excellent method for extending the outreach of an agency to the citizens that it serves. Over half of U.S. households now have some kind of Internet access, and that number is increasing. Citizens are turning to the Internet for information in the way that they used to look to telephone directories, the public library, and the newspaper. Many law enforcement agencies have created web sites to make citizens aware of the services that they offer. Crime prevention information can be posted on a department's web site, along with instructions on how to report a crime or a complaint against a member of the department. The medium is essentially no-cost, so every member of the agency can have a web page to highlight his or her backgrounds, accomplishments, and interests, putting a better face on the police department. Citizens with an interest in seeing the latest goings-on with the agency can view reports of crimes or the department's activity logs. Some agencies have even piped a relay of their radio traffic onto the web, so that scanner buffs can listen in from all around the world.

Electronic mail is a great way to do long-distance networking, but it can also be used effectively for internal communications. It is often much more inexpensive to disseminate a new policy or other document by electronic means, instead of by the old-fashioned method of printing enough copies for every affected employee, most of which will wind up in wastebaskets. When a document is received electronically, it can be printed or just saved to storage, depending on the individual's preference.

For those in the job market, there are several web sites that are nothing but listings of jobs available in law enforcement, and most agencies with an online presence list their recruiting opportunities online at their web sites. There are also many online job listing boards, which offer employment outside the public sector. Most of these operate at no cost to the job hunter, and one can browse openings, post a resume for potential employers to see, and get job search and interviewing tips online.

The web is also helpful when looking for a particular item. Many merchants sell their wares online, and often at a substantial discount, since they do not have to go to the expense of maintaining a brick-and-mortar retail presence. There are also several online auction sites where both retailers and private parties offer unused items for sale.

There are any number of opportunities to enrich oneself personally or professionally online and ample opportunities for fun as well. We will look at some of the available options and how to use them to our advantage in the following chapters.

HARDWARE

If the only reason for buying a computer is to go online, then the most powerful or the latest model will not be necessary. The only requirement is that the machine be able to run the **operating system** that will be used. Frequently, a computer that has been discarded or set aside in favor of a newer model is still capable of performing basic communication functions, although it may not perform them as fast or as efficiently as a newer model.

Computers evolve very quickly, so a machine that is more than three years old is nearing obsolescence. One that is five or more years old and is still using the same software and hardware that came with it may not be able to handle present-day tasks. This is only a guideline, and there will always be exceptions, but it should help determine whether or not a legacy machine can be used to get online.

When intending to purchase a new computer, there are some big and potentially expensive decisions to make. It would do no good to include in this book specifications for what computer to purchase; they would be outdated before the book went to press. One of the best ways to determine what constitutes the top of the line in available computers is to purchase a copy of a major computer magazine and look at the advertisements there. Some good magazines include *PC Magazine*, *PC World*, and *Computer Shopper*. Any of these will have a number of advertisements for computers from major manufacturers such as Gateway, Dell, and Micron. A sample ad is found in Figure 3–1. It is important to pay careful

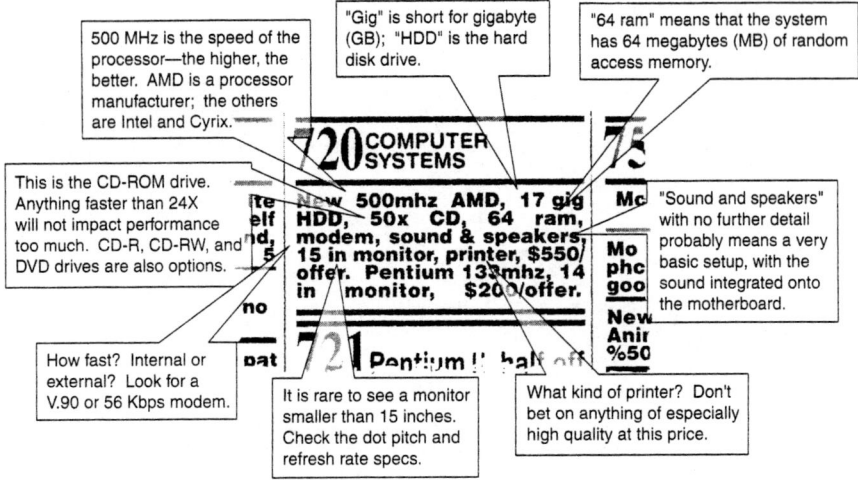

Figure 3-1   How to Read a Computer Ad

attention to the specifications of the high and low ends of their product lines. These high- and low-end models represent the benchmarks of what should be considered for purchase. Getting something below the low end of the spectrum may mean that it will not run software presently available or that it will become obsolete too quickly. Looking above the high end of the product line, if there is anything superior to these models, usually means that a premium price will be charged for computing power that only very sophisticated users are likely to need.

Popular computer games often determine the upper end of the personal computing market. Games require a considerable amount of computing power, especially with regard to graphics and sound. A newly released game might not run at all on a computer more than a year old. A computer intended for gaming should be on the on the high end. However, for surfing the web, sending and receiving e-mail, and performing basic office tasks, just about any new machine will do, although some are better than others.

Processors

The heart of any computer is its **Central Processing Unit**, or **CPU**. The large case that holds all of the computer's circuitry is also called the CPU sometimes, so it is important to understand the context in which this term is being used. At any given time, one class of CPU generally dominates the personal computer market. This means that most new machines offered for sale will have that processor or some variant of it. As this is being written, the ideal processor is the

Pentium 4, which is made by the Intel Corporation. Intel used to be virtually alone in the processor market, but there have been some competitors in recent years, namely AMD and Cyrix. Within a few weeks or months of one company releasing a new chip on the market, the others respond with something comparable, if not faster.

Each class of processor has associated with it a data width, the number of bits that it can handle at one time. Modern processors are capable of handling either 16 or 32 **bits**, so they are sometimes called 16-bit or 32-bit processors. The path over which the data travels is called a bus, and the capacity of the bus also determines processor speed.

Within a class of processor there will be various clock speeds, usually measured in megahertz (MHz). A megahertz is one million cycles, so a 600-MHz microprocessor is capable of completing 600 million cycles every second when running at full capacity, which they almost never do. Each instruction from the software and operating system requires a specific number of cycles to complete, so to an extent this speed determines how fast the processor completes each task given to it.

As an oversimplified example, think of the bus as being a highway and the bits of data on it as cars. A 16-bit bus has sixteen lanes, so that sixteen bits can move down it simultaneously. A 32-bit bus has thirty-two lanes, so it can move twice as many cars, provided they are all traveling at the same speed, which is the clock speed. A 16-bit processor running at 100 MHz can only process half as much data as a 32-bit processor running at 100 MHz.

In most cases, there is only one choice of bus capacities, since this standard changes much more slowly in the market than clock speeds. Bus capacities are normally measured in increments of eight, and there are some 64-bit processors running in some high-end graphics computers; there will almost certainly be desktop computers running 64-bit processors within a year or two. However, clock speeds are the standards that change far more rapidly and are what cause computers to become dated so quickly. At the time of this writing, the fastest microprocessor available to the average consumer is a 1500 MHz Intel Pentium 4 chip; however, at the moment it is quite expensive. Within eighteen months, the 1500 MHz chip will probably be heavily discounted in favor of whatever hot chip will be on sale at that time.

AMD and Cyrix, the competitors of Intel, make quality products, but they do not have the advantage of Intel's primacy in the marketplace. Even though an AMD or Cyrix chip might actually run faster than its Intel counterpart, software that is optimized for the Intel chip may not contain the code to recognize the full capacity of the AMD or Cyrix chip and may "see" a slower chip. This could keep some software from running at peak efficiency. However, Cyrix and AMD chips generally cost significantly less than Intel chips of similar capacity. It is important that software for a computer with a chip made by a company other than Intel will operate under the AMD or Cyrix chip.

Memory

Another consideration in purchasing a computer is the amount of memory that is installed in the machine. It is important not to confuse memory with hard disk capacity. **Random Access Memory**, or **RAM**, is the workspace of the computer and is usually measured in megabytes (MB). When a program is loaded from a disk drive, some or all of it is stored in RAM. This gives the processor immediate access to it so that the instructions contained in its code can be processed. When the capacity of the RAM is exceeded or a new program needs to be run, the information contained in RAM is either written to the hard disk for later use or deleted entirely. For this reason, RAM is considered **volatile** memory. If this information has not been recorded in a more durable, **nonvolatile** medium, the information is lost.

The volatile nature of RAM explains how people lose files while working on computers. A letter that has not been saved to the hard drive or floppy disk will be lost if the power goes off. If the letter has been saved, however, the portion completed at the last save will be retrievable even after a power failure. Many word processors and other programs have autosave features that can be set to save work automatically at predetermined intervals, such as ten minutes. If this feature is activated and there is a power failure or a system crash, the part of the work completed at the time of the last autosave will be available.

Not too long ago, RAM was very expensive, costing around $50 per megabyte, but costs have fallen dramatically. Now most computers come equipped with at least 32 MB of RAM, and 128 MB is not unusual. Depending on the intended use, speed, and manufacturer, RAM can now be purchased for $1 or less per MB.

When shopping for computers, note the high and low RAM numbers on various models, and shoot for somewhere in the middle. Too little RAM will make a computer lethargic, and too much is a waste of money; large amounts of RAM generally will not cause a great difference in performance. Also, RAM can be purchased and added later if the machine has any empty RAM slots. These chips are called SIMMs or DIMMs (Single or Dual Inline Memory Modules). If there are no empty slots, the chips installed will have to be discarded to make room for higher capacity chips in order to add more RAM.

Disk Space

A good computer can never have too much hard drive space. Like RAM, the typical hard drive capacity of personal computers has increased markedly in recent years. The seemingly hard-to-fill 40 megabyte hard drive was eventually replaced by a 10 gigabyte (GB) hard drive (1024 MB = 1 GB). That is far too little space by today's standards.

Part of this need for storage capacity has come with the greater use of multimedia on personal computers. A single complex graphics file can consume several MB of hard disk space, as can music in formats such as MP3. Software for basic tasks takes up far more room than before; there are many new features that require complex, space-filling code. Early word processors shipped on a single floppy disk with a capacity of 640 KB. Microsoft Office 2000 Premium requires four CD-ROMs, each holding 650 MB of data, much of which is stored in a compressed format.

The most common type of disk storage is the Hard Disk Drive, (HD or HDD). Hard drives were also called *Winchester drives* at one time, mainly because most of the companies that manufactured them were headquartered on Winchester Drive in San Jose, CA. A hard drive is composed of one or more platters of spinning metal disks, which typically rotate somewhere between 5600 and 10,000 RPM, enclosed in a hermetically sealed container. When the hard drive contains more than one platter, they are stacked one on top of another, like records on an automatic turntable but with an air gap between each platter. Each platter has a read/write head, a sensor that floats just above the platter and moves in and out from the edge to the center of the platter as it reads or writes data to the disk. These disks are magnetically sensitive, and data is recorded on them by changing the polarity of the tiny magnetic particles on the disk, in the same way that sound is recorded on a cassette tape. In fact, a magnet with enough power can wipe a hard disk in the same way that a tape recording can be erased, although this does not happen very often.

The price of hard disk drives is determined by three factors: capacity, spindle speed, and interface. Capacity is pretty easy to gauge—the more GB, the greater the capacity of the drive. Few computers, usually laptops, are shipped with less than 4 GB of hard disk space, and 40 GB drives are fairly common. At this writing, the largest drives available hold around 75 GB. Spindle speed is the number of revolutions the drive turns each minute. Most turn at 5600 RPM, some faster ones move at 7200 RPM, and some very fast SCSI drives speed along at 10,000 RPM. The faster the spindle speed, the faster that data can be written and read from the drive. Unless the computer will be used for some task that requires very fast read and write capacity, such as nonlinear video editing, the 5600 RPM drives will work just fine.

Interface is another issue because there are so many interface protocols. The most common drive interfaces installed in personal computers are **Integrated Drive Electronics (IDE), and AtTAchment interface (ATA)**, which are often used interchangeably, and **Small Computer Systems Interface (SCSI**, pronounced "skuzzy").

ATA and IDE connect directly to the **motherboard** of the computer. They are, by far, the most common hard drives, and if there is no other drive interface specified, it is either an ATA or IDE drive. These are also fine for most computing tasks.

SCSI is used for computer peripheral devices that need a very high rate of data transfer—up to 80 MB per second. In most cases, a SCSI device will require a separate SCSI interface circuit board installed in the computer and adds significantly to the cost of installing the device. SCSI devices can be daisy-chained to one another, so that the circuit can run from the SCSI board to a hard drive, which in turn runs to a scanner, which might then run to some other device. Once set up, SCSI devices are very efficient, but they can be difficult to configure. IDE/ATA hard drives are recommended, unless a given application really needs SCSI.

Large hard drives can be partitioned into two or more virtual drives, each with its own drive letter. The drive letter is the computer's designation for the drive. Most computers have drives A and B reserved for the floppy drives installed on the machine (although most computers now only have one floppy drive), C for the hard drive, and D for the CD-ROM drive installed on most machines. Other drive letters can be assigned to other devices or to virtual drives. A virtual drive is a section of a hard drive that is set apart from the others so that the computer "sees" more than one drive, even though there is only one physical device. A 15 GB hard drive might be partitioned into three drives of 5 GB each, designated C, E, and F.

The main reason for this strategy is that some operating systems are not capable of addressing very large hard drives. If a computer is incapable of recognizing a hard drive partition larger than, say, 5 GB, then a drive larger than that can be partitioned into smaller drives that it can handle. Also, some users like to keep their programs on one drive partition and their data on another. When they back up their hard drive to preserve the data from loss, they need only to back up the data portion. If the partition containing the programs is lost, the programs can always be reinstalled. For the most part, setting up drive partitions is a matter of how the hard disk is managed. Some people prefer a partitioned hard drive; others keep everything in small individual files and folders. The choice is up to the user.

Up until the mid-1990s, floppy drives and hard disk drives were the only choices for storing data, but there are now several other available options. CD-ROM (Compact Disk Read-Only Memory) drives, which were at one time very expensive, have now become commonplace and are priced very reasonably. Virtually every new computer comes with a CD-ROM drive, and most new software is distributed on CD-ROMs. CD-ROM drives also play music Compact Disks (CDs), and except for the label, a music CD looks just like a data CD-ROM. Some disks contain both data and music. A standard CD-ROM drive, as the spelled-out name implies, is a read-only device; a computer cannot record on a CD-ROM. A file can be copied from the CD-ROM to the hard drive, which is how most software is installed on a computer, but files cannot be saved back to the CD-ROM.

Most computers will have a hard drive, a floppy drive, and a CD-ROM installed as standard equipment. Listed below are types of storage devices other than hard or CD-ROM drives that may be available as options or extras.

Device	Description
floppy drive	This is the oldest and most common storage medium on personal computers. The early floppy disks were either 8 inches or 5.25 inches across and were flexible, hence the name *floppy*. These have been replaced by 3.5-inch floppies, which have a rigid plastic shell and are not "floppy" anymore. The data capacity of a 3.5-inch floppy is either 720 or 1440 KB, the latter being far more common, and they are very inexpensive, costing less than $0.25 each when bought in bulk. They can be rewritten as many times as necessary until they wear out, and they are easily erased, accidentally or on purpose, with any magnet. Nearly every computer comes with at least one installed floppy drive.
CD-R	This stands for Compact Disk-Recordable. Blank CD-ROM media can be purchased for less than $1 each, and data or music can be written on them. Once data or music is written to the CD-R, it is permanent. There is no way to destroy it, short of destroying the CD-R. CD-Rs are a good and fairly inexpensive way to archive data for safekeeping. CD-R drives can also be used like any other CD-ROM drive.

Device	Description (continued)
CD-RW	This stand for Compact Disk ReWriteable. These are just like CD-R drives and can be used in the same way, except that by using a slightly different and more expensive type of blank media, the created CD-ROMs can be erased and rerecorded. In order to rerecord onto a CD-RW, all of the data on the CD-RW must be deleted. These are not as versatile as some other storage devices, because CD-RW disks cannot be read in non-CD-RW drives. CD-RW drives can also be used like any other CD-ROM drive.
DVD	Depending on whom you ask, this stands for Digital Video Disk or Digital Versatile Disk. DVDs are best known as a medium for distribution of movies, and computers with installed DVD drives usually come with the software necessary for viewing DVD movies. A few software titles are available on DVD, taking advantage of their much higher capacity (4.7 to 17 GB). DVD drives can also read CD-ROM and CD-R disks.
Zip drive	**Zip disks** look like fat floppy disks and hold either 100 or 250 MB each, depending on the model. 250 MB Zip drives will read the lower capacity disks, but the 100 MB Zip drives will not read 250 MB disks. The disks cost about $10 each, and they can be rewritten like floppy disks.
LS-120	Also called the SuperDisk, these drives use special disks that look just like 3.5-inch floppy disks but will hold up to 120 MB per disk and can be rewritten like floppy disks. The same drive will read and write to regular floppy disks. This technology is more versatile than that in the Zip disk, but Zip drives are more common, having gained earlier and greater acceptance.
tape drive	Tape drives use cassettes, similar in appearance to audio cassettes. Most drives use a type of cassette unique to that line of drives. Tape drives are most commonly used to make backup copies of data to forestall against a catastrophic loss. In order to restore the data after a loss, the information has to be copied from the tape cassette back to the hard drive. Cassettes can be reused hundreds of times before they wear out and need to be replaced. The cassettes are relatively expensive, at $10–$50 each, depending on the model. They are also fairly slow, requiring 1–2 hours to copy the contents of a drive, depending on the amount of data to be copied.

Monitors

When examining a wonderful deal on a desktop PC, look carefully for fine print that says either "after rebate" or "monitor not included." The rebate issue will be addressed in the chapter on Internet service providers. The "monitor not included" issue is a kind of loss leader, which is a product offered at a loss to bring customers into the store and encourage other purchases. Loss leaders, however, may work favorably for the customer. Monitors are fairly expensive and may be the most costly single component with a PC. They may look like television sets, but they are quite different. A computer monitor is capable of displaying much higher resolution and detail than a television set of similar size. Monitors are intended to be used at fairly close distance, whereas televisions are usually viewed from across a room, and small distortion problems are not as apparent. They are similar only in that both use a cathode ray tube in their basic design.

For many years, monochrome monitors were standard equipment on PCs, and it was rare to see one with a display larger than 14 inches from corner to corner. Now monitors are almost always color models and range in size from 14 inches to 21 inches and larger. Larger monitors are much more expensive.

With Windows-type operating systems, large monitors are valuable because the user can keep more than one application open and visible on screen at one time. This is possible with smaller monitors as well, but the detail becomes so small that it is difficult to distinguish. Monitors are categorized in terms of size, dot pitch, resolution, and refresh rate. These terms are defined as follows.

Feature	Description
screen size	Screen size is measured diagonally from corner to corner. In some cases, this entire area may not be viewable, in which case the manufacturer will include a disclaimer, something like "19 inch (18.5 inch viewable)." This is a problem only if there is a large discrepancy between the rated size and the viewable size.
dot pitch	**Dot pitch** is the size of the **dots** or **pixels** that make up the image. Smaller is better. Do not buy anything with a dot pitch of more than 0.28; it will not be a good experience. Selling monitors with big dot pitches (0.32 and greater) is a common way for merchants to offer substandard components at what appear to be bargain prices. Dot pitch is called **stripe pitch** by some manufacturers, but the two measurements mean essentially the same thing.
resolution	The number of pixels that the monitor is capable of displaying at one time, expressed as width vs. height, e.g. 640×480. 640×480 is the basic minimum resolution. Resolutions below that are unacceptable for working with anything but simple text. Resolution increments after that are 800×600, 1024×768, 1152×1024, 1280×1024, and 1600×1200. Only very high-end monitors will have resolutions above 1024×768. Monitor resolution is related to the capabilities of the computer's video card, which is discussed on pages 23–24.
refresh rate	This is the number of times that the image on your monitor is updated or refreshed. Cheap monitors have slow refresh rates. Refresh rates also get slower as resolution increases, since there is more information on the monitor to update. If a monitor refreshes at a rate slower than 75 Hz (75 times a second), it will seem to "flicker" like an old silent movie. This can be a very subtle but annoying characteristic.

One consideration in choosing a monitor is the space it will occupy. A large monitor consumes a lot of desktop space, and if the proposed computer area is restricted in size, the user may be uncomfortably close to the screen. Big displays are viewed from the front, but keep in mind that most of them have considerable depth to them. A 19-inch monitor can have a depth of 17.5 inches, deeper than most comparable television sets.

One option for those who have limited space is a flat panel monitor. These displays are very similar to those that usually come with laptop computers, although they tend to be slightly larger. They are also smaller in display size than a traditional cathode-ray tube monitor because the displays are difficult to manufacture, and the difficulty increases as size increases. Flat panel monitors are much thinner, usually one to two inches thick, and run cooler, since there are not a lot of electronics to heat up. However, they are also much more expensive. Flat panel monitors for desktop computers usually start at around $1000 for a 15-inch panel, and large displays are even more expensive. Some of these displays do not refresh as fast as a comparable cathode ray tube monitor, so it is recommended that anyone interested in purchasing one to play games or watch video should try one out before buying it.

Some desktop computers now being marketed have an extremely low physical profile, since all of the electronics are built into the flat panel monitor and pedestal, and the only remaining peripherals are the keyboard and mouse. These are very appealing visually and work as well as any other computer of similar capacity. However, if any of the components need to be upgraded, it may be impossible because of the proprietary design.

Sound and Video Cards

Within the box that holds all of the computer's internal components there are a number of circuit boards, often called *cards*. Many of these are modular and can be replaced or upgraded as desired to give the computer greater capabilities. Video and sound cards are almost always included in a complete desktop setup, although the quality and capacity of these cards varies tremendously.

Sound cards allow the user to hear music and other sounds included in most software packages, play music CDs, and get streaming and downloaded audio content from web sites. At one time, the only sound capability routinely included on a PC was the speaker wired to the motherboard (the one that beeps when the computer is first turned on), and that is an altogether separate system from the one that sound cards provide. Many modern sound cards come packaged with speaker sets designed to be used with that card. Some of these are very sophisticated and include subwoofers, which generate very low bass sounds and can even vibrate, and multiple speaker arrangements that can surround the user with sound. The sound card is also the place to connect a joystick or gamepad.

The basic sound card has outputs for two speakers, often coming from a single cable, and the speakers will be wired so that one accepts the cable from the sound card and is connected to the other speaker, to which it feeds the signal for the second stereo channel. The power for the speakers may come from the speakers themselves or from the sound card. If power comes from the sound card, the volume is greatly limited because the amount of power that can be sent through the sound card is minimal.

More advanced sound cards have a digital output to be connected to a set of digital speakers. Some prefer digital speakers over the analog variety, but this is up to the individual user. It is possible to spend a great deal of money on just the sound capabilities of a computer. Most of the more sophisticated sound setups are owned by gamers and those who enjoy downloading music. If the owner's interests are less esoteric, then this might be a good place to economize.

The video card is another story. No matter what the computer is used for, most time is spend looking at the display, and a low-end video card will make for a less crisp and less colorful display. The display resolutions and refresh rates that we discussed previously come to the monitor from the video card, and if the video card cannot supply the data fast enough for the monitor to display it, then it does not matter how expensive the monitor is. In addition to resolution and refresh rates, video cards also add in another factor—the number of colors that they can display. Early computer monitors were monochrome. They had, in essence, one color, versus the blackness of the display. The next generation could display 16 colors, which seemed like a lot as long as they were used only for cartoons and simple graphics. Most modern video setups will display at least 256 colors, and then the increments go to 65,536 (16^4) and 16 million colors (actually 16777216, or 8^8 colors, in multiples of eight, just like bus capacities). This might seem like more color than necessary, but a comparison of three full-color photos rendered in 256, 65536, and 16 million colors will show a marked difference. These colors are necessary to get photo-realism.

A video card tells the monitor what color and brightness to assign to each pixel. The more pixels there are and the more colors that can be assigned to each one, the more that is required of the video card. Full-screen moving video and games that show fast movement on the screen put an even greater demand on the video card, since the image has to be updated much more often. Of all of the changes that take place among computer components, the evolution of video cards is possibly the hardest one to follow. Besides everything previously mentioned, there are issues like antialiasing, the way that jagged lines are smoothed artificially, and polygon rendering, which has to do with the way that computer graphic images are constructed and composed. This technology is too advanced to be discussed in this book.

The quality of a video card is generally proportional to its price. If the computer will be used for viewing complex graphic images, playing any kind of newer game, or any other visually artistic endeavor, it is important to get the best and newest video card. Video cards typically carry their own memory chips on board, and more is better. At least 8 MB of video memory is recommended; however, 64 MB is not too much.

Cheaper computers have sound and video cards integrated with the motherboard. This is an economy measure that usually produces poorer performance. For this design, however, it is generally difficult to upgrade any of the integrated components later on, and if any of them fail, the rest of the sound and video system fails with it. Integrated video and sound on the motherboard seems like a big plus, but it is really a handicap. Stay away from computer configurations that are set up this way.

Modems

Most computers come with modems installed, because most people who use their computers to go online do so via a dial-up connection. When accessing the Internet via a DSL or **cable modem** connection (see Chapter 4 on Internet service providers), a special cable or DSL modem, usually provided by the ISP, is used instead of a conventional telephone modem. In most cases, though, a modem is needed to connect, and the computer is probably going to come with one installed anyway. Some modems are external, plugging into one of the serial ports on the back of the computer. Most modems supplied with desktop machines are internal, meaning that they are one of the circuit cards that plug in to the motherboard.

Modem stands for MOdulator-DEModulator. A modem is the interpreter between the computer, which deals in **digital** information, and the telephone line, which is optimized for **analog** data. One way to illustrate the difference between analog and digital is to consider the two most common types of clocks. Analog clocks have hands that point to numbers that indicate the time. With an analog clock, the user is never certain about the *exact* time. The hands are always in transit from one position to the next. With a digital clock, the reading at any given moment is as exact as the precision of the clock, which is determined by the number of digits displayed. Analog information is in a more or less continuous flow, whereas digital data is incremental.

Modems are rated in terms of how much data they can handle per second. The unit of measure for this data is **Kbps**, or **KiloBits Per Second**. Note that this is not kilo*bytes* (which would be abbreviated KB, instead of Kb), but kilo*bits*, which is one-eighth of a kilobyte (8 bits = 1 **byte**). Early modems handled 300 Kbps, which meant that the text that appeared on the display could be read as fast as it could be sent. The fastest modems presently available, and the fastest that are likely to be available, are rated at 56 Kbps.

As technology progresses, modems are not likely to get any faster. The reason has to do with the capacity of a telephone line to carry information. Most telephone wires are part of **Plain Old Telephone Service**, or **POTS**. Barring some revolutionary development in communications technology, no one has managed to get data pushed through a standard phone line any faster than 56,000 bits per second. In fact, it is seldom that fast.

The flow of data transmission is comparable to plumbing. Water, like data, will only travel as fast as the narrowest pipe in the system will allow it to. If a five-inch line is connected between a house and the city water supply, and the pipe that it connects to is only three inches in diameter, then the extra capacity of the five-inch line is wasted. The same logic applies to the transmission of data. The data source may be able to produce five megabytes per second, but it will only get to its destination as fast as the slowest link in the network, which is usually the telephone line, will allow it.

Telephone lines vary tremendously in quality. Areas served by older wiring may have noisy telephone service, and this will degrade data transmission as well. Newer neighborhoods may be served by fiber optic lines and have very fast and clear transmission all the way up to the box near the house—where the service switches to the plain old copper stuff.

It would seem that the newest, most modern telephone equipment would be able to transfer data at a speed greater than 56,000 bps, but this is not the case. Most authorities agree that 56,000 bps is about the capacity of POTS, and that is when everything is working right. In practice, the connection speed of 56,000 bps will not attained. There are ways to get faster Internet connections, but they require special equipment and services, which will be covered in Chapter 4 on Internet service providers.

A modem may be rated in Kbps or according to a V.*x* standard. *V* stands for "version" and the *x* is the version number. V.*x* (e.g. V.32, V.90, etc.) would for most purposes, represent the modem's fastest speed under ideal conditions. However, these V.*x* numbers are protocols that define how data is compressed and sent, among other technical issues. Protocols are conventions or agreements made between equipment manufacturers and software developers so that their products will all work together. The protocols that determine the speed of modems that are likely to be sold in today's market are as follows.

Protocol	Maximum Data Rate
V.32bis	14,400 bps
V.34	36,600 bps
V.90	56,000 bps

Thus, a modem labeled "V.90" and another labeled "56 Kbps" have the same capabilities.

It is important to get the fastest modem that is affordable, even though the connection might not be capable of feeding it data that fast. If a 56,000 bps modem connects to a service that can only handle speeds up to 36,600 bps, the modems on each end of the connection will determine the connection speed during a "handshaking" process that takes place at the start of the call. This negotiation produces the tones and whistles that have become very familiar to online service users as the sound of their dial-up call being completed.

A modem connects to the telephone line between the wall connection and the regular telephone, much like an answering machine does, and the phone will still be available for use when the modem is not. Some people choose to have a second phone line installed if they are online a lot. This line can also be used for a fax machine, or the computer can receive faxes, although it will have to be on all the time to do this.

Input Devices

Input devices allow the user to interact with the computer. The most common input devices are the mouse and keyboard. The choice of input devices is a up to the user, since different people like different setups. It is possible to spend a great deal of money on a keyboard and mouse setup or to get them almost for free.

Just about any computer comes with a mouse and keyboard, but this is an area where merchants tend to economize by buying the cheapest components possible. If the mouse and keyboard will be used for no more than a few minutes a day, then the low-end components are probably going to work just fine. Users who spend a lot of time working on their computers generally want better quality components.

Keyboards look more or less the same, but there are variations. The function keys (the ones that start out with "F," e.g. "F1," "F2") can be on the side or the top of the keyboard, or both. The numeric keypad can be to the left or right of the keyboard, or the keyboard may have special buttons to activate certain programs, functions, or to go to specific web sites on the Internet. Another less apparent quality is the feel of the keyboard. This is something that can be determined only by using it, but this does not take long. An office or computer superstore will have keyboards on display that can be tried. There is a tremendous difference in the feel of them and even in the noise that they make. A $20 keyboard may have a better feel than one going for four times that amount. Keyboards are inexpensive, so a new one can be purchased to replace one that is not satisfactory. This also applies if the user spills something into the keyboard that causes the keys to start sticking. The keys can be pried off the key tops and cleaned out, but it is usually more economical to buy a new keyboard.

If an ergonomic keyboards seems to be a good idea, try one out first. Some people, for example, find the Microsoft Natural Keyboard, which has the keys for each hand aligned for the natural angles of the hands and wrists, to be very beneficial, but others have difficulty using it. The same applies with keyboards with a cushioned wrist rest at the edge closest to the user. The usefulness of these new designs depends solely on the user. Furthermore be advised that the ergonomic designs usually cost considerably more than a standard keyboard.

Because there is some question about the plural of *mouse*, meaning the input device, and because not all of them are mouses/mice, they will be referred to as *pointing devices*. The pointing device became necessary when most of the computer world started using a **Graphics User Interface**, or **GUI** (pronounced "gooey"). Apple Computer was the first producer of a GUI for consumer use, and Microsoft began using it with their Windows operating systems. Prior to that, computers had only keyboards, and that was sufficient to communicate with the machine. The GUIs have become so pervasive that it is now possible to run some software without ever touching a keyboard.

The mouse is by far the most common type of pointing device, but there have been many designs. The standard mouse operates via a ball that protrudes slightly from its underside. As the mouse is moved across a surface that gives it traction, such as a mouse pad, wheels that are in contact with the ball measure the distance and direction that the ball travels in two dimensions. The screen cursor, or mouse pointer, moves in the same direction and velocity as the mouse. Newer mouse designs use an optical tracking device to sense movement of the ball, which eliminates the mouse pad.

A standard pointing device has two buttons. The left button, which is under the index finger of most right-handed users, is the primary button and is used to click on icons or text in order to execute a command or otherwise make something happen. When an instruction tells the user to click on something, this means to click the left mouse button. The right mouse button is used to bring up context menus, a list of alternate commands that pertain to the object under the cursor. The context menu seen in Figure 3–2 might include options to cut, copy, paste, attach to a mail message, rename, move to a different directory, or delete the item under the pointer.

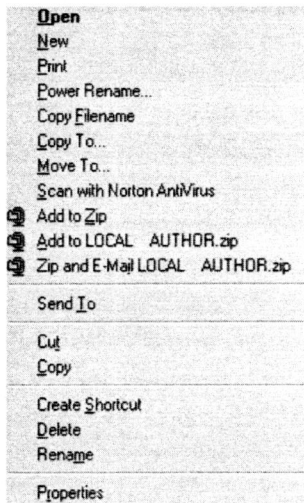

```
Open
New
Print
Power Rename...
Copy Filename
Copy To...
Move To...
Scan with Norton AntiVirus
Add to Zip
Add to LOCAL   AUTHOR.zip
Zip and E-Mail LOCAL   AUTHOR.zip

Send To                            ▶

Cut
Copy

Create Shortcut
Delete
Rename

Properties
```

Figure 3–2   A Context Menu

Left-handed users will be relieved to know that it is possible to reassign the pointing device buttons so that the right button is the primary and the left button will bring up context menus. It is also possible to find keyboards that have the numeric keypad on the left side of the keyboard (it is customarily on the right) or even a keyboard whose sections are modular and can be attached and rearranged in almost any configuration desired.[1]

There are other pointing device options to consider. A trackball is essentially an inverted mouse. The mouse ball is pointing up, and the user rotates it with a finger or thumb, using buttons positioned around the trackball to click. There

---

[1] One source for these is New England Computer Supply, 89 North Main Street, P.O. Box 1991, Andover, MA 01810, (978) 474–0088, or on the web at <http://www.ergosupply.com>.

are many designs of trackballs, and trying them out before buying is critical. Like keyboards, these are often on display in computer stores, so that customers can see which one is most comfortable. An advantage of the trackball is that it does not require the use of a mouse pad, so it takes up slightly less space on the desktop. This has a second, less apparent advantage. Over time, a mouse pad picks up oils from the user's skin and becomes slick. The mouse ball gradually loses traction, and the cursor appears sluggish, not moving when the mouse moves.

This can be remedied by cleaning or replacing the mouse pad, but the problem is one that comes up slowly and irritatingly until what is causing it finally becomes apparent. There are now trackballs that eliminate this problem. By the way, mouse pads are popular giveaway items for businesses that place their logos on the surface. It is not necessary to spend a lot of money on a mouse pad when they are available for free.

Pointing devices frequently include a wheel as an option. The wheel is a disk, about the size of three quarters, that the user can rotate with a finger or thumb, and sticks out of the pointing device somewhere. The wheel is very handy for scrolling up and down through a document or web page. The wheel can often be reprogrammed to zoom in or out on the display. Each manufacturer offers a different set of options for the wheel.

Finally, touchpads or pens can be used as pointing devices. These are most commonly found on laptops and palmtop computers, but they can be purchased for desktop machines as well. A touchpad is a smooth, flat surface, usually about nine inches square, that is touch sensitive; the user can direct the cursor by moving his or her fingers across the surface in the direction that he or she wants it to go. Clicking can be accomplished by either pushing one of the buttons mounted around the touchpad or by tapping on the touchpad with one's fingers. Pen pointing devices use the same basic technology, except that an inkless pen, or stylus, rather than the fingers, is used.

Touchpads are popular on laptop machines because they have no moving parts expect for the buttons, and they do not take up much space. A common complaint of touchpad users is that any accidental contact with the touchpad is interpreted as a command to move the mouse or insertion point and therefore interferes with typing. This is especially problematic for people with large hands. They are seldom available as standard equipment on desktop machines, but they can be ordered as replacements for the standard mouse.

All of these devices can be purchased at a wide range of prices. At large computer superstores, it is not uncommon to find pointing devices and keyboards offered for sale as *freebates*, meaning that a mail-in rebate is available that will roughly equal the purchase price, making the device essentially free. This, of course, is a loss leader, and the store is hoping to generate sales of other items. These devices will work, but they are not going to be as comfortable as a higher-quality device. For computers that are in environments where dust, dirt, and spills are an unavoidable hazard, it is probably wiser to buy cheap input devices and plan on replacing them as they get damaged; the expensive ones will not last any longer under these conditions than the cheap ones. For more pristine environments, more costly devices are recommended for their comfort and ease of use; users are likely to produce more work with high-quality equipment. The differences between the cheap and the expensive gear are subtle, but they become apparent when a user spends most of the workday with them. Determine which input devices have the best feel for the user and then invest in those. If the devices are used often, there will be no regret at having spent the money.

Printers

It is not essential to have a printer to go online, but sooner or later it will prove useful for printing pages, letters, envelopes, and address labels.

However, an investment in a printer can be avoided. Some print shops have computers or printers for rental use. Data can be saved to a floppy disk and printed out there. This is also a good option since some printer cannot provide necessary formats.

There are four principal categories of printers with a lot of variations in between.

Printer	Description
dot-matrix	Each character is made up of either nine or twenty-four dots, which are made by pins in the printing head. They are very commonly used at points-of-sale, because they are fairly inexpensive, reliable, and will print through onto a carbon copy or NCR paper form to make duplicates on a single pass. However, they are also noisy, making a sound a little like a miniature chainsaw when they print. They can produce monochrome graphic images, but these are generally not very good.
daisywheel	These printers work most like typewriters. A disk with many small arms radiating from the center is rotated until the appropriate character is under the printing head, and then the character is snapped onto the paper. Print quality is generally higher than dot matrix printers, but it is limited to the font of the daisywheel, which is replaceable. Like dot matrix printers, daisywheels print onto carbons and NCR paper. This kind of printer is expensive, noisy, and tends to need a lot of maintenance. They are no longer widely produced.

Printer	Description	(continued)
inkjet or bubblejet	These are by far the most common printers purchased for consumer use. They print by spraying ink from a cartridge onto the paper and can print in full color, if desired. Some printers can produce photographic images that rival conventionally printed photos. If the printed copy is not allowed to dry properly, or if certain papers are used, their images are subject to smearing and sometimes run if they come into contact with water. They can be somewhat slow, requiring as much as a minute per page. Time increases if complex images are on the page. They will not handle multiple part forms; if more than one copy is needed, additional pages must be printed or photocopied. They are quiet even when printing complex images. Initial purchase prices are low as compared to laser printers, but the ink cartridges that they use can be very costly, making their per-page costs higher than a laser printer.	
laser	These are the most popular choices for office environments, where printing is generally limited to business documents and simple charts and diagrams. Purchase price is about 50% more than a comparable inkjet printer, but the toner cartridges that they use last much longer, making per-page costs considerably lower. They generally print in only black and shades of gray. They are extremely quiet when operating, making only a low hum. Print speed ranges from around four to as many as sixteen pages per minute, depending on the model. They will not handle multiple-part forms.	

There are other types of printers, such as dye-sublimation machines, that will print in dazzling color, but these are very expensive, high-end devices that are beyond the scope of this book.

When printers are included in package deals with a computer, they are almost always inkjet printers. This is because these have the lowest production cost of any of the commonly available types. They are well-suited for the home user who prints an occasional letter or school report, but heavy users will find themselves running to the office supply store a lot for new ink cartridges for the printer. Inkjet printers use up to four ink cartridges (one black, and one in each of the primary colors), and these cartridges generally cost from $15–$35 each, depending on the brand and the distributor. Usually, each printer is tied to a specific cartridge manufacturer for supplies, depending on the maker of the printer.

Black is the only color necessary for business documents, and that will be the cartridge that is most commonly replaced. A typical inkjet cartridge will produce several hundred pages, compared to the life of a typical laser toner cartridge, which is typically several thousand pages and costs from $50–$80.

The other significant consumable with printers is paper. Dot matrix printers will usually take standard single-sheet paper, but they work most efficiently with continuous-form paper that has perforated tear-off strips on each side for the tractor feeds that they use. Daisywheel printers work more or less the same way. Inkjet and laser printers use single sheets only. For photo-type images, it may be necessary to buy paper with a special photo surface in order to get the best result. For almost everything else, multipurpose paper intended for photocopiers is usually fine and is available cheaply just about everywhere.

Laptops

Laptops or **notebooks** have a number of advantages, especially if the computer will be used in more than one place. Moving and setting up a desktop computer is a chore that takes a couple of hours, whereas moving a laptop is no more difficult than moving a book.

Portable computers have become as capable as their bigger desktop companions, but at one time there was a question of capability versus portability. They are sturdy, reliable, and easy to use, but there are still some considerations in choosing a laptop over a desktop machine.

The single biggest concern is price. Expect a laptop to cost at least 50% more than a desktop machine of similar specifications. This is because the fabrication of a laptop is somewhat more exacting and labor-intensive than what is required for a desktop. A typical desktop computer is a collection of components connected to a motherboard, which is in turn bolted into a case. Given the necessary tools and components, a reasonably handy person can put one together in half an hour or so, and it will actually work. This is how large made-to-order computer companies like Dell and Gateway stay in business. They typically do not manufacture anything, although they may ship components with their labels on them, made for them by a supplier. When an order is received, the builder gets the specifications and pulls the necessary components from parts bins. He or she then screws them into place, loads the necessary software onto the hard drive, and puts the whole thing into a box. Unless one of the off-the-shelf, ready-to-ship machines is specified, which are just as reliable as the ones that are custom built, one of these computers is actually assembled just for the customer.

Laptops are generally made on an assembly line, and there are not as many options to choose from. Models that have a larger hard drive or more memory are typically from a different product line, and when one is ordered it has already been built and is waiting in a box to be shipped. The components in a laptop are much more closely packed together and are frequently not interchangeable, as are most desktop components. Getting a different video card, for example, consists of purchasing a new one at the computer store, pulling out the old one, installing the new card, and running a supplied disk to get the drivers installed. Upgrading the video on a laptop will most likely entail buying a new laptop, because the video function is almost always integrated with the motherboard.

Some laptop components can be upgraded, but it is usually expensive to do so. For instance, a new 10 GB hard drive for a desktop computer can be purchased for considerably less than $200. A 10 GB hard drive for a laptop might cost $500 or more. The moral here is when buying a laptop, buy one that will not have to be upgraded frequently; replacing it is probably going to be more cost-effective than upgrading it.

One of the biggest factors in determining the price of a laptop is the size and design of the display. The best displays are **Thin-Film Transistor**, or **TFT** displays, also called **active-matrix** displays. They usually range in size from around 9 to 15 inches diagonally. These are very bright and can be read from a wide viewing angle, meaning that the display can be seen when the user is standing to one side of the computer. They are also very difficult to manufacture, and the larger they get, the more difficult they are to make. As a result, they cost a lot more than their cheaper counterparts, the **passive-matrix** or **HPA (High Performance Addressing)** displays. The difference between an active-matrix and a passive-matrix display is apparent when they are viewed side by side. An active-matrix display is bright when the viewer is standing directly in front of it and loses very little brightness and legibility as he or she moves to one side. A passive-matrix display can be read best while viewing it straight on, and the colors are not as vivid as those on an active matrix. As the viewing angle changes from center, the image falls off rapidly. Assuming displays of comparable size, a laptop with an active-matrix display can be $300–$600 more than one with a passive-matrix display.

Other considerations in choosing a laptop are weight and size. There are laptop computers that are less than one inch thick and weigh less than three pounds and still perform very well. These machines achieve this reduction in size and weight by externalizing or eliminating components such as a the floppy disk drive or CD-ROM drive and/or by reducing the size of the internal battery, which reduces the time that the laptop will operate on battery power. Users who need to access a floppy or CD-ROM drive will have to plug in an external module, which sometimes has to be purchased separately and usually is not cheap. The battery issue is only a problem if the user routinely runs the machine away from a power outlet. If the machine is to be used on a bus, plane, train, or outdoors, then battery power gets to be a consideration. Spare batteries, although costly, can be purchased, but the laptop must often be shut down to change the battery, which is a nuisance.

Batteries are commonly available in nickel-metal hydride (NiMH) and lithium-ion (LiI or LiIon) configurations. NiMH batteries are cheaper, but they are prone to developing a memory—if the battery is recharged before it is completely drained, it may deliver less running time—and they will hold less energy than a LiIon battery of similar weight. LiIon batteries do not have the memory problem, but they tend to endure fewer charge–discharge cycles before they will no longer hold a charge and need replacement.

If one component in a laptop breaks or otherwise malfunctions, it generally takes the whole machine with it. Repairs are usually more expensive because the machine must be sent to a competent repair station and more troubleshooting and repair time is required. When a component in a desktop machine fails, it is usually easiest to swap out the faulty component with a replacement and continue to work. This can be done by most users with a little coaching.

Most laptops come with touchpads for the reasons mentioned previously. A few models are available with a pointing stick, a little nub about the size of a pencil eraser that sticks up between the G, H, and B keys on the keyboard. The cursor is moved by pushing the pointing stick in the direction that the user wishes it to go, and clicking is done with two buttons mounted below the keys. However, the only major laptop manufacturers that routinely include this option are Toshiba and IBM. Most laptops will accept an external pointing device, but the touchpad will remain active, lending to problems of unintended cursor movement.

Laptops are extremely theft-prone items. They are costly, easy to transport, and highly marketable. Over 300,000 laptops are stolen each year. As a rule, treat a laptop like a firearm. Do not leave it unattended unless it is secured, lock the premises where it is stored, and know its serial numbers and other identifying characteristics. Most laptops have security ports that will accept an inexpensive cable lock that can be looped around a desk or other unwieldy object.

Finally, a good option for a user who buys a laptop but uses it at a desk much of the time is a **port replicator**, sometimes called a *dock*. This is a device that plugs into the back or side of a laptop and duplicates the ports, or plug-ins, that are otherwise available on the machine. A port replicator might have attached to it a full-size regular keyboard, a standard pointing device, a printer, a power supply, a network card or port, and some type of external drive. When the user arrives at his or her desk, he or she attaches the port replicator, and all of the external components are attached to the laptop with a single action. This saves a great deal of time, as well as wear and tear on the ports, since it avoids attaching and detaching various plugs and wires and allows the user to get the advantage of a full-size keyboard and other equipment available to the office.

Port replicators are generally machine- and even model-specific, so that a port replicator manufactured for one laptop probably will not work with another model. There are some new universal port replicators now available to attach to either a **USB** (**Universal System Bus**) port or a **PC card** slot, both of which are common features on laptops, and thus can be used on more than one model.

Chapter

4

INTERNET SERVICE PROVIDERS

Before anyone can go online, he or she will have to obtain an Internet service provider—a conduit to the Internet. There are a number of factors involved in the selection of an ISP, including, but not limited to, location, whether or not the user will need to access the Internet from a place other than "home base," the connection speed to maintain, costs, equipment, and capabilities. An ISP provides people with a way to connect to the Internet. In most cases, ISP services will also include one or more e-mail accounts and may include web site space, newsgroup server access, technical support, and access to proprietary services, such as forums and online discussions. It might appear that those service providers offering the most services at the lowest price are the smartest choice, but this is often not the case.

The best example of this principle is with the world's largest ISP, **America Online (AOL)**. AOL has gone from a tiny start-up that was not taken seriously by anyone in the computer industry to a megacorporation that has acquired other media and high-tech companies. Much of this growth was attributed to AOL's aggressive marketing program, where every household in the country was inundated with AOL installation floppy disks and CD-ROMs. Disks were included with magazines, mail-order merchandise, computer components, and in mailers direct from AOL. The literature that came with most of these disks invited their recipients to a free trial of AOL for up to 500 hours before they were charged any connect-time fees.

AOL also provided a method of connecting to its service that was almost foolproof. Running the installation program on the disk or CD-ROM automatically installed AOL's proprietary e-mail client, web browser, and directory of dial-up numbers. The user had only to fill in the blanks on the onscreen displays and enter his or her credit card number (even though the trial was free, AOL was expedient in debiting the user's credit card once the free hours or trial period had run). Then the software would connect to the AOL service and provide the user with his first e-mail message, an automatically generated welcome from Steve Case, president of AOL. Few things having to do with computers could be simpler, and part of AOL's appeal was that nontechnical users could gain access to the Internet.

The problem with AOL is that, in the process of automating so many functions, it also serves as a barrier to many of the resources of the Internet. For instance, AOL's e-mail software is the only one that will work with AOL mail. A user who wants to use Outlook Express, Eudora, Pegasus, or another e-mail client will have to obtain a second, nonAOL e-mail account to do so, and even then may have to connect to that account with a nonAOL ISP. AOL users may also have difficulty using any web browser than the one that comes preconfigured with AOL. AOL installation programs are also infamous for changing the settings on a computer with an existing Internet connection so that the original connection will no longer function without some tinkering.

AOL is an excellent choice for users who want the basic tools for connecting to the Internet, but who do not want to deal with the details of configuring their connection and are willing to accept some limits on what they can easily access. For the masses, this works out fine, and AOL's wide acceptance and customer base is a testimony to how easy it is to use. However, be forewarned that many of the methods and resources covered in this book are not available on AOL, since AOL has its own idiosyncrasies that preclude the use of some services on the Internet.

ISP and Content Providers

Some of the more well known ISP content providers include CompuServe, the **Microsoft Network** (**MSN**), and, of course, AOL. CompuServe, AOL, and MSN offer their own content which is either unavailable to those who do not subscribe to their services or is available to nonsubscribers only on a limited-access basis (e.g. those not subscribing to a service that provides a particular type of content may be able to view the content but not participate with subscribers).

As an example, AOL, MSN, and CompuServe all have forums or message boards for users interested in law enforcement and public safety. These forums have their own message boards where members can post messages containing questions or topics for discussion. Other members can read and respond to these messages. MSN calls these forums *communities* and allows participants to create their own specialized community for nearly any reason. A search for the keywords law enforcement on MSN communities showed 217 different forums that had something to do with policing. CompuServe has Safetynet for members involved in all fields of public safety work, and there is a section on the United Kingdom forum for British police officers.

Why does MSN have 217 police-related forums, and CompuServe only two? This is because CompuServe regulates the forums that are allowed there. CompuServe subscribers who wish to start a forum must apply to CompuServe to do so and demonstrate that there is enough interest in the subject area to keep the forum alive. Forums that have low message traffic are eventually discontinued. On MSN anyone can start a forum, and it is evident that lots of people have done exactly that. However, a large number of forums with similar topics dilutes the usefulness of a forum. For example, say that a police officer/Internet user had noticed that a particular lot of factory ammunition appeared to produce a number of misfires. By posting a message on a law enforcement forum, where it was likely to be seen by other users of that ammunition, the problem could be more readily identified. If the user chose to post his message on the Safetynet Forum, then it stands to reason that all of the CompuServe subscribers with an interest in law enforcement who subscribed to and monitored Safetynet would see the posting and be able to respond if they had a similar or different experience. However, the same message would have to be posted on as many as 217 different forums on MSN in order to ensure that all law enforcement MSN members saw it.

Forums and communities, which are essentially synonymous, provide functions other than message boards. Each forum may have one or more chat rooms functioning at any given time, where members can converse with other members in real time. In a chat room, a member types text into a message window, and when the Send key is pressed or clicked, the text is posted in the chat window for all to see and respond to. Chat room sessions can be saved and posted for later reading, but this method of communication is essentially synchronous, as members need to be logged onto the forum at the time of the chat to participate. Message boards are asynchronous; messages can be viewed and responded to at any time and in any order. Some forums and communities schedule chats on specific topics, or a member can log into a chat room and just see if anyone else is there who wishes to converse.

Some forums also maintain file libraries that can be downloaded by members. A file library may contain transcripts of chat sessions, graphic images, photos of forum members, text files, software, and anything else of common interest to forum members. File libraries are good vehicles for sharing material that is too voluminous to post on a message board or that may not be of interest to everyone there. When a file is added to the file library, an announcement is usually made on the forum's welcoming screen or on the message board, alerting members that a new file is available. Members can also search the file libraries for keywords or browse the listings for files that they may wish to download.

Content provider ISPs like their members to use the forums, especially if they are charging the member for the time that they spend connected to the service. Some, if not most, ISPs have an unlimited connect-time rate, but they may also offer a monthly allocation of hours for a reduced fee. For instance, CompuServe has one pricing plan that provides twenty hours of connect time for $9.95 per month, or an unlimited number of hours for $19.95. They also contract with various online businesses to offer that business' services to their customers, even though one can usually patronize the business if he or she is not a subscriber to that content provider ISP.

As an example, say that a CompuServe subscriber is looking for a new car and resorts to the Internet to make use of one of the numerous pricing and buying services offered for car buyers. She can do a search for something like auto-buying services and get one set of web sites or go directly to a site that she has seen advertised on television or in a magazine. However, the CompuServe browser will open to a page that is filled with links, one of which will lead directly or indirectly to a car-buying service of some type. The car-buying service has paid dearly for that preferential routing, and the content provider ISP is going to do its best to see that the user find that one first.

Subscribers to the content provider ISPs can also obtain service through a bring-your-own-access plan. With this strategy, the user accesses the content provider via another ISP account (e.g. any method of connecting to the Internet) and gets the benefit of the content without having to use the content provider's dial-up network. This is a good option for users who do not have home Internet access, a local dial-up number point of presence, or access to the Internet by means of a dial-up connection.

Some content provider ISPs have attempted to increase their customer base by providing substantial rebates on computers and other electronics in exchange for one- to three-year service contracts.

A typical deal might be that the consumer gets a $1500 computer for $900 or so, and then is obligated to subscribe to CompuServe, AOL, or MSN at $19.95 per month for three years. The customer actually pays $1618.20 ($900 + $718.20, the cost of the $19.95 monthly service fee for 36 months) for that $1500 computer and is obligated to use an ISP that may not be ideal. Sometimes the ISP does not have a point of presence that is a toll-free call from where the customer lives, and it is always wise to consider the possibility of moving in the future. Evaluate these rebate programs carefully.

Nationwide ISPs

Nationwide ISPs are those that have a network of dial-up **points of presence** or **POP**s (not to be confused with **POP3**, or **Post Office Protocol version 3**, which is used to retrieve e-mail) that span a region, the entire country, or even the world. Nationwide ISPs are an especially good choice for access if the user travels and needs to be able to access the Internet from a location other than home base. However, they may also be a good choice for someone who never travels but does have a point of presence that is a local call from wherever he or she accesses the Internet. These differ from the content-provider ISPs discussed previously, in that the service they provide is more generic. They provide Internet access, usually some software, an installation program, and sometimes web space for a web site, but the content is whatever is found on the Internet.

The specific location of a point of presence is critical, since local calling areas for many phone subscribers have become so complex. The advent of overlay area codes, where multiple phone lines at the same address may have different area codes, and competing telephone service providers has made it fairly difficult to assess which calls are considered local and which will incur toll charges. Before choosing an ISP, either call the customer service number or look at the web site to see what local access numbers/points of presence are nearby, and then check with the phone company to see if those numbers are local calls. Often, the ISP will be able to determine if the call is local by running the user's phone number through its database, but check with the phone company to make sure anyway. The ISP and phone company databases are not always in sync.

To access the Internet from a location other than home base, such as a vacation home or a branch office, verify that the ISP has a point of presence that is going to be a local call from there as well. For the occasional time when there is no local point of presence, most nationwide ISPs have 800 numbers that can be accessed without incurring toll charges. However, the ISP will usually surcharge the connect time on these calls. A typical surcharge is $.10 per minute, or $6.00 per hour. This is not an exorbitant amount of money to pay for occasional access, but it adds up if there is a regular need to connect through the 800 service.

The largest ISPs also have international numbers that can be dialed from foreign countries. However, be aware that some foreign countries surcharge data calls and have measures in place to ensure that telephone users do not place data calls over voice lines without paying the surcharge. Further, many countries have such poor telephone service that any data call will connect at a very low data flow rate, even though the ISP may provide high-speed access modems. Further complications include having the hardware necessary to connect to foreign telephones, which often use connectors very different from the **RJ-11** standard phone jacks used in most of the United States and Canada. Vendors that specialize in hardware for "road warriors" who need to connect while traveling can supply converter kits for most phone systems, but still expect that every foreign trip with a computer will be something of an adventure.

Leased-Line Service

Large bandwidth users, such as corporations and universities, often lease direct connections to the Internet backbone, called **T1** or **T3** (there are no T2 lines). T1 and T3 lines are always-on, dedicated direct connections to the Internet and are usually supplied by the local telephone service provider. T1 and T3 users will usually have a central server for their operations with data cables running on an internal network to the workstations of the various users.

When a user plugs his or her machine into a T1/T3 connection, the computer does not need to dial up into a telephone network. In fact, the computer using a T1/T3 connection does not need a modem. It does need a **Network Interface Card** (**NIC**, pronounced *nick*), which connects the computer to the network. The network connection is usually via an **RJ-45** plug and jack, which looks like the RJ-11 plug-and-jack combination that most household telephones use but is slightly larger; it carries eight wires to the RJ-11's six.

With a desktop PC, the NIC is usually an internal circuit board that is plugged into one of the machine's open slots. It can be identified by the RJ-45 jack that will be visible among the computer's other connectors. Because RJ-45 and RJ-11 jacks look so similar, they are often confused, and computer modems also have RJ-11 jacks, making the identification task even more difficult. However, the task is simplified by looking at the arrangement of the jacks. A modem will have two RJ-11 jacks side by side, usually (though not always) labeled "phone" and "line." A NIC will have only a single RJ-45 jack, as it needs no pass-through connection to allow use of the telephone on the same line as the modem.

T1/T3 connections are very fast; downloads that require hours via a dial-up connection are reduced to minutes over a leased line. The cost of these, however, makes them impractical for individual users. A T1 line costs from several hundred to several thousand dollars a month to lease, while a T3 can run into four and even five figures per month. They make sense for businesses that have many Internet users with high bandwidth needs, and this is the primary market for T1/T3 providers. Access to a leased line connection is almost always through a school or employer. This does not mean that other services, such as AOL or CompuServe, cannot be accessed through the leased line, but doing so will cause traffic to be routed through the company or school network, which means that it can be monitored. Many employers and schools continually or randomly monitor users' Internet activity for inappropriateness, and sanctions can be severe, ranging from loss of online privileges to termination and even criminal prosecution. Use of a leased line for personal activities is viewed by some businesses as a theft of services, and is treated the same way as someone who makes personal long distance calls on the company's bill. If the network is used to access materials that the employer or school finds to be objectionable, the penalties can be even harsher.

Leased-line service is wonderful for business or school use and it usually comes with the job or student registration. Just understand that leased-line service usually means that activities can be monitored, and use of this resource for anything but strictly authorized activities can carry a high price.

ISDN and DSL

Home and small business users are not limited to using T1/T3 lines for high-speed Internet access. For these users with intermediate bandwidth demands, ISDN and DSL service is far more economical and available.

ISDN stands for **Integrated Services Digital Network**. ISDN lines are high-quality telephone lines that are capable of carrying two data streams or conversations at the same time, each at about 64 Kbps. The two bearer (more commonly called "B") channels of an ISDN line can be combined to obtain a data transmission rate of 128 Kbps, or one can carry a voice conversation on one while the other channel maintains a data connection at 64 Kbps.

ISDN service availability is determined by the local telephone service provider and is usually limited to locations within three miles or so of the telephone central office. This is because the signal strength on an ISDN line starts to degrade after the length of the cables carrying it extends much over three miles. Length is determined by the way that the telephone lines are run and not strictly by direct distance from the central office. Thus a location only two miles from a central office might have a telephone cable run of considerably more than two miles.

ISDN service requires a **terminal adapter**, analogous to a modem, for a dial-up connection. The difference is that the data on an ISDN line does not have to be converted from analog to digital and back again, because the data on the ISDN line is already in digital form. There are ISDN telephones that combine the terminal adapter and a regular telephone, so that the ISDN line can be used to make voice and fax calls.

Not all ISPs support ISDN, although it is common for a branch of the telephone company that provides the ISDN service to offer compatible ISP service as well. This often means either changing ISPs from the one that provided dial-up service or paying for a second ISP in order to preserve the ability to dial up when traveling or during outages of the ISDN service. Accessing Internet services via an ISDN line still requires dialing up the ISP over the ISDN line, but the call goes to a node that has sufficient bandwidth to handle the increased amount of data.

Small businesses and those who work from home or otherwise need medium-high bandwidth connections can resort to ISDN, but it can still be relatively expensive. Installation of an ISDN line can cost hundreds of dollars, plus the cost of the terminal adapter, although some telephone companies will furnish the telephone adapter or waive installation fees as an incentive to potential subscribers. ISDN service is usually charged on a per-minute-of-use basis. This rate can be different depending on the time of day. For instance, there might be a charge of five cents per minute during peak business hours, but the service might drop to one cent a minute, or not be metered at all, during nonpeak hours. The rate might also change depending on whether one or both B channels are being used for data.

An alternative to ISDN for heavy bandwidth users is **DSL**, or **Digital Subscriber Line** service. DSL is becoming more popular than ISDN and has replaced it in many areas, given that the availability of service has similar restrictions. With DSL, users get an always-on connection to the Internet that is not metered for per-minute use. The same phone line that carries the data can also be used for voice or fax traffic with no loss of transmission speed.

DSL requires a dedicated wire pair from the user's location to the telephone company switching office, and the run of the wire pair cannot normally exceed 20,000 feet, which is a little more than three miles. In addition to these requirements, the wire pair must often be of the same medium along the entire run of the connection. If there is a section of fiber-optic cable or some other switch in between the user's location and the switching office, then the DSL service will often be unavailable.

The wire pair that is used for DSL will be reserved for the exclusive use of the DSL subscriber. Normal telephone service (POTS) is intended to be used only a small fraction of the time. When a POTS subscriber picks up the phone to make a call, the system senses that the device is "off hook" and searches for an available circuit. When one is located, the subscriber hears a dial tone and can make the call. Under normal conditions, this happens so fast and so regularly that we do not think about it much. However, during periods of very high call volume, such as during a disaster, the number of users wanting to make calls may exceed the number of available circuits, and the user will get either no dial tone at all or a recorded message requesting that the call be placed at a later time.

The proliferation of home Internet users has placed a considerable strain on the availability of phone circuits, since users may remain online for hours at a time or try to use their POTS line as an always-on connection, tying up the circuit continuously, as opposed to most voice calls, which typically conclude in a few minutes. Telephone companies are expanding the number of circuits that are available through the use of fiber-optic cable and computerized switches that can handle a much greater quantity of traffic than the traditional system, which used copper wire and mechanical switching equipment almost exclusively. If this were not the case, most Internet users would be paying a surcharge for data calls, as many telephone services in Europe do now.

DSL users have a DSL modem that is the interface between their computer and the telephone line, as well as a NIC that connects to the cable that runs out of the DSL modem. As with ISDN service, many DSL service providers will waive installation fees or supply a free DSL modem as an incentive to obtain the DSL service. This largesse frequently carries a commitment to maintain the DSL service for at least a year, at a monthly service rate significantly more than one would pay for POTS.

A big advantage of DSL is that only one phone line is required for normal household use. Voice/fax traffic is carried on the same line as the DSL connection since as the digital data uses a different frequency than the analog voice/fax traffic. The DSL service provider will supply small RJ-11 "pigtail" filters that plug in between the wall jacks and any telephones that are connected to the line. Without these filters, telephone users will hear annoying interference on the phone line. The filters make the presence of the DSL service audibly transparent.

Most DSL service is **ADSL, or Asymmetrical Digital Subscriber Line,** service. *Asymmetrical* refers to the difference in the rate of data flow **upstream** (from the user's computer to the Internet) versus **downstream** (from the Internet to the user's computer). Upstream speeds are usually a fraction of the downstream speeds. A data rate for basic ADSL service would be typically 128 K/ 768 K, or 128 Kbps upstream and 768 Kbps downstream. Since most users have more traffic flowing from the Internet to their machines than going the other way, this works well for most people. Depending on the service being offered at home or place of employment, **SDSL (Symmetrical Digital Subscriber Line)** service may be available, but it will usually be considerably more costly than basic ADSL.

DSL service is usually available in several classes of service, almost always based on data transmission capacities. For instance, a high volume user might want 768 K/1024 K service and will be willing to pay the premium fees that this class of service requires. DSL lines can be shared over a simple network, so this provides a method where a small office can provide each employee with an always-on and reasonably speedy connection to the Internet without having to resort to the expense involved in obtaining direct T1 access.

When a potential subscriber asks for ISDN or DSL service, the service provider, which is usually but not always the local telephone company, will need to test the telephone lines to ensure that the service can be made available. This process usually requires several steps. First, the potential subscriber will provide his or her zip code or telephone number, and sometimes both, on a web-based form or to a customer service representative. This information will be compared against a database to determine if service is available in that area. If that hurdle is overcome, then the DSL or ISDN provider will conduct a test of the existing telephone lines to see if service can be extended to that precise location. Depending on the way that the wire network is set up in the potential subscriber's area, the service may be available at one address and not available across the street or even next door. In some cases, a technician will have to go to the potential subscriber's home or place of business to conduct more line tests. Once all of these conditions have been satisfied, the potential subscriber is advised that he or she can obtain DSL or ISDN service.

The hardware necessary for these connections (the DSL modem or terminal adapter for ISDN) is commonly supplied by the service provider, or the subscriber can furnish his own. In the latter case, it is important to make sure that the equipment that the subscriber provides is compatible with the service he or she is getting. In the case of provided hardware, providers frequently offer promotions where they require a service contract of a year or more in turn for the necessary hardware. The hardware is fairly simple to set up even if the subscriber is not technically oriented.

This process is usually complicated. ISDN and DSL installation and configuration problems are very common and frustrating. Customers commonly complain about the difficulty of obtaining this service and getting it to work properly, but once the service is established, it is generally problem-free. Unlike ISDN service, DSL service is continuous, or "always on," can be used over the same phone line as is used for regular voice or fax traffic, and can have more capacity than ISDN. A DSL connection can be used to connect a web server to the Internet because the connection is live any time the computer is on.

Because a DSL connection is always live, it creates a potential security hazard. In order for a computer to make a connection to the Internet, it must have or establish an **Internet Protocol** or **IP address**. The IP address is the Internet equivalent of a telephone number and is unique for each device connected to the Internet at any given time. IP addresses are most commonly assigned dynamically, or on an as-needed basis. Typically, an ISP will have a block of IP addresses reserved for assignment to its users. When a user dials into an ISP to make an Internet connection, one of the available addresses is assigned to that user's computer and is maintained for the duration of that online session. If the connection is broken for any reason, the IP address is freed up and reassigned to the pool of available addresses. This process is called **dynamic IP addressing** because the addresses assigned to various computers are always changing.

Online system **crackers** attempt to invade others' computers by locating their IP addresses, then using a variety of techniques to get access to their resources (drives, files, processor, etc.). If the computer is not protected by a **firewall** or some other security measure, the invader's job is made easy.

When using dynamic IP addressing, the possibility that a cracker can invade a computer is reduced, though not eliminated, because the online session is relatively short. A cracker would have to stumble onto a user's IP address and gain access to the system all during a single online session, because when the online session is terminated, it closes the conduit that the cracker would have to the computer, and when the next online session is initiated, the IP address would most likely be different.

With **static IP addressing,** which assigns a permanent IP address, half of the cracker's task is done as soon as he or she locates the target computer. Then all he or she need do is gain access, because the online conduit is usually long term or permanent, and the IP address will not change, even if the target computer goes offline for a time. When the computer goes back online, the IP address will be the same as before.

DSL service may use either static or dynamic IP addressing. Generally, static IP addressing is reserved for the higher speed, premium accounts purchased by larger users for connecting their servers to the Internet. It is not unknown for standard DSL service to use static IP addressing, however. Even DSL users with dynamic IP addressing should protect their machines from invaders; those IP addresses are often valid for many hours at a time, making it possible for a cracker to try to invade the machine.

A user who plans to acquire DSL service should install and maintain security software, such as Norton Internet Security 200*x* (a new version is issued every year), ZoneAlarm, or Black ICE Defender, to protect his or her machine. Crackers use software that poll IP addresses in sequence to see if any are live, then try to access that computer when a live connection is found. Without some kind of effective security software, invaders will be able to access and probe a computer without the user's knowledge, reading, copying, and even deleting files. This software is not expensive, and versions for individual consumer or trial use are often free for the download.

With the addition of a **router**, a DSL or ISDN connection can be shared between two or more computers, even if the DSL account has only a single IP address. A router is a switching box, about the same size as the DSL modem, which accepts the input from the DSL line and then uses a system of **headers** to assign the data to the appropriate connected computer. It can be purchased for a minimum of $150 and allows home or small office users to establish a small network and to economize by requiring only a single Internet connection.

Cable

Television cable companies have been slowly replacing their copper wire systems with fiber-optic cable, since this medium is capable of carrying far more bandwidth than the old system. When cable TV first became available, viewers who had been tied to over-the-air reception via rooftop or "rabbit ears" antennas were ecstatic to be able to get ten or twelve channels via cable, all interference-free. Modern consumers are more jaded and view any cable system that is incapable of delivering less than 100 channels of entertainment to be substandard.

Fiber-optic cable can deliver all of the channels that the entertainment industry is likely to produce in the foreseeable future and more. It also provides for two-way communication; the viewer can send signals back to the cable company's offices. The original intended use for this technology was to enable interactive programming choices, such as pay-per-view programs, ordered directly from a console attached to the set. The carrying capacity of fiber optic is so massive, however, that many cable companies are using it to carry data from user's computers to the Internet and back again.

From the user's perspective, cable Internet access works very much like DSL service. The connection is live whenever the computer is on the cable connection is plugged in. A special cable modem, usually supplied by the cable company, sits between the wall connection and the computer, and the cable connection can be shared through a router in the same way as a DSL connection. The speed of the connection is asynchronous and similar to most DSL service, with upstream speeds at around 128 Kbps and downstream speeds of "up to 100 times faster than a 28.8 Kbps modem,"[1] (presumably around 2.8 Mbps) according to one major cable Internet service provider. It is here, however, that the similarities between cable and DSL/ISDN service end.

The architecture of television cable systems is such that cable connections do not run directly from the cable company to a home or office. Instead, the cable network uses a system of distribution points or junction boxes, to which the main feed runs from the cable company. From these distribution points run the cables that actually connect the service to the subscriber. This system in effect creates a network of users who are sharing the bandwidth provided to the distribution point that serves them.

Most users will never notice the effect of sharing their Internet connection with other users in their neighborhoods for a number of reasons. First, it is entirely possible that only one user connected to a given distribution point is subscribing to cable Internet service, and that the other subscribers are just receiving regular cable programming. If that is the case, then using the cable data connection will probably be very fast and free of security problems. As other Internet users join the same distribution node, however, performance may fall off, since all of the data that all of the subscribers are sending and receiving has to be pushed through the same **broadband** "pipe," and there is a finite amount of data that can be carried on that circuit at any moment.

Many cable modem users have been delighted when their cable Internet service is first installed, only to see a marked drop off in performance as other neighborhood users join in and subscribe to the same service. If any of the users on that distribution node place excessive demands on the available bandwidth, then everyone suffers. Users who are routinely downloading large video or **MP3** files drain away the available bandwidth from other users, slowing the **throughput**

---

[1] @Home, 1995–2001, <http://www.home.com/speed.html.html> (March 8, 2001).

speeds to a crawl. Subscribers have even been known to operate active web servers over a cable Internet connection, although this is usually a violation of their subscription agreement and will cause their service to be terminated once it is discovered.

An even more critical problem is one of security over a cable Internet connection. The users who share the bandwidth from a common distribution node are, in effect, on a **Local Area Network** (**LAN**). Breaking into someone else's computer over the Internet is something of a challenge, at best; breaking into a computer on a local network is relatively easy. Networks, by definition, are structures where users can share resources among one another. Files, printers, network connections, and other assets are all shared over networks. If a computer is not properly secured against other network/cable modem users who are using the same distribution point, others may be perusing, editing, and even deleting files on the machine.

There are a number of methods for securing one's computer against this kind of intrusion, some of which are mentioned in the previous section on ISDN/DSL connections. However, one of the most basic methods is to ensure that disable file sharing is installed on the machine. To check and set file sharing option, first click on the **Start** button, then choose **Settings|Control Panel** from the flyout list. From the list of icons in **Control Panel**, double-click on **Networks**. A dialog box similar to that in Figure 4–1 should appear.

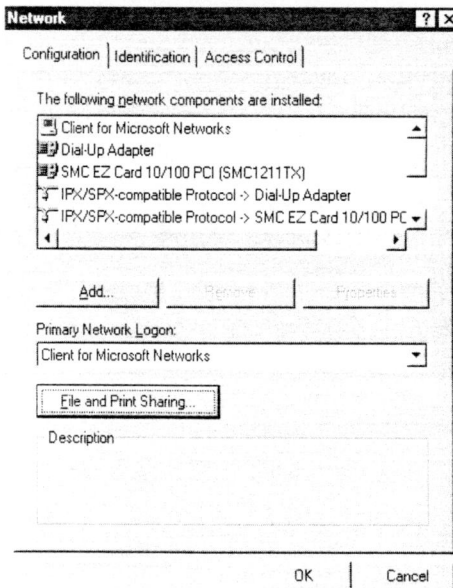

Figure 4-1   Network Configuration Dialog Box

Click on the button marked File and Print Sharing (see Figure 4–1). Another dialog box will open, similar to that in Figure 4–2. The options for this dialog box should be set just as they are in the illustration. If a user checks either option, this will allow others with network access to browse his or her files and even to send print jobs to any printers connected to his or her machine. If either box is checked, then uncheck it, and click on the OK button. If the boxes are unchecked to begin with, then click on either OK or Cancel; the file sharing options are already set as they should be.

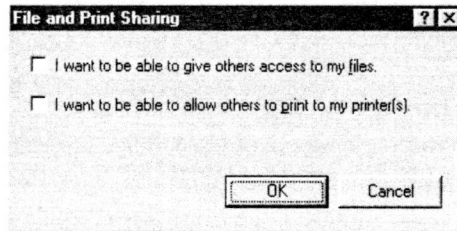

Figure 4-2   File and Printer Sharing Options

Cable Internet access may be the best solution for home users who have access to it, as it is relatively inexpensive, reasonably dependable, and much faster than a comparable dial-up connection. Business users may have their application for cable Internet access denied on the basis that too much bandwidth will be used, slowing the connection for other users on the same circuit. In most cases, there is no choice in the provider for cable Internet service, because each household is typically served by only one cable television service company. To determine if this service is available, check with the company that provides cable television access to the location where the Internet connection is desired.

Satellite-Based Connections

In rural areas that are out of reach of DSL or ISDN lines, users without either cable television service or service that does not include cable Internet service will usually be dependent on a dial-up connection for Internet access. Under ideal conditions, the connection speed will peak at 56 Kbps, but conditions are seldom ideal, even in city centers where telephone wiring is state-of-the-art. In most cases, dial-up connections rarely exceed 40 Kbps. In rural areas where phone lines tend to be old and noisy, the connection may be much slower and may drop off unexpectedly. If the other access options are impossible, there is another option—connecting to the Internet via a satellite dish.

A satellite dish connection works off of the same system as that for satellite television systems, using the smaller, pizza-size dishes mounted in a yard or on a rooftop. They require an unobstructed view to the southern sky for most of the United States, and the farther north a location is, the closer to the horizon that the dish has to point in order to get the necessary line of sight connection to the satellite. This means that satellite users to the north have to be more concerned with tree lines, surrounding structures, and other geographic and man made terrain features that may obstruct the signal. This service is offered to consumers through DirecPC, which is a branch of the same company that provides the DirecTV service, and a newer company called StarBand.

Satellite Internet systems are a hybrid of wired and wireless connections. Traffic upstream from the user travels on a POTS telephone line to an ISP of the user's choosing. E-mail is handled as it would be over any other dial-up connection, but requests for web pages and other information in an interactive mode are sent to a DirecPC ground station after they have come back from the Internet. There, the information is sent via a satellite uplink station to the satellite in geosynchronous orbit.

The data stream is sent over a channel of the satellite's signal to a backyard or rooftop dish where the interface box picks out the necessary data and displays it on the computer. It is a long way for all this information to go (50,000 miles, give or take a few thousand), but since it travels at about the speed of light, the distance is almost insignificant.

The distance that this data must travel is *almost* insignificant because satellite Internet service hookups are well known for their **latency** problems. If the data only had to travel without delay through the various components of this system, then the distance that it had to travel might not be too evident. However, just as there are delays when surfing the web through conventional hookups, there are also delays and bottlenecks at many of the DirecPC way stations, in addition to the ones that everyone else has to tolerate. Even though the data stream from the satellite to the user is very fast—around 400 Kbps—the other delays along the network can slow up delivery of the information to a frustrating pace.

User reports from DirecPC subscribers seem to be very uneven. Some users report consistently fast download speeds and reliable service, while others complain about service outages, interference with the satellite signal due to snow and other weather conditions, and what they view as unfair application of DirecPC's **Fair Access Policy (FAP)**.

The FAP is directed at users who, in DirecPC's view, monopolize the available bandwidth. The bandwidth pipe supplied by the orbiting DirecPC satellite has considerable but finite capacity. The satellite can push through only so much data in a unit of time before users start experiencing data loss and delays in delivery. DirecPC monitors the online activity of its users in terms of the amount of data delivered to their dishes and will temporarily restrict the data flow of users who exceed what they have determined is more than their fair share in order to give other users more reliable access. The users most dramatically affected by this are those who download very large files, such as MP3 music files through services like Napster or full-motion video files from movie, sports, or pornographic sites. When DirecPC has restricted a subscriber's download rate, he or she is said to have been FAPed, and the download speed can slow to as little as 8 or 10 Kbps, a fraction of what he or she would experience over a typical dial-up connection. Until the subscriber's rate of use looks normal for his or her service plan, the slowdown will continue. According to subscribers who have posted messages on a newsgroup for DirecPC users, this period ranges from a few hours to a day or two, and there is no known formula that DirecPC uses to determine how long the restriction will be in force.

Many DirecPC subscribers obtain the service so that they *can* download large files quickly, and the fair access policy causes them great dissatisfaction. Although DirecPC does explain their fair access policy on their corporate website, they do not advertise it, so new subscribers hoping to get access to those big downloaded files might have an unpleasant surprise when the bandwidth is unexpectedly reduced.

DirecPC has a number of service plans, based on whether the user is a business or a residential customer, the hours of use included each month without a surcharge, and whether ISP services are furnished by DirecPC or by the subscriber. Using DirecPC's ISP is cheaper only if they have a point of presence that is a local call for the user. Otherwise, users will have to find a local ISP, or they will incur long distance charges while they are connected to the service.

Users have to have a satellite dish that is compatible with DirecPC's service, a modem designed especially for the service, and software supplied by DirecPC, as well as a working telephone line and modem for the upstream link. With the addition of a satellite receiver, the same satellite dish can be used for reception of DirecTV satellite programming, and DirecPC/DirecTV offers a small discount for the combined services.

DirecPC and a competitor, StarBand, are now orbiting a truly wireless, satellite-based service, but as this is written, the product is too new to evaluate.

Wireless Service

Wireless technologies have seen a tremendous upsurge in recent years, both in terms of number of users and in applications for them to use. A pager was once a status symbol of someone who was too important to be out of touch with his or her home base at any time. These devices and the services that enable them have dropped dramatically in price, so it is now common for every member of the family to have a pager account. Cellular telephones have become similarly ubiquitous and are threatening to supplant pagers because of the inexpensive two-way communication that they offer.

Deskbound users have not created nearly as much demand for wireless technologies, but as can be seen from the profiles of other available methods of connecting to the Internet, the availability of a telephone line does not necessarily mean carefree, fast Internet access. Some offices have telephone systems that cannot be readily adapted to modem connections, and routing an extra phone line to a desk or wherever the user happens to be working may not be easy or inexpensive.

Transmission of Internet-type data over a wireless connection has, to date, been a matter of bandwidth. The radio spectrum has become very crowded, with commercial television and radio, public service and private enterprise two-way radio, pager and cellular phone companies, and many others all competing for space. If radio frequencies are allowed to overlap, then interference will make everyone's wireless access useless. The expansion of radio communications into higher ranges that were previously out of reach and greater use of digital techniques to compress and piggyback data onto fewer channels have made commonplace wireless data transmission possible.

Mobile users have the largest share of choices for choosing wireless Internet services. It is now possible to send and receive e-mail and some web content over a handheld computer, such as the Palm® or Visor® devices, with a cellular phone, or even via a properly configured pager. For most users, though, these are stopgap solutions that are less than satisfactory for full-length, routine communications.

Handheld computers can create, send, and receive e-mail, and some users even receive their e-mail through a regular PC, then transfer it onto a handheld device to read and respond to it. When they are done, they transfer the replies back to the PC, which sends them through the PC's e-mail client. This is not true wireless communication, since the actual transmission occurs over a conventional connection, but it does allow the user greater freedom, such as the ability to handle e-mail during a train or bus commute. Handheld computers equipped with radio transceivers eliminate the need for the PC in the process, as they can send and receive their messages directly. There are two methods that wireless handheld computers use to communicate: proprietary data networks and CDPD.

Proprietary data networks are set up specifically for wireless data services, such as two-way pagers, wireless handheld computers, and special-needs data services, such as those that deliver real-time route updates to parcel delivery services. They are dependent on a system of transmission towers and relay stations, which can be anything from a box mounted on a utility pole to a rooftop antenna, linked to a central system by conventional landlines. Generally, they provide coverage only in the more densely populated areas of the country, since that is where most of their users are. It would not be cost-effective for the companies that build these networks to construct a truly nationwide or worldwide system; this would require too much infrastructure and be too expensive to support, given the number of subscribers. Users who spend most of their time in urban environments, such as business travelers, seldom notice any loss or gaps in coverage, as they spend the majority of their time in the areas that the wireless networks intend to target. However, law enforcement users, especially those in smaller and more rural communities, often spend the majority of their time outside of these coverage zones. The ideal system depends largely on what devices are going to be used and where they will be used. Examples of proprietary data networks include the Palm.net service, which is used by the wireless varieties of Palm® handheld computers, and SkyTel, which provides one- and two-way pager service, including interactive e-mail.

The other principal method whereby wireless data is transmitted over the cellular telephone network is called **Cellular Digital Packet Data**, or **CDPD**. With CDPD, messages are broken up into packets of uniform length, the number of packets in a message being dictated by the length of the message. These packets are coded with header information that identifies the message with which they are associated and their sequence in the complete message. The packets are sent over unused cellular channels, sometimes in between other data being carried on the same channel. The computer on the receiving end identifies each packet as it is received, performs a **checksum** calculation to ensure that the packet was not garbled in transmission and stores it in memory. When all of the packets in the message have been received, the computer assembles them in the appropriate order and stores the unencrypted message to be read by the device's operator.

CDPD offers potentially faster (up to 19.2 Kbps) communication, and is more widely available than most proprietary data networks. This is because

CDPD is generally available anywhere that a digital cellular network is available, and those networks are being expanded constantly to answer the demand of cellular customers. Wireless modems from various manufacturers use CDPD-based communication, although some use proprietary networks. Obviously, it is important to know which method any wireless device being considered for purchase uses, to ensure that it will work in the area where it is intended to be used.

Both proprietary network and CDPD technology are dependent on the use of a finite amount of wireless bandwidth, and the owners of that bandwidth have to ensure they do not overburden their own networks. They typically regulate the amount of traffic on their networks by setting their fees based on the amount of data transmitted per month. This is distinct from cellular airtime, which is measured in minutes or fractions of minutes. Telephone conversations are more of an analog-type communication, and lend themselves to per-minute billing. Digital data communications may be interleaved with other messages, so it is the amount of information sent and received, not the time that it took to send or receive it, that is critical in metering this resource.

Rates for wireless digital communication will always be changing, but in late 2000 an "unlimited" account on both a CDPD-based and a proprietary wireless network was charged at around $40–$50 per month. Rates for users with lesser demands were comparably less but still started at around $20 per month.

It is possible to use a wireless device as the only e-mail conduit, but most users will find the experience unsatisfactory. Composing e-mail on a two-way pager involves using a tiny keyboard. Most users tap out messages with only their thumbs, holding the pager with their other fingers. This method works fine for short messages, which is what the designers had in mind anyway, but anything more than a few sentences proves tiresome. Composing messages on a cellular phone that is capable of creating text messages is even more tedious, as each button on the phone keypad represents three letters, plus a number. For instance, typing the letter *C* usually means three presses of the *2* button, as the display cycles between *A, B,* and finally *C.* Moreover, the display of most cell phones will show only twenty to fifty characters at a time, so viewing either outgoing or incoming messages means a lot of scrolling back and forth.

Handheld computers are much better adapted for creating and sending e-mail than cellular phones and pagers, but they still do not work as well as a PC. Handheld computers use either a virtual keyboard or some version of handwriting recognition to create text. The virtual keyboard is one that is superimposed on the small display, and tapping each virtual key with a stylus enters characters. There are a number of software approaches to this method of text entry, most of which combine a proprietary arrangement of letter keys and auto-completion of words. As each word is typed into the device, the software searches for words in its list that are the most likely to be the one that the author is trying to enter, and presents a suggestion list. When the correct word appears in the list, tapping on it will cause the complete word to be placed in the message. With experience, users can become extremely adept at entering text this way.

Fitaly uses a keyboard arrangement that is optimized for use with a stylus, rather than with fingers (see Figure 4–3). When the manufacturers of the Fitaly held a competition for the fastest user of their product, they found a user who could enter text at better than eighty words per minute.

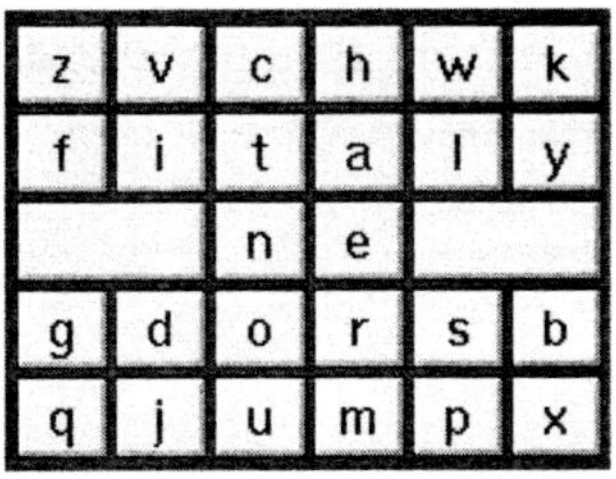

z	v	c	h	w	k
f	i	t	a	l	y
		n	e		
g	d	o	r	s	b
q	j	u	m	p	x

Figure 4-3   The Fitaly Keyboard (graphic courtesy of Textware Solutions)

Some handheld computers will plug into near-full size keyboards with the traditional **QWERTY** arrangement of keys, making text entry nearly as easy as typing into a regular PC. The drawback to this method is that it requires carrying an additional piece of equipment, and one that will not easily fit into a pocket or on a belt case. One keyboard, however, called the Stowaway, folds up into a package about the same size as the Palm computer that it connects to.

Handheld computers, pagers, and message-capable cellular phones will also not accept file attachments, which can be the core of some e-mail messages. To sum up, wireless solutions for messaging are, for most people, only a supplement to messaging on a regular PC or laptop. They can handle short messages to and from users who are within the service boundaries of whatever carriers they are subscribed to, but they are not likely to replace more traditional e-mail solutions.

Handhelds do have other uses for law enforcement officers, however. Since instant access to criminal justice databases, such as **NCIC (National Crime Information Center)** and motor vehicle records came about in the 1960s, the typical method of access for police officers has been via a communications operator. The officer dictates a request into his or her radio, and the dispatcher enters it into the hardwired terminal at the communications center or police station. The communications operator then reads the reply back over the air to the officer, who writes it down in a notepad if necessary. Vehicle-mounted **Mobile Data Terminals** (**MDT**s), where they have been installed, have drastically cut back on the need for these long verbal exchanges; officers can enter their own inquiries into the terminal and read them on their displays, saving or printing the information if needed. Depending on the software installed with the terminal, the same device can also be used for routine dispatching chores, sending calls for service to the officer's vehicle, rather than broadcasting them over the air. Since many law enforcement agencies have dramatically increased the size of their departments without a concurrent increase in the capacity of their dispatch centers or radio channels, this innovation has made it possible for some departments to continue to provide services with the same communications personnel resources.

Mobile data solutions that use handheld computers or two-way pagers as their interface devices are now available. These devices are built on the same technology as other two-way pagers and wireless handhelds, but they use encryption systems and specially written software to send inquiries and receive responses from criminal justice online databases. One of the more costly aspects of these systems is that they often have to be specially adjusted to function in each state, as there is no data standard for state criminal justice information systems. Virtually everyone uses NCIC, but requests to NCIC and to comparable databases administered by most states must usually flow through a switch at the state level, and the design of these switches varies tremendously from one state to another.

As these systems become more refined and standardized, mobile data and messaging will no longer be tied to the officer's headquarters or even to his vehicle but will remain with the officer wherever he goes—out of the vehicle, on foot, bicycle or mounted patrol, or even while off duty.

Free ISPs

The most common method of getting access to the Internet without having to pay for it is through one's employer or school. Some employers provide Internet access to their employees because it is necessary or helpful to them in performing their duties. Many employers are reluctant to do this, however, because of the impact that Internet access can have on overall productivity. There are many attractive time wasters available over the Internet, but there is also the hazard that the access will be used for illegitimate purposes. It is bad enough when workers play games, browse auctions, or chat over company e-mail accounts, because they are not doing the tasks that they are being paid to perform, but this problem is aggravated when the content being viewed is objectionable, such as pornography or content that is critical of the company's operations. Another misuse of the Internet is when it is used to disseminate confidential or proprietary information outside of the company's walls.

Using a free e-mail service such as Hotmail mitigates this problem somewhat, at least in the eyes of the employee, because the company's e-mail is not carrying the objectionable content. The employer, however, still has an interest in seeing that the company's resources are used to advance corporate goals. An analogy would be using a city police vehicle to run personal errands, but filling it up with gasoline paid for by the employee. Doing this might make the action a little less wrong, but it still is not something that the employer is likely to condone.

Law enforcement officers can often profit by having access to the Internet, which is the basis for this book. If the employer provides access, however, please ensure that it is used for legitimate purposes of which the employer would approve, even if they are not likely to find out about it. Using the resource for other purposes can result in loss of access for everyone.

Many colleges provide Internet access to their employees and students, and some will even provide access to alumni for free or at a reduced rate. Because many students and college employees frequently work from home, colleges often have dial-up access from off campus as well as high-speed connections on campus. They are often accessible in semipublic areas, such as the library, where users can plug into the system with their own machines.

Also, some public libraries offer Internet access at fixed terminals in their common areas. These terminals cannot be used for typical POP3 e-mail accounts because the client software on each terminal has to be configured for each user's account, but web-based e-mail services like Hotmail can be accessed from these stations. Some libraries use monitoring or filtering software to ensure that obscene or otherwise objectionable material is not displayed on their terminals, so this solution may not be the best for all users.

There are ISPs that provide free dial-up Internet access to anyone who requests it. Companies like Juno and NetZero provide dial-up service that operates like any other ISP. Both of these companies make their money through the sale of advertising, and they package their service so the user cannot avoid seeing the ads that their sponsors post. Most free ISPs require that customers use software that they provide for access to their service. The software is usually downloaded for free from the web site, or in some cases they will mail potential users a CD-ROM with the software.

When the software is loaded onto the user's computer, users get a new surprise—their display does not look like it used to. With most free ISPs, typically 20–25% of the display is taken up with a "frame" that contains display ads for various customers of the ISP. There is no way to hide these ads or turn them off, unless, of course, the user wishes to change ISPs.

Moreover, depending on the methodology of the free ISP, users have to click on one of the display ad banners to load the full advertisement into their web browser every fifteen to twenty minutes, or the dial-up connection will automatically terminate. This is to keep people from using the free service as an always-on connection. It also prevents the user from downloading very large files without babysitting the download process; the user must click on one of the banners every once in a while.

Some of the free services also attach a short advertisement to the beginning or end of every e-mail or newsgroup message that the user creates. A typical message might be as follows:

> Get a [corporate name deleted] Visa with rates as low as 2.99% intro APR!
> 1. Fill in the brief application
> 2. Get approval decisions in 30 seconds!
> [URL of advertiser's site]

The advertisements are chosen as to be inoffensive on moral grounds, e.g. no ads for adult services, but they lend a decidedly unprofessional look to any e-mail message. The messages also usually include a blurb for the free ISP service, in addition to the other ad.

For casual correspondence between friends, small ads are easily ignored, and a free ISP might be a good, cost-effective way to get basic access. But for business correspondence or even moderately heavy Internet use, free ISPs are not a good decision. Free ISPs also tend not to have the biggest choice of POP dial-up numbers, so most users in sparsely populated areas will be able to use the service without incurring tolls.

Once an ISP is chosen, it is likely that the e-mail address will be linked to it, e.g. user@msn.com, user@aol.com, or user@juno.com. An e-mail address and account can be easily changed, but it is not so easy to get the old address out of the address books of correspondents and businesses. If a subscriber cancels an old ISP account and does not have an updated address, mail sent to the old account will **bounce** back to them. ISPs will not usually forward mail of former subscribers onto their new accounts, like the telephone company will do with callers to an old phone number. So it is important to choose an ISP carefully and consider using an e-mail account that can be accessed from any of them, rather than the one that the ISP provides. Once a method for connecting to the Internet has been chosen, the browser, e-mail client, and newsreader can be set up to retrieve and send information.

INSTALLING OUTLOOK EXPRESS

Microsoft's Outlook Express is one of many **clients** or applications that allow the user to read and create electronic mail, browse **newsgroups**, and perform other functions online. It is not necessarily the best application to use, and in fact some prefer to use other software to perform online tasks. However, Outlook Express is included in complete installations of Internet Explorer, which is one of the most widely used web browsers. It can also be downloaded from the Microsoft web site at no cost, so it is available to everyone. For these reasons, we will use Outlook Express and Internet Explorer as the example platforms for this book. Anything illustrated here can be accomplished by using other software packages as well.

Outlook Express installs automatically when Internet Explorer installs. In many cases, this occurs by default when a Windows operating system is installed, such as Windows 95, Windows 98, or Windows 2000. If Internet Explorer does not install automatically, it can be retrieved from most distribution CD-ROMs for Windows (the CD-ROM that is used to install the operating system) or downloaded from the Microsoft web site.

Once the program has installed, at least two icons should appear in the Quick Launch portion of the Taskbar, which is the portion of the display that contains the Start button. For most users, the Taskbar will be along the lower border of the display. The Quick Launch portion of the Taskbar is immediately adjacent to the **Start** button and contains one or more icons. Clicking on one of these icons will immediately start the program associated with it. Figure 5–1 shows the Outlook Express icon.

Figure 5–1   Outlook Express Icon

There will also be a similar icon on the Desktop and a new program entry under **Programs** on the Start Menu. Clicking on any one of these will activate Outlook Express.

Setting Up Outlook Express

Getting Outlook Express configured to send and receive e-mail is not a complex process, but it is an exacting one. The procedure is not forgiving of errors, and making any one of the many possible mistakes will prevent the e-mail account from working.

There are several pieces of information to have ready in order to set up Outlook Express to retrieve and send e-mail.

♦ User name
♦ Password
♦ **SMTP (Simple Mail Transfer Protocol)** server name
♦ POP3 mail server name
♦ Dial-up or point-of-presence phone number if a dial-up account will be used

The ISP should supply all of these. They are usually included in a **readme.txt** file with the setup information, in the accompanying literature, or on the ISP's web site. If any piece of this information cannot be found, call the ISP's technical support line and ask. Ensure that they spell all terms very carefully, or that each character is recognized for what it is. If the user name or password is something like flot01d, make sure to distinguish between the numeral one (1) or alpha character ells (as in *Lincoln* or *Lima*) and the numeral zero (0) or alpha character Os (as in *Oscar*). These may look the same, but they are very different to the computer.

Upon opening Outlook Express, the first screen should look something like Figure 5–2.

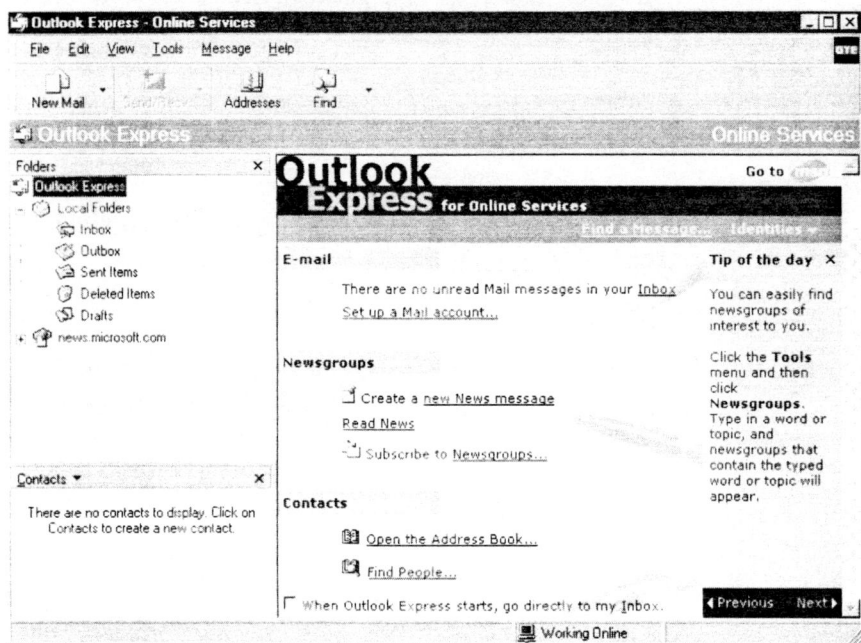

Figure 5-2   Outlook Express Opening Screen

To set up an e-mail account, click on the underlined text that reads **Set up a Mail account** . . . This will start the Internet Connection Wizard, which performs most of the set up.

There will be a choice between **Create a new Internet mail account** and **Use an existing Internet mail account**. If e-mail is being set up on this computer for the first time, then choose the **new account** option. If there is already an e-mail account on the computer, and Outlook Express will be the new e-mail client, then choose the **existing** option. If the **existing** option is visible as a choice and not grayed out, this indicates that the software has located an existing e-mail account installed on the computer already.

There is also the option to sign up for a new e-mail account from Hotmail, which can be done from the Hotmail site itself; this provides another method to get a Hotmail account. This series of instructions for setup assumes that the user is *not* setting up a Hotmail account right now. However, the process of setting up a Hotmail account is controlled by a wizard, a self-explanatory series of dialog boxes, and is a fairly straightforward process. A Hotmail account is useful for sending messages from one account to another to practice the examples described here. Choose the appropriate option, and enter the necessary information, then click on the **Next** button at the bottom of the screen.

The next task is to choose a **Display name.** In most cases, this will be the user's real name, such as **John Smith.** However, depending on the nature of the e-mail account, something more formal might be appropriate, such as **Detective Sergeant John Smith,** or something more mysterious, such as **The Shadow.** The display name is what people will see in the **From** field, in addition to the actual e-mail address. This can be changed anytime by revising the account information. It is necessary to put *something* in here, so choose a name and click on the **Next** button.

Next a dialog box appears that asks for the user's e-mail address. This is the entire e-mail address, not just the user name. For instance, if the user name is **John99** and the ISP is **myisp.com,** then the complete e-mail address is **John99@myisp.com.** This is the information that Outlook Express will use to show correspondents how to reply to messages.

This entry can be reconfigured depending on the user's needs. If there is a need to send an e-mail messages from one account but to have replies to those messages come to another, a different e-mail account can be specified in this box, and replies to messages will go to the account specified. Someone might do this if he or she is using an e-mail alias or if he or she is using a personal account for both business and personal messages. When a suitable e-mail address has been entered for replies, click on the **Next** button.

The next screen has fields for the POP3 and SMTP information mentioned earlier. Note the choice at the top of the dialog box in Figure 5–3.

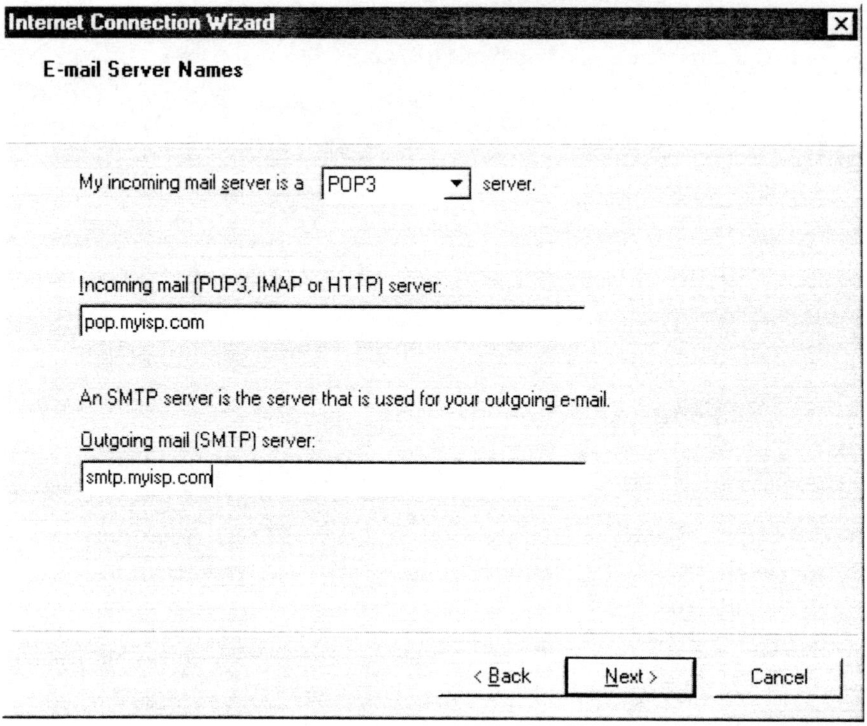

Figure 5-3   Outlook Express Mail Server
              Setup Screen

In the vast majority of the cases, the mail server will be a POP3 server, as this is the standard of the industry. If the server is an **HTTP** (**HyperText Transfer Protocol**) or an **IMAP** (**Internet Message Access Protocol** server), the ISP should inform the user so that he or she can set the appropriate option.

Enter the POP3 and SMTP server names from the information supplied by the ISP into the appropriate blanks. Double-check these entries; they are not tolerant of errors.

When an Internet account, such as myisp.com, is set up to retrieve mail from another account, such as one on CompuServe, and the ISP's settings are used for both SMTP and POP3 servers (something like smtp.compuserve.com and pop.compuserve.com), mail can be retrieved, but when replies or new messages are sent, an error message will come up. This is because the computer is not properly logged into the SMTP server, which is the one that handles outgoing mail.

If myisp.com is the Internet service provider, the CompuServe account should be configured on this screen as shown in Figure 5–4.

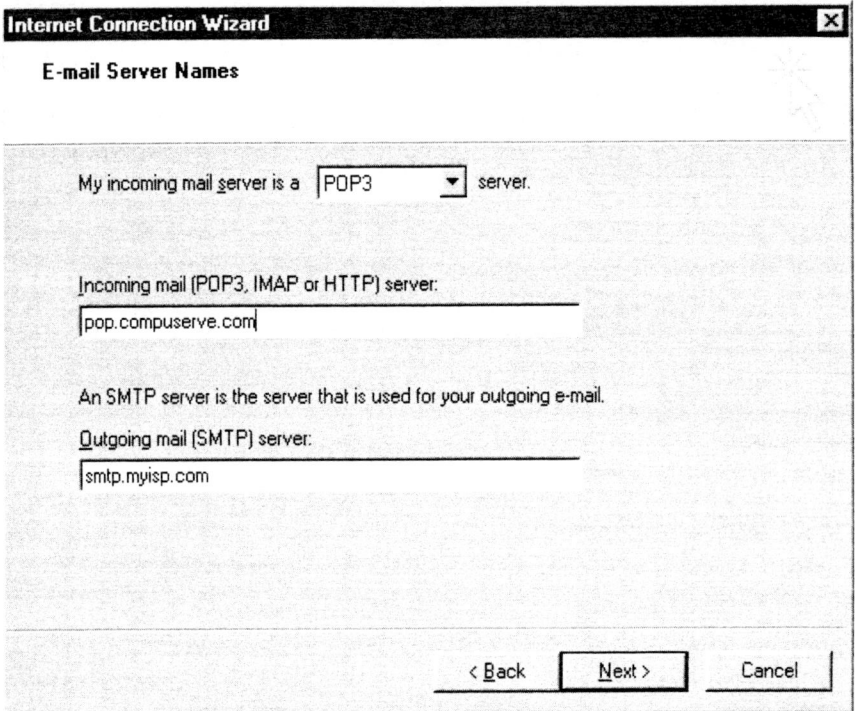

```
┌──────────────────────────────────────────────────────────────────────┐
│ Internet Connection Wizard                                         [X] │
├──────────────────────────────────────────────────────────────────────┤
│    E-mail Server Names                                                 │
│                                                                        │
│                                                                        │
│        My incoming mail server is a  │POP3       ▼│ server.           │
│                                                                        │
│                                                                        │
│        Incoming mail (POP3, IMAP or HTTP) server:                      │
│        │pop.compuserve.com│                                            │
│                                                                        │
│        An SMTP server is the server that is used for your outgoing e-mail. │
│        Outgoing mail (SMTP) server:                                    │
│        │smtp.myisp.com                                                 │
│                                                                        │
│                                                                        │
│                                                                        │
│                              < Back  │   Next >   │    Cancel          │
└──────────────────────────────────────────────────────────────────────┘
```

**Figure 5-4   Server Setup for Third-Party Access to
E-Mail Accounts**

Thus CompuServe mail can be retrieved from the server where it resides. However, sending mail from the same server requires that the user log into CompuServe directly. This is because CompuServe, like most other large e-mail providers, does not accept "proxy" or third-party access to its servers. The user does not have to fully understand this mechanism, but he or she should know that mail could be received from as many accounts as desired; however, it may be impossible to send mail from multiple accounts in a single session. When this is configured and any necessary test runs have been completed, click on the Next button.

The screen shown in Figure 5–5 is where the user name and password are entered. Note that no matter what is entered into the password field, all that appear are asterisks. This is to keep someone from reading the password; if someone learns another person's password he or she has unlimited access to the e-mail account. Be very careful when entering the password, because none of this will work until it is right. If the password is entered incorrectly, it can be changed later. This also applies if the ISP allows users to choose a new password or if the user wants to change the for security reasons. Passwords are usually, though not always, case insensitive, meaning that FIDO007 is equivalent to fido007. Just to be safe, use the same case that the password has in the instructions.

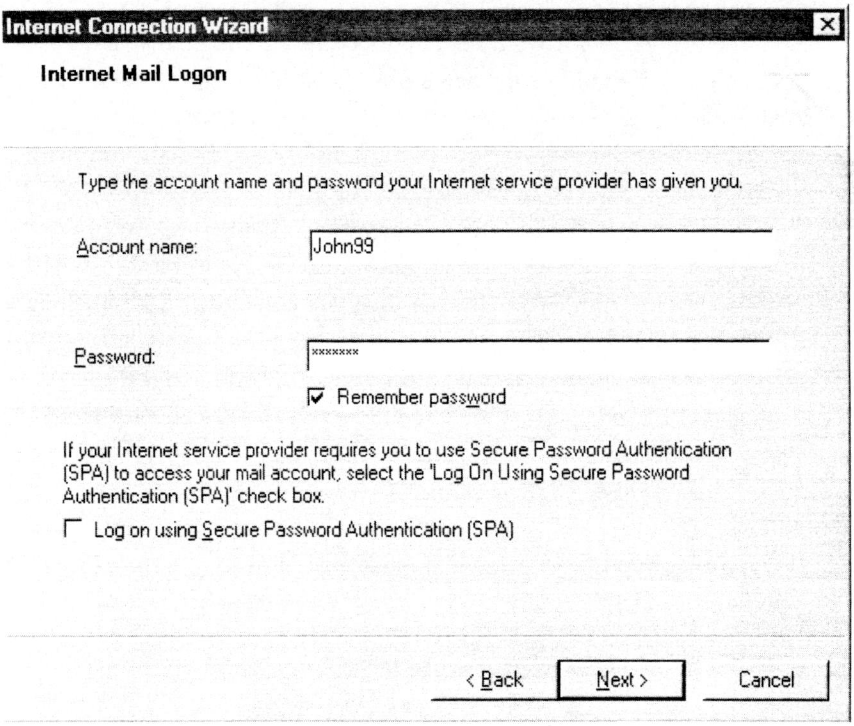

Internet Connection Wizard   ☒

Internet Mail Logon

Type the account name and password your Internet service provider has given you.

Account name: John99

Password: ×××××××
                   ☑ Remember password

If your Internet service provider requires you to use Secure Password Authentication (SPA) to access your mail account, select the 'Log On Using Secure Password Authentication (SPA)' check box.
☐ Log on using Secure Password Authentication (SPA)

< Back   Next >   Cancel

Figure 5-5   User Name and Password Entry Screen

Checking the **Remember password** box keeps the user from having to enter the password manually every time the account is accessed. Otherwise Outlook Express will require the password with every log-in attempt. If only one person uses the computer and no one else has access to it, then it is probably safe to check this box. However, if several other people have access to the machine, they will be able get into the e-mail as easily as the primary user—without knowing the password.

The box labeled **Log on using Secure Password Authentication** should only be checked if the ISP supports this feature. This information should be included in the setup package.

When the password and user name are entered correctly, click the Next button and set up is done. This process will have to be repeated for any other e-mail accounts that are to be accessed through Outlook Express.

Setting Up the Internet Connection

If service has already been established with an ISP and their installation software was used, the connection may already be set up. To determine this, first look on the Desktop to see if there are any new icons that indicate that clicking on them will establish an Internet connection. In most cases, clicking on these will dial the modem and connect the machine to the ISP. There is also another place to be checked. Double-click on the My Computer icon on the Desktop to open the My Computer window, then on the folder within that window that reads Dial-Up Networking. There will be icons for each Dial-Up Networking connection that has been set up on the computer. If there are none other than Make New Connection, then the connection will have to be set up from scratch. It is possible to do this from within Outlook Express, but setting up the Dial-Up Networking connection from its native window will ensure that the connection is available for other activities as well.

To set up a Dial-Up Networking Connection, refer to Figure 5–6 and double-click on the icon labeled Make New Connection. This will start the new connection wizard, which will guide the user through the process.

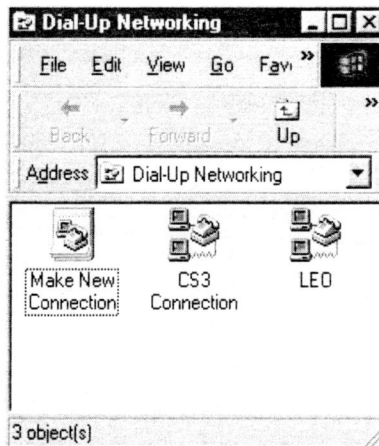

Figure 5–6   Dial-Up Networking Window

Under **Type a name for the computer that you are dialing**, the user should supply a name that is meaningful to him or her, such as **Anytown ISP**. The name itself is irrelevant, as long as it is not already in use and can be recognized later. For the "device," the default entry will almost always be the right one. In most cases, the local modem will be listed there. If the computer has more than one modem or some alternative method for connecting, then choose it from the drop-down list.

The next window asks for the phone number that the modem is to dial. It is necessary to input the area code and the phone number, even if the call is within the user's area code and is a local call. Windows takes into account the local area code in dialing numbers and may refuse to dial if the area code is omitted. The number that goes in this box is supplied by the ISP as the local dial-up node or point of presence. Ignore the **Country Code** selection unless the user is dialing a number outside the United States or Canada. Clicking the **Next** button completes the process.

A new icon will now appear in the Dial-Up Networking window, labeled with the name given to this connection. It maybe useful to have a shortcut to this connection on the Desktop; otherwise the Dial-Up Networking window will have to open to dial the Internet connection. Creating the shortcut is easy. Right-click on the new connection icon, and choose **Create Shortcut**. The computer will say that it cannot create a shortcut here (meaning the Dial-Up Networking window) and will ask to create a shortcut on the Desktop instead. Answer **Yes**. The new icon appears on the Desktop when the Dial-Up Networking window closes.

Double-clicking on the new Dial-Up icon makes the computer try to dial the number, and if it connects with another modem, a dialog box appears that asks for the user name and password. A curious "feature" of Windows asserts itself here. If the connection fails the first time, the computer will not "remember" the user name and password; these will have to be re-entered on the next try.

Once a dial-up connection is created that Outlook Express can use, the next step is configuration of Outlook Express to send and receive e-mail.

Setting Options

Outlook Express can be customized, and any of these options can be changed at any time. If something is not set up as desired, it can be reconfigured.

To enter the Options configuration screen for Outlook Express, click on the Tools portion of the Menu Bar at the top of the program window as shown in Figure 5–7, and then on Options.

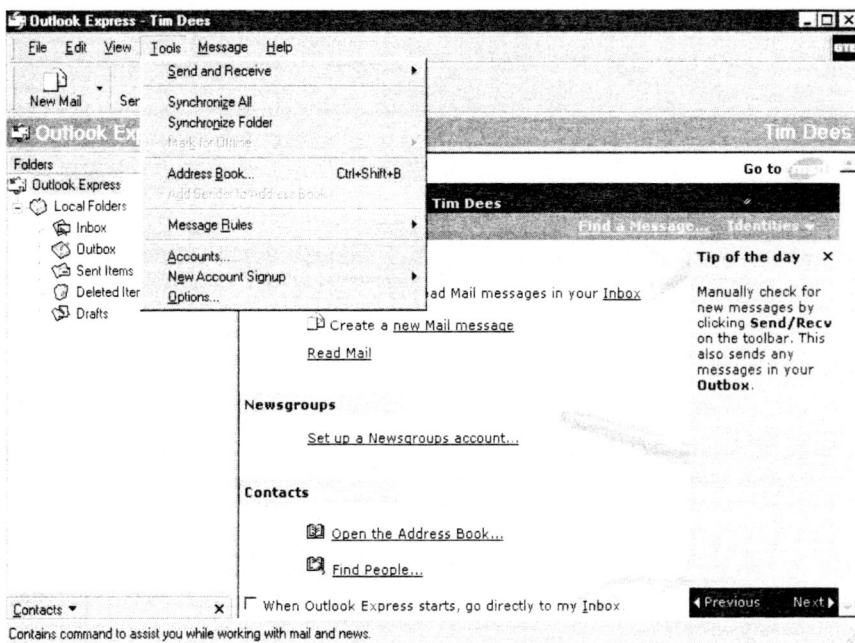

Figure 5–7   Getting to the Outlook Express Options Window

The Options dialog box looks complicated because Outlook Express has many customization options. However, most of the choices involve choosing the desired options and clicking them.

The tabs at the top of the Options dialog box each pertain to a specific set of choices. The opening screen under the General tab, as seen in Figure 5–8, allows the user to choose the way that Outlook Express behaves when it starts and how it will check for messages. The effect of each option, checked or otherwise, is shown on the chart on pages 71–72.

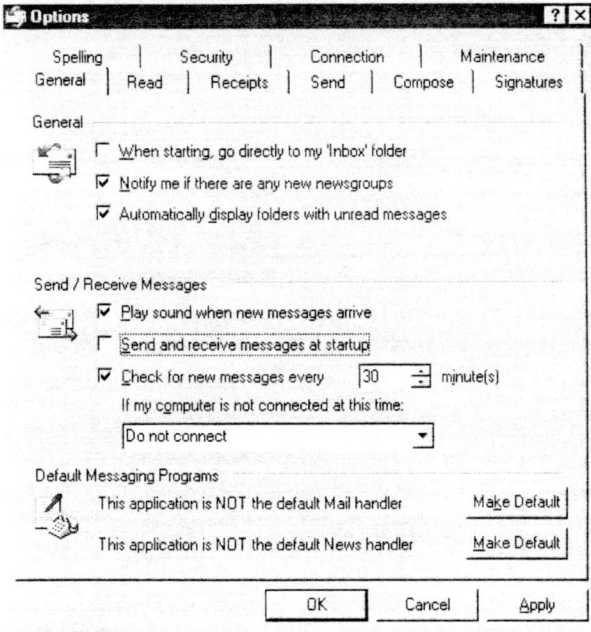

Figure 5-8   Outlook Express Options: General Tab

Option	Effect
When starting, go directly to my "Inbox" folder	If checked, Outlook Express will start with new messages listed in the opening window. If left unchecked, the same basic setup window appears that came up the first time Outlook Express was started. Most people prefer to start with the Inbox open after the program has been configured.
Notify me if there are any new newsgroups	This option pertains to the reading of messages in Usenet, which is covered in another chapter. For now, leave this unchecked.
Automatically display folders with unread messages	Outlook Express allows the user to create as many message folders as desired, as well as rules that act to automatically file certain messages in the folders designated. If this box is checked, any folder with an unread message will be displayed in the folder list, no matter how many levels down it might be buried. This is a good option to check.

Option	Effect (continued)
Play sound when new messages arrive	This plays an audible alert (the default is a kind of musical tone, but you can change this with the Windows **Control Panel/ Sounds** option) whenever new messages arrive. Those who prefer a more interactive computer should choose this option.
Send and receive messages at startup	If this is checked, Outlook Express will try to connect to the ISP, send any messages waiting in the Outbox, and retrieve any messages that might be waiting. If the user starts Outlook Express to compose mail offline or to look at a message that was sent previously, this may be an annoyance. Messages can be sent and received manually by clicking on an icon.
Check for new messages every *x* minutes	If this box is checked, then Outlook Express will poll the mail server at the interval selected for mail and send any mail waiting in the Outbox at that time. The drop down list below this item indicates what action Outlook Express will take to connect to the ISP. If the computer connects to the ISP via a dial-up account, set this to automatically connect and use a single phone line; it is very easy to interrupt someone's phone call with the computer trying to log on. A phone line dedicated to online work or an always-on connection, such as a DSL or ISDN line, will probably be most convenient when set to one of the "connect" options.

A short polling interval may result in a drop in efficiency because computing resources are required to log on and check for mail. For most people, checking every 15–30 minutes is often enough. |
| Default Messaging Programs | If Outlook Express is selected for e-mail and newsgroup work, then it might as well be set as the default handler. This means that when an e-mail or newsgroup "event" is triggered in an external application, such as clicking on a mailto: link of a web page, which opens a window to compose an e-mail message, Outlook Express will open automatically, if it is not running already. If another program handles mail or newsgroups, then Outlook Express should not be the default. |

Clicking on **OK** or **Apply** at the bottom of the dialog box will save the choices. This dialog box can be reopened and changed whenever necessary.

The options in the **Read** dialog box shown in Figure 5–9 affect how the program behaves when the user is reading messages from mainly newsgroups, but it also affects e-mail messages. The options and their effects can be seen in the chart following Figure 5–9.

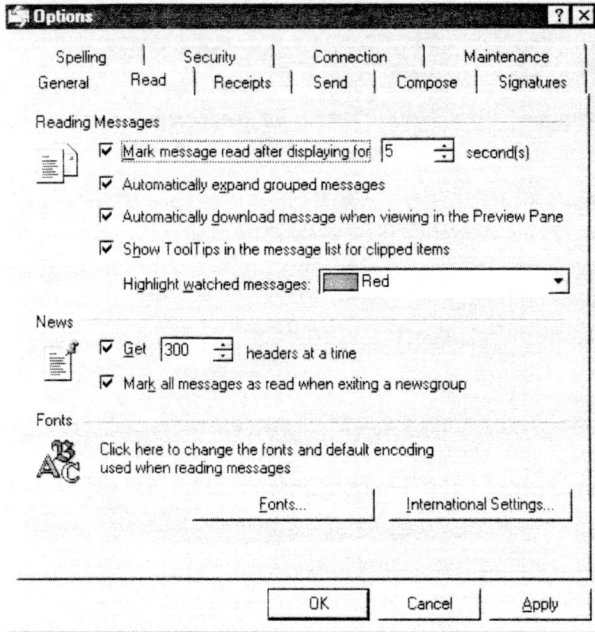

**Figure 5-9   Outlook Express Options:
Read Tab**

Option	Effect
Mark message read after displaying for *x* seconds	New messages in both e-mail and newsgroups usually appear in boldface. Checking this option will automatically change the boldface to the default font *x* seconds after the message header is clicked. If the user routinely gets a lot of mail or newsgroup messages that are left unread, this box should be checked and set to zero. Then as soon as the message header is clicked, the text will change to the default. To make sure the messages have been read before they are marked, set the interval to something like ten seconds, so that it will be marked only after it has been viewed for a while.
Automatically expand grouped messages	This option applies more to newsgroup messages than to mail. Newsgroup messages are usually arranged in a hierarchy or outline format, so that replies to a message are indented slightly from the "parent." Messages with replies are marked with a tiny + symbol, and clicking on this will expand the hierarchy. If this box is selected, the hierarchy will expand as soon as the message header is clicked.

Option	Effect (continued)
Automatically download messages when viewing in the Preview Pane	It is possible to keep both newsgroup and mail messages on the mail server until the user decides to download them onto the computer. Downloading newsgroup messages can require a lot of time and disk space, so it is usually best to check this box; then the newsgroup messages will be received one at a time. It takes a little longer, but it prevents cluttering the inbox with unwanted messages.
Show ToolTips in the Message List for clipped items	Some e-mail and newsgroup messages have very long subject lines, which do not fit in the display. This item causes a little yellow box with the full subject to pop up when the cursor is over a "clipped" (not fully displayed) subject line. It is a pretty useful option to have checked.
Highlight watched messages (color)	In newsgroups, a message can be placed on a "watch" list. This function places a little pair of eyeglasses in one column and changes the subject line color. This is helpful when trying to follow an ongoing dialogue or **thread**, which is fairly common in newsgroups. Checking this box makes those watched messages easier to find.
Get *x* headers at a time	This is strictly a newsgroup option. Some very active newsgroups might generate thousands of messages a day. When a user logs onto one, it will retrieve the *x* most recent message headers (subject lines) for him or her to examine. The higher this number is set, the more time and bandwidth will be consumed each time the user clicks on a newsgroup. Three hundred messages is a good starting point, but the number can be changed up or down as necessary.
Mark all messages as read when exiting a newsgroup	Unread newsgroup messages appear in boldface. Messages that have been read appear in the default font. In most cases, the user does not want to read every message in a newsgroup. Checking this box sets them all to the default font when the user exits the newsgroup, so that he or she knows that there is nothing new there of interest.
Fonts	These options should not be changed unless the user really dislikes the fonts or messages appear to be blank or gibberish. Most of the time, the default settings will be just fine.

It is possible to get an acknowledgment that a mail message has been received, even if the recipient does not reply. Unfortunately, some e-mail clients handle these badly, so the system does not work quite as smoothly as it otherwise might. Unless there is a need to know when sent and received messages have been read, set these options as they appear in the **Receipts** tab illustration (Figure 5–10).

The **Send** dialog box shown in Figure 5–11 sets the options that control how sent messages will appear and otherwise be handled. Refer to the chart following Figure 5–11 for the options and their effects.

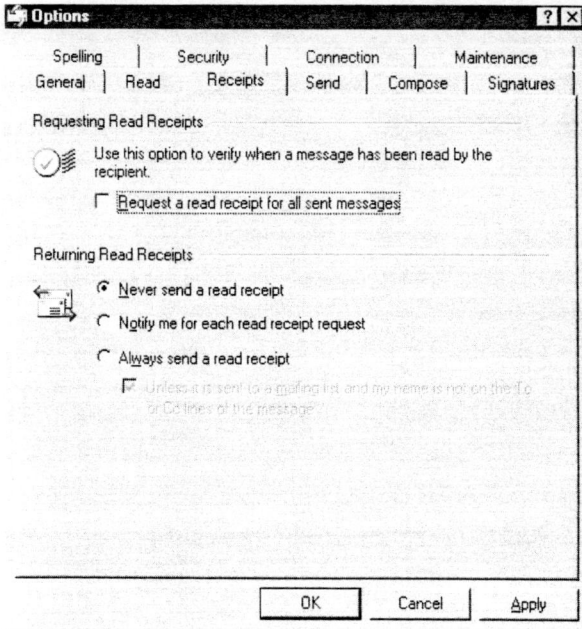

Figure 5-10   Outlook Express Options: Receipts Tab

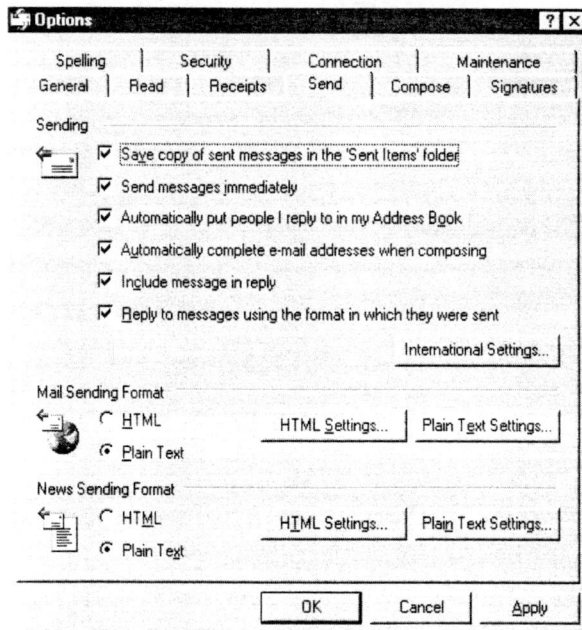

Figure 5-11   Outlook Express Options: Send Tab

Option	Effect
Save copy of sent messages in the "Sent Items" folder	When a message is composed and is not sent or marked to be sent, it gets placed automatically in the Drafts folder. When the user marks it for delivery, it goes into the Outbox until it is actually sent, at which time it goes into the Sent Items folder if this box is selected. As it is frequently nice to be able to go back and reread messages, checking this box is a good idea. Otherwise, once a message is sent, it is gone from the machine.
Send messages immediately	Selecting this box means that messages will be sent upon clicking the Send button. If the user is not online, the program will try to connect. Some users do not like the modem dialing out every time a message is completed. If the box is left unchecked, the program will place the completed outgoing messages into the Outbox and will only connect when the Send/Receive icon is clicked.
Automatically put people I reply to in my Address Book	This option saves the user the trouble of manually saving the e-mail addresses of correspondents in the computer address book. However, if the correspondent has a screen name of Wild Man and his true name is John Smith, he is going to be listed in the address book as Wild Man until it is revised. This is a handy feature, but it is important to know how it works.
Automatically complete e-mail addresses when composing	When the user starts to type an e-mail address in the To blank of an outgoing message, this option instructs the computer to look for matches in the address book and complete it. This is handy if typos are a problem, but it can result in confusion of two people with similar e-mail addresses.
Include message in reply	Checking this tells the computer to include the original message in any replies that the user writes, with each line prefaced with an angle bracket (>) character. This is useful for trying to respond to certain topics in an e-mail message, because the correspondent may otherwise forget the topic of discussion between messages. Judicious use of this feature is discussed in the portion of this chapter on e-mail etiquette.
Reply to messages using the format in which they were sent	Some e-mail programs compose in HTML (web-type) format and others in plain text. Not all e-mail clients can read all formats. As a rule, check this box and reply to people in the same format as their messages.
Mail Sending Format/ News Sending Format	Unless there is a compelling reason to do so, leave these both at Plain text. This makes the format legible to all machines.

The Compose dialog box (Figure 5–12) sets the way that outgoing messages will appear, and the options and their effects are shown in the chart following the figure.

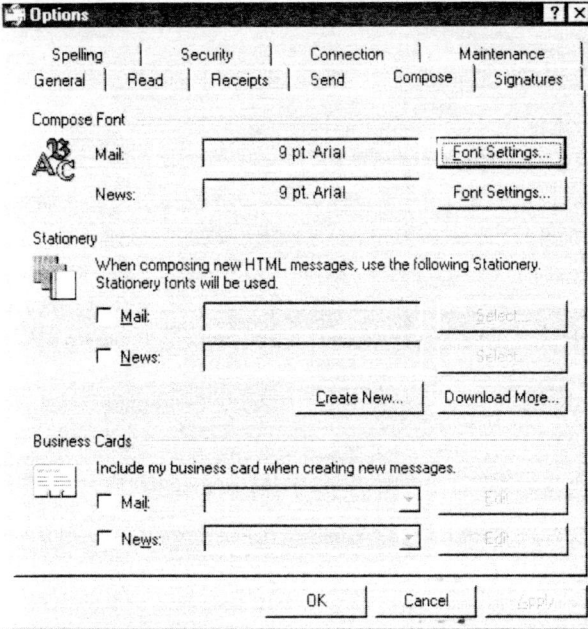

Figure 5–12   Outlook Express Options:
Compose Tab

Option	Effect
Compose font	The user can choose the font and size to compose messages in both newsgroups and e-mail, but they may not necessarily look the same when they get to their destinations. If the recipient's computer does not have that font installed, it will try to approximate the font with a substitute that is installed, and the result may be less than pleasing. As a rule, stick to common fonts, such as Arial, Times Roman, or Courier.
Stationery	This option affects only messages that are composed in HTML format. Predesigned stationeries are available, but the user can also create them. Stationeries include background and margin images, special fonts, and other decorative effects. These seldom appear businesslike, and some users without HTML capabilities will not be able to see them, either. Unless there is a special need to use stationery, it is best to avoid it.

Option	Effect (continued)
Business cards	A business card file can be created from any entry in the address book. The business card file, which will have a name something like **John Smith.vcf**, will contain all of the information in the address book entry, including business and home addresses, phone numbers, e-mail addresses, web page locations, notes, etc. How much or how little information is contained there is entirely up to the user, and it is not mandatory to create one. When a *.vcf file is attached to a message, the recipient, if he or she is using an e-mail client that has a compatible address book file, can import the *.vcf file directly into the address book and have an entry there containing all of the information without retyping. Creation of the address book entry will be covered later in the chapter.
	When this box is selected, a prompt requires the user to choose the address book entry from which the *.vcf file is created. The *.vcf file will then be automatically appended or attached to every e-mail or newsgroup message that is sent. The file can be manually deleted from each message if desired.

The tab shown in Figure 5–13 helps the user create signatures, which are the blocks of text that appear at the end of e-mail or newsgroup messages. Typically, they include the composer's name, address, title, and so on, but they can include just about anything. Some e-mail users are fond of attaching favorite quotations or clever bumper sticker-type slogans to their signature blocks.

A user can have as many signature blocks as he or she chooses and can attach them manually or have one automatically appended to each message when it is composed. Discretion should be used when composing a signature block; attempts at being humorous may not be favorably regarded by all recipients. The content of the signature block will be determined by the environment in which it is used.

To create a signature, click on the **New** button, and then type the text that will appear in the signature block in the lower pane of the dialog box. The information can also be pulled from a text file by clicking on the **Browse** button and navigating to the text file. Once the signature block is completed, the **Rename** button allows the user to give it a name more descriptive than **Signature #1**, and if the signature is to be appended to all composed messages, check the appropriate box in the upper pane. Creation of more than one signature activates the **Set as default** button, and any one of the signature files can be automatically appended. A signature can be used for another message by clicking a button. This will be covered in the section on composing messages.

Outlook Express can automatically check spelling in each message. For most people, this is a good option to set; making typos is very easy when composing e-mail. The options shown in Figure 5–14 are fairly self-explanatory.

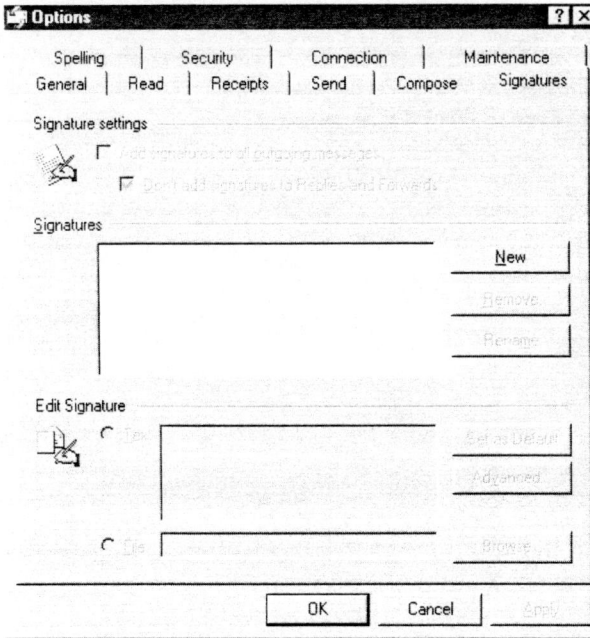

Figure 5-13   **Outlook Express Options:** Signatures **Tab**

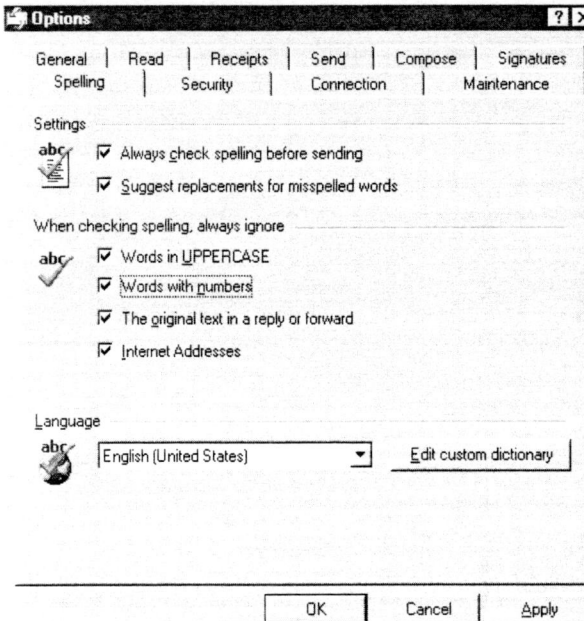

Figure 5-14   **Outlook Express Options:** Spelling **Tab**

If the **Suggest Replacements** box is checked, Outlook Express will provide a list of words that come close to whatever was typed, which can save time. The **When checking spelling** section has to do with what words the spell checker will check and ignore. Unless the user is working outside of the United States, do not reset the **Language** option. Setting the option to, for instance, **English Canada** will cause words like *color* to be recognized as misspelled, and *colour* will be suggested as a replacement.

Most users leave the settings in Figure 5–15 at their defaults. Digital encryption and signing of e-mail messages will be covered later in the chapter.

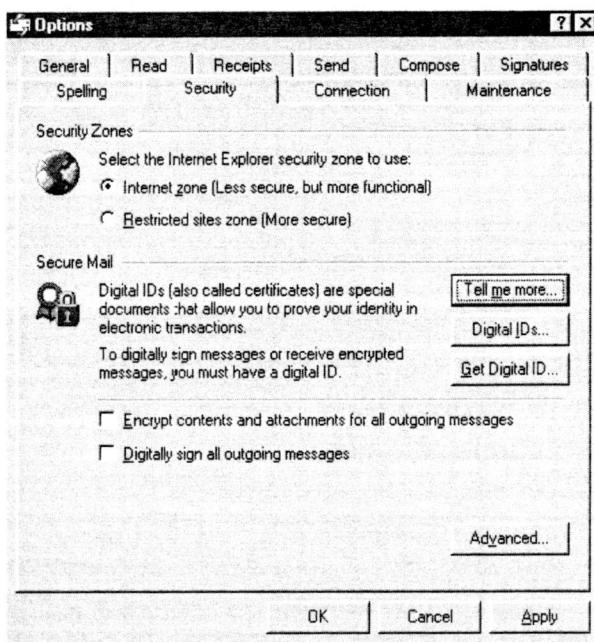

**Figure 5-15   Outlook Express Options:
Security Tab**

In the screen shown in Figure 5–16, the user selects which dial-up or other Internet connection Outlook Express will use to retrieve e-mail and newsgroup messages. Clicking on the **Change** button will show a list of Dial-Up

Networking connections that are already established. Checking the **Ask before switching dial-up connections** will cause the program to make sure that it is okay to disconnect from one connection before going to another, assuming that there is more than one configured. Checking the **Hang up after sending and receiving** box will terminate the connection after mail has been dealt with, which is not ideal if the user wants to surf the web or otherwise use the Internet while Outlook Express is running. However, it is a good option to check if Outlook Express will be running on an otherwise-unattended computer and is set to check for mail at designated intervals; the phone line will not be tied up until the connection times out.

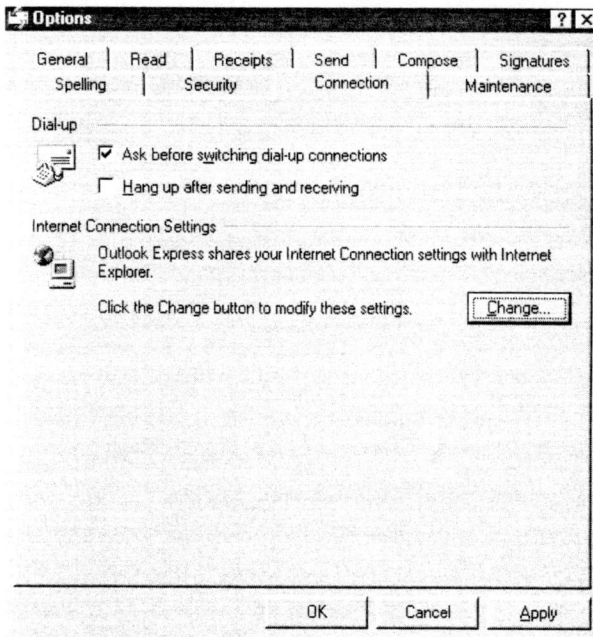

Figure 5-16   Outlook Express Options:
Connections **Tab**

The dialog box in Figure 5–17 sets the options that determine how long and how many messages will be saved on the machine and where they are saved.

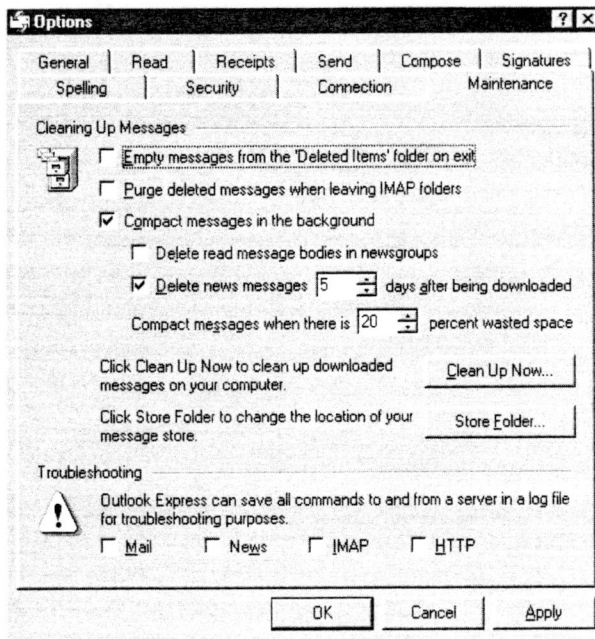

**Figure 5-17   Outlook Express Options:
Maintenance Tab**

For the most part, old messages are saved until they are deleted. One exception might be with newsgroup messages, which can be purged at a selected interval. Most of the time, though, users do not keep old newsgroup messages.

Option	Effect
Empty messages from the "Deleted Items" folder on exit	Messages that the user deletes are automatically transferred to the Deleted Items folder. If this box is selected, the folder is purged every time the program is closed. If it is left unmarked, the Deleted Items folder will grow in size until it is purged manually. There is always the option of deleting individual messages from the Deleted Items folder, in which case they are truly gone.
Purge deleted messages when leaving IMAP folders	A lot of users do not use IMAP, so this does not affect most people. Leaving this box unchecked will cause the IMAP folders to gradually grow in size until messages are purged manually.

Option	Effect (continued)
Compact messages in the background	Compacting messages makes them take up less space on the machine while preserving them intact. This box should normally be checked unless the computer is short on memory or other resources. If this is the case, there will be a drop off in efficiency when computer resources are shared with the compacting feature. If the disk drive is churning from time to time and the rest of the machine is slowing down when Outlook Express is running, uncheck this box and see if it improves the situation. The messages can always be compacted manually.
Delete read message bodies in newsgroups	Newsgroup messages can consume a lot of disk space. Checking this box indicates that Outlook Express will delete messages from the machine after they have been read. They can still be retrieved from the news server to the extent that the server retains them.
Delete news messages *x* days after being downloaded	Again, this is a disk-space saving strategy. Whether or not this option is selected and the length of the prescribed interval depend on how and why newsgroups are used.
Compact messages when there is *x* percent wasted space	This option determines when Outlook Express will automatically compact message files. If the machine is churning unexpectedly and downloading a lot of mail and news messages, set this to a higher number, or uncheck it entirely.
Click Clean Up Now to clean up downloaded messages on your computer	This is the manual command to compact files and purge folders that need to be purged. This is a good option to choose when the machine will be idle for a while, such as overnight. Some of these processes can take quite a long time.
Click Store Folder to change the location of your message store	Messages can be stored anywhere, although Outlook Express defaults to a folder buried deep within the Windows file hierarchy that has a name that is not immediately recognizable. This option allows the user to save e-mail to a created folder. Before clicking this button, create an empty folder somewhere on the machine and give it a name that can be easily remembered. Then click the **Store Folder** button and navigate to the new folder. For security reasons, a storage folder on a floppy disk or other storage media can be created, which can be removed and taken along, but the disk may fill up quickly and may not have room to save messages.
Troubleshooting	These are options that technical support people may use when trying to isolate a problem; most people never bother with them.

Folder Structure and Functions

Back at the main screen of Outlook Express, there is a listing of folders in the left pane of the main window. If a display similar to Figure 5–18 cannot be found, then click on View|Layout at the top of the screen, and check the boxes that correspond to the portions that are missing. The view can always be customized with this option, and the portions that are not selected to display will not be lost, but will be hidden from view until they are selected.

As shown in Figure 5–18, the principal folders in the list under Local Folders are as follows.

♦ Inbox
♦ Outbox
♦ Sent Items
♦ Deleted Items
♦ Drafts

Figure 5-18   Outlook Express Default Mail Folders

Mail messages move around these folders more or less automatically depending on the nature and status of the message. A new message starts off in Drafts. An unsent message stays in Drafts when the programs is closed and will be available for completion or deletion the next time the program runs. A sent message goes to the Outbox folder and waits to be transferred to the mail server. This, however, may happen immediately upon clicking Send/Receive if there are messages to be sent and the machine is connected to the Internet.

When the message has been sent, it moves to the Sent Items folder. Any time a message is deleted from any folder, it moves to Deleted Items. And, finally, incoming messages are stored by default in the Inbox folder. The contents of each folder can be displayed by clicking on the folder icon in the left display pane.

The program must have these five folders by default, but folders can be created to hold and file messages by any strategy. Outlook Express even provides a method whereby messages can be automatically placed into folders with no further intervention.

For instance, suppose there is a project called "Diamond," and all correspondence regarding Diamond must be kept separate from other messages. To create a "Diamond" folder, first click on the folder, which will be the "parent" of Diamond (the folder that will appear above it in the hierarchy) and then on the File|New|Folder pulldown menu in the menu bar (holding down the Control, Shift, and E keys at the same time will open the same menu option). Enter the name that the folder is to have, in this case, Diamond (see Figure 5–19), and hit the Enter key. A new folder called Diamond appears displayed in the folder hierarchy (see Figure 5–20).

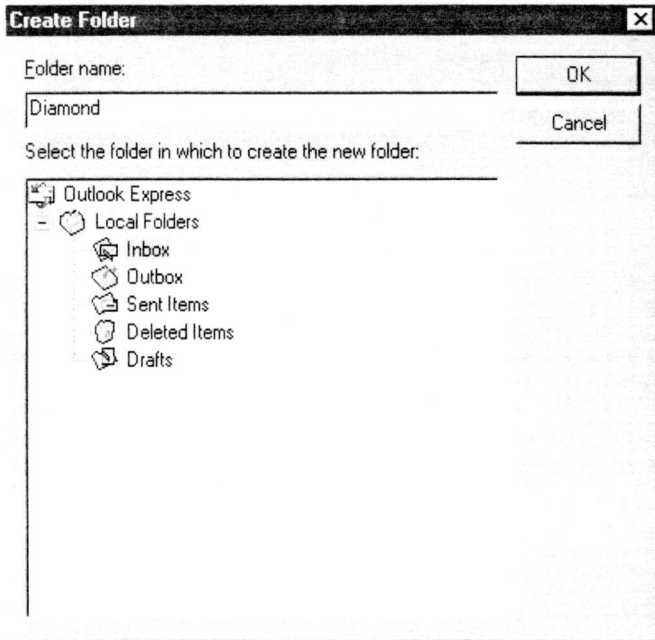

Figure 5-19   Folder Creation Dialog

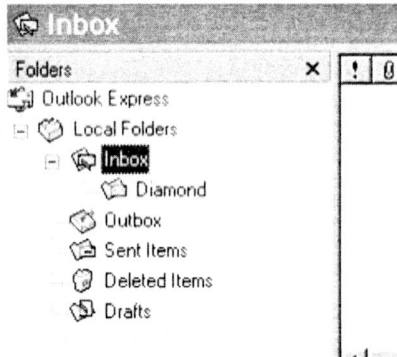

Figure 5-20   New Folder Created

Moving messages between folders is a simple drag-and-drop operation. Click on the folder that contains the messages to be filed under **Diamond** so that they (and the others in the same folder) show in the message list. Click on the messages to be refiled, and drag them to the **Diamond** folder icon. They will be moved to that folder.

Message Rules

Message rules can be set that will cause the program to take predefined actions when the program receives messages that meet prescribed criteria. Message rules are useful for automatically flagging messages of special or lesser importance, keeping other correspondents aware of certain ongoing e-mail discussions, and ensuring that the Inbox (the default storehouse for all incoming messages) does not get clogged with long lists of messages that ought to be filed elsewhere.

The previous example involved creation of a folder called **Diamond**. Suppose it is necessary to ensure that all messages pertaining to the Diamond project are automatically filed in that folder. First, all of these messages have to have some characteristic that Outlook Express can recognize. An easy one might be the word **Diamond** in the subject line, but that is dependent on everyone involved in the project adhering to that policy. If there are certain correspondents who will be communicating with one person only about Diamond, then that person can set Outlook Express to file all messages to or from them in that folder.

To create a message rule, click on the **Tools|Message Rules|Mail** pulldown menu from the Menu Bar. In the lowermost box, title the rule **Diamond**, and check the box next to **Where the Subject line contains specific words**. This will cause this text to appear in the third box, with the words **contains specific words** underlined in blue. Click on this underlined text, and another dialog box will appear. Type **Diamond** in this box (see Figure 5–21).

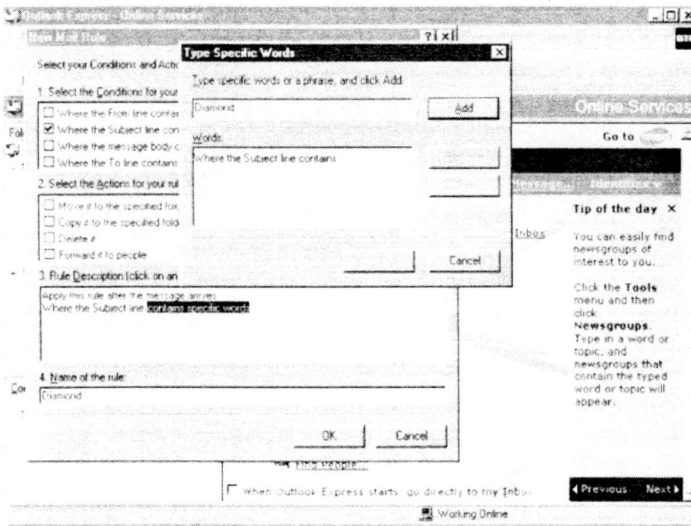

Figure 5–21   Creating a Message Rule

In the **Type Specific Words** dialog box, click on the **Add** button, and then look at the second box in the **New Mail Rule** dialog box labeled **Select the Actions for your rule.** Click the box next to **Move it to the specified folder.** This text will appear in the **Rule Description** box with the word **specified** underlined. Click on this word and then on the **Diamond** folder that appears in the diagram. If the **Diamond** folder has not been created, click on the folder that is to be its parent, then on the **New Folder** button. Click on **OK** button until the **Message Rules** box appears with **Diamond** listed and checked. Clicking the button labeled **Apply Now** tells the program to search for all messages meeting that criterion and move them as directed.

Message rules can be used to move, copy, delete, forward, or highlight messages or even to trigger the processing or the cessation of other rules. Message rules are invaluable for someone who receives many messages or is trying to manage multiple projects at one time.

Having seen how to set up and use Outlook Express, the next step is to create and send electronic mail.

ELECTRONIC MAIL

E-mail, short for electronic mail, is probably the most useful and widely used function of the online world. Some sources estimate that 15 billion e-mail messages are sent each year.[1] Before e-mail, communication was, for the most part, limited to synchronous methods.

Of course, it has always been possible to send a letter through the postal service or "snail mail," but there is a fair amount of time, trouble, and expense associated with this, not to mention the delay in getting the message into the mail system, waiting for it to be delivered, and standing by for a response. This has been the traditional method of communicating asynchronously, but it is not nearly as efficient as e-mail.

E-mail works more efficiently than snail mail or synchronous communications for a number of reasons:

♦ It is almost instantaneous. In most cases, an e-mail message is available to the addressee within seconds or minutes of its transmission.

---

[1] Internet.com Corporation. Webopedia, 2001. <http://webopedia.internet.com/TERM/e/e_mail.html> July 31, 2000.

- The composer can be as verbose as he or she pleases; the cost of sending a long e-mail message is usually the same as the cost of a short one.[2]
- E-mail software permits the sender to enter the addressee's name in the address blank and then takes care of the full addressing process automatically.
- Multiple recipients can be sent the same message at the same time by simply including more than one address in the To: blank or using a distribution list.
- In some cases, the message can be set for delayed delivery and will be sent at a future time of the sender's choosing with no further intervention.
- Messages can carry file attachments of anything in electronic format, as well as embedded links to sites on the World Wide Web.
- Messages can be filed for future use or discarded much more efficiently than is the case with paper-based communications.
- Replying to the sender of an e-mail message requires even less effort than sending the initial message.

E-mail can also be misused, and this is frequently the case. Unwanted e-mail is referred to as **spam,** which is the name of a canned meat product. The word was used repeatedly in a song by British comedy troupe Monty Python's Flying Circus, and the song gave rise to the new usage, indicating anything that is repeated annoyingly and needlessly. Recently there have been lawsuits against **spammers,** people who collect e-mail addresses from every source they can and then send advertisements and other unwanted information to those addresses.

E-mail can also be used as evidence in civil and criminal proceedings. Both the Reagan and Clinton White Houses, Microsoft, and many other corporations have been the recipients of subpoenas for archived e-mail files that demonstrated that witnesses had been less than forthcoming in their sworn testimony. Some of these resulted in costly verdicts and criminal convictions.

E-Mail Addresses

E-mail addresses have three parts: the user name, the *at* symbol ("@"), and the domain name. In the example anyuser@isp.com, anyuser is the user name,

---

[2] Some users, especially those in less-developed countries, get their e-mail through carefully metered and expensive connections. For these users, long messages and large file attachments are an expensive and often unwelcome proposition.

followed by the @ to separate it from the domain name, which is isp.com. That domain name is actually in two parts. The last part, which includes only the characters to the right of the period or dot farthest to the right in the address, refers to the **top-level domain.** As shown in the following chart, top-level domains indicate the type of organization that owns or sponsors the domain, or at least what country it is registered in.

Top-Level Domain	Organization
.com	Commercial businesses
.edu	Universities and colleges
.gov	Units of the federal government
.mil	Military organizations
.net	Network organizations
.org	Nonprofit organizations
.us, .jp, .de, .uk	Domains registered in specific countries e.g. the United States, Japan, Germany (Deutschland) and the United Kingdom, in that order

Registration of domain names has become such a fast and furious enterprise that any verification of the actual status of the registrant has been nearly abandoned in favor of expedience. This allows just about anyone to be able to register any domain name, although there are still some restrictions. Most private citizens would find it difficult to register a domain with the top-level suffix of .gov or .mil, but there are lots of .org domains that are owned by profit-making businesses, as well as .net domains that have nothing to do with networks. This is because people who register domains want something short and catchy that people can remember. Businesses try to get memorable phone numbers, like 555-1234 and 555-BEDS, for the same reason.

Domains can have subdomains that serve as branches to simplify addressing and allow common user names to coexist on the same server. For instance, say that a large company called MegaCorp has the domain megacorp.com registered and has hundreds of thousands of employees using e-mail under that domain. Employees' e-mail addresses at MegaCorp consist of the user's first and last names separated by a period, e.g. John.Doe@megacorp.com. For someone named Aloysius Thunderbutt, the user name is exclusive; however, people with more common names, such as Mary Jones and John Smith, will be competing for the same user name. MegaCorp can avoid this problem by creating sub-domains for various units, such as operations.megacorp.com and accounting.megacorp.com. This would allow two Mary Smiths to have the same user name, so long as they were working in different divisions, e.g. Mary.Smith@accounting.megacorp.com and Mary.Smith@operations.megacorp.com.

It is important to know that the sponsor or owner of a domain is represented only by the portion of the address immediately preceding the top-level domain name (the .com, .edu, .net, et al.). Anything in front of that is a subdivision set up by the domain owner. In the previous examples, MegaCorp owns the domain and has divisions and subdomains for accounting and operations personnel. They can have as many subdomains as they can devise terms for. This is also a way of making a very small business look large. MegaCorp might consist of people working out of a basement, but they can create all sorts of user names and make themselves look large, even though all of the mail sent to those accounts goes to the same single mailbox.

E-mail addresses cannot contain spaces or certain characters that are reserved for special functions in computer commands and file names. The following chart lists characters that are forbidden in e-mail addresses.

Forbidden Characters	
forward slash (/)	question mark (?)
backslash (\)	quotation mark (")
greater than sign (>)	pipe symbol (l)
less than sign (<)	colon (:)
asterisk (*)	semicolon (;)

This is why the e-mail addresses that people use are usually something other than their names with their traditional punctuation. John Doe cannot have the e-mail address John Doe@isp.com because the user name has a space in it, which is not allowed. However, he can have John_Doe@isp.com, John-Doe@isp.com, John.Doe@isp.com, or JohnDoe@isp.com, so long as those user names are not already taken. Incidentally, e-mail addresses are not **case sensitive**, meaning that it does not matter whether the letters are in upper or lower case.

E-mail addresses with underscores in them are often interpreted as spaces, because some software automatically underlines an e-mail address or web address (called a **URL** or **Uniform Resoruce Location**), so that the user can click on it and have the program open a blank e-mail message, pre-addressed to that address, or go to that web site without retyping the URL. Thus John_Doe@isp.com can look like there is no underscore character there when there really is. If there is an e-mail address that appears to have a space in it, the space is probably an underscore character.

There can be a John Doe at every domain that hosts an e-mail server, but only one. Typically when someone registers a user name on an e-mail host, that name is forever taken out of circulation, even if the user cancels the account shortly after registration. This is to prevent a subsequent user with the same user name from receiving messages and other possibly objectionable materials that were intended for the original registrant. Very large e-mail hosts, like America Online, have distributed millions of disks inviting new users to try out their service for a month, and people who cancelled them as soon as the first bill was due registered many of those accounts. As a result, most of the simple user names are taken on AOL. This explains why most AOL addresses are either nonsense words or words with numbers following them, like JohnDoe123@aol.com.

How E-Mail Works

Assuming that one has an e-mail account to send a message from, creating a message is not much more complicated than addressing it properly, entering the text that makes up the body of the message, and sending it. The technology that allows this to work is very complex, but the user interface has been simplified to make it easy.

If the computer on which the message is composed does not have a continuous connection to the Internet, and the connection is not "live" when the message is sent, (when the Send key or button is clicked), then the message will more than likely be stored in a message **queue** (pronounced "kyoo"). A queue is a line of messages awaiting further action. They cannot be sent to their destinations until there is a conduit for them to travel, in this case an Internet connection. While the messages are in queue, they can be deleted or modified, but once they have been sent, they cannot be retrieved.

When the computer holding the messages is connected to the Internet, usually by a dial-up connection to an ISP, and the e-mail program is started, the program will attempt to establish a connection with the mail server that is registered with the e-mail software or client. The client will connect to that server, log into the server with the user name and password associated with that account, and check for messages waiting on the server. Those messages will be downloaded to the client. The client will then send messages waiting in queue to the server, which will send them to the servers hosting the accounts where they are addressed. Depending on the e-mail client, this process may be reversed, i.e. the outgoing mail may get sent first, then incoming mail is processed.

If more than one e-mail account is registered on the client, the client will then go to the next server or account in line and repeat the process. Some e-mail clients will handle only one account at a time, and others will check as many accounts as the user cares to register there.

Sometimes a message is sent to a server, and the server does not find an account corresponding to the user name in the message. Also the server itself may be down (not working) for any number of reasons. Either one of these problems will cause the message to bounce. Determining whether the address is incorrect or the server is temporarily down is usually a matter of resending the message after a few hours to a few days to see if it bounces again. Repeated bounces generally indicate that something is wrong with the address, not with the server.

To use the metaphor of a typical postal service, creating the e-mail message is like typing a letter, addressing it, and putting it in the out basket. It will not go anywhere until someone takes it to the post office and puts it in the slot (similar to connecting to the mail server and sending it). If the address on the envelope is incorrect, the message will be returned to the sender (similar to a bounced e-mail).

The author has had repeated episodes with students who insisted that they had sent their assignments to him via e-mail in a timely manner; however, he had not received them. More often than not, as soon as they would boot up their computers and activate their e-mail programs, the message containing the assignment was found waiting in queue on the student's machine. The student had composed the message but had never connected with the mail server and sent it on its way.

In order to receive e-mail, one must first have access to an e-mail account. Most people get their e-mail accounts through their employers or from their ISPs. There are also web-based e-mail accounts that can be accessed from any computer with web access. This means that e-mail can be checked from a terminal at a public library, at work (assuming that such activity is permitted), on a friend's computer, or at an Internet café.

There are many providers that offer e-mail accounts for free, although these do not provide a method of connecting to the Internet to access it. Free e-mail accounts generally fall into two categories. Web-based e-mail accounts allow users to read their mail from a web site (and only from a web site) that the provider sponsors. The other free e-mail method forwards any message sent to that account to another e-mail account that is specified when the user signs up. Of course, this requires the user to have one regular e-mail account. Forwarding services require users to have an established e-mail account, but web-based e-mail accounts do not.

Web-Based E-Mail Accounts

Hotmail, possibly the largest web-based e-mail provider, is owned by Microsoft. Hotmail is more versatile than some other web-based e-mail providers, because Outlook Express (the e-mail client that will be used as an example in this book) can also access a Hotmail account like a POP3 account. In order to establish a Hotmail account, the new user uses a web browser to go to http://www.hotmail. com (or uses the Hotmail New Account Wizard in Outlook Express) and follows the procedure detailed onscreen to set up the new account. The new user will have to choose a user name not already registered and a password. The setup procedure takes just a few minutes. Once the account is established, the new user can send and receive mail at the new Hotmail address, which will be something like username@hotmail.com.

To use the account, the user goes to the Hotmail web page, enters the user name and password, and is presented with a listing of messages that have been sent to the account. Clicking on a message header will open the message for reading. The user can click on an on-screen icon to reply and will be given a blank message form with the address already entered or can create a new message to be sent to anyone.

With a web-based e-mail account, there is no e-mail client on the user's computer. All of the software except the web browser, which is necessary to view a web page, resides on the **web server** that also handles the mail. Because the user cannot compose or read messages without being connected to the Internet, messages do not wait in queue to be sent, thus they cannot be recalled or deleted if sent in error.

Web-based e-mail accounts can, depending on the provider of the service, be used to access regular e-mail accounts, also called POP3 or POPMail accounts. Using this method is useful for those who are away from their usual computers and are able to use another computer with web access.

Web-based e-mail accounts usually provide a rudimentary filing system where the user can create virtual folders in which to file messages. The messages are still held on the web server, but they are visible only when the user opens that folder. The user can also set up address books, which are listings of correspondents and their e-mail addresses. As with a software-based e-mail client, using an address book means that a message can be sent to anyone in the address book by just entering his or her name, instead of having to look up his or her e-mail address. The software finds the e-mail address and inserts it automatically.

Web-based e-mail accounts are notorious for attracting spam or unsolicited junk mail. Spammers collect e-mail addresses from every source imaginable and also send blind messages to addresses that they think might exist. For instance, if the user name Rambo is already taken, then reasonable alternatives might be Rambo1, Rambo2, and so on. The spammers will set up programs to create as many of these addresses as they think might produce any results and send mail to all of them. Most of the messages will go to nonexistent mailboxes, but the spammer does not care because it did not cost any more to send those thousands of messages than it cost to send one. Many spam messages contain sexually oriented subject matter, and for that reason, it is unwise to set up a free web-based account for a young person or to access the account from an employer-provider workstation.

Web-based accounts have also gained a reputation for their lack of security. Not too long ago, a security flaw was discovered on the Hotmail server that left users' passwords accessible to anyone who knew how to read them. No serious breaches were reported, but it is also possible that many users were unaware that their accounts had been accessed.

Web-based e-mail users who access their accounts from shared terminals are at risk for another reason. Most web browsers store recently viewed pages in a **cache folder** of memory reserved for this purpose. This is to speed reloading of the pages if the user returns to them, so that the page does not have to be retrieved from the web server. If the user fails to empty the cache after a web surfing session, the next user may be able to peruse it and see what the previous user was looking at, and even see their passwords. Once someone has another person's username and password, he or she can use the account just like the primary user, read his or her messages, and send mail that will appear to have come from that person. This problem can be remedied by emptying the browser cache after a web session. Instructions on how to do this are included in the chapter on the World Wide Web.

POP3 E-Mail Accounts

The other type of e-mail account is called a POP3 account, also called POPMail. POP3 stands for Post Office Protocol, and is a format for handling e-mail messages that are stored on a server before being downloaded to local machine. The difference between a web-based e-mail account and one based on POP3 has to do with the type of e-mail client and where messages reside. With a web-based account, no software other than the web browser is necessary to use the account. Also, messages are never stored on the user's machine. When using a POP3 account, the user has to have some type of e-mail client, such as Eudora or Outlook Express, loaded on the machine he or she is using to access the e-mail account.

E-mail sent to a POP3 account is stored on a mail server, a remote computer run by the company that handles the e-mail account, which connects to the user via the Internet or a telephone line. When the user connects to the mail server and verifies his or her identity via the user name and password, the mail server transfers any waiting messages to the user's computer. The server then deletes those messages from the user's mailbox, but this option can be changed to provide for messages to be stored on the server indefinitely. At more or less the same time, the e-mail client sends any outgoing messages to the server to be sent on the way to their designated addressees. Outbox messages are stored on the user's machine until they are transmitted to the server, and then a copy is preserved in a folder called **Sent Items** or something similar. The options regarding what is saved and stored and where it is saved and stored can be configured to the preference of the user.

The user can then log off of the server, disconnect from the Internet, and work offline. This is a useful function if the connection to the Internet cannot be maintained at all times, such as while traveling or using a computer in a car. Messages can be downloaded to the user's machine and then read, answered, and filed at a time convenient to the user.

Most users have POP3, as opposed to web-based, accounts. For those who are not sure which type they have, it is almost certainly a POP3 account. The larger the organization sponsoring the account, the more likely it is that they have an in-house mail server, as opposed to using a third-party provider, such as an ISP. The largest ISPs, like CompuServe, America Online, Earthlink, and

Mindspring, all have their own POP3 servers, and the e-mail accounts that most of their users have are POP3 accounts. However, most of these services also have an option to retrieve e-mail via a web-based interface, which is convenient when their users are traveling or otherwise away from their home machines.

E-Mail Aliases

It is possible and easy to have many e-mail addresses and only a single e-mail account. Creating an e-mail alias does this. Many commercial enterprises will offer their customers an e-mail alias through their registered domain. They do this because each e-mail sent under the alias gets their domain name noticed by someone new and because it does not really cost them anything. Messages sent to an e-mail alias are simply forwarded to whatever mailbox has been registered under the alias. If a user goes to MegaCorp and registers an e-mail alias, say, user@MegaCorp.com to be associated with his regular e-mail account JohnDoe@isp.com, then mail sent to user@MegaCorp.com gets sent on immediately to JohnDoe@isp.com and is stored on the server only momentarily. Most domain name hosts (the companies that actually own the servers that store the web pages, e-mail messages, and such) allow for an unlimited number of e-mail aliases to be associated with a domain, although the number of true POP3 mail accounts is usually limited. This is because the messages sent to a POP3 account *will* be stored on their server until retrieved, and those messages are going to take up space and server resources.

There are several reasons to have an e-mail alias. It may be useful to adopt an alter ego for some online activities. A number of sexual predator cases have been made by police officers using email aliases to accept invitations to meet from would-be child molesters. An online predator is not likely to respond to someone with the return e-mail address of JohnLaw@AnytownPD.org but might readily send an invitation to Julie15@isp.com, which will then go to John Law's e-mail account.

When using an e-mail alias for covert purposes, setup of the e-mail client is critical. Although one can reply to an e-mail message sent via an alias, the reply may carry the user's "parent" e-mail address in the message header, which will reveal the deception. There are ways to configure the e-mail client to keep this from happening, but it is important to send a few test messages first and have them analyzed by someone familiar with extracting information from message headers before starting an investigation that will depend on the user's anonymity.

E-Mail Clients

As stated previously, an e-mail client is the software or program that helps create, read, send, and otherwise manage e-mail. Commonly used e-mail clients include Microsoft Outlook and Outlook Express (these are two separate but related programs), Eudora, Pegasus Mail, and Netscape Messenger. The choice of email clients is a matter of individual preference. This book, however, uses Microsoft's Outlook Express as the example and standard to illustrate the techniques discussed.

Outlook Express is one of the only e-mail clients that will work with Hotmail, which is one of the most popular web-based free e-mail services. Most e-mail clients do not work with web-based e-mail at all. Rather than an e-mail client, web-based e-mail uses the web browser and the native software on the web site that provides the e-mail to navigate the account. However, since Microsoft owns both Outlook Express and Hotmail, they are compatible.

There is also a Microsoft product called Outlook, without the *Express*. Outlook is commercially packaged and sold in stores, rather than bundled with Microsoft Internet Explorer. It comes with all versions of the popular Microsoft Office package and is widely used in enterprise settings where corporate workgroups have access to one another's calendars, contact lists, and such for coordination purposes. Outlook is also a very powerful, multifaceted program that does much more than manage e-mail, and entire books are devoted to the various features of Outlook. Many of the methods described here will be similar to Outlook, but they will not be exactly the same, so be aware of which software is being used if trying to follow the instructions in this chapter closely.

Creating E-Mail Messages

After setting up Outlook Express, it is time to create an e-mail message. Some people like to test their e-mail by sending a message to themselves. If that test email comes through and looks okay, the account is ready to send messages to other people.

To create an e-mail message, click on the New Mail button at the top of the Outlook Express display (see Figure 6–1), or click on File|New|Mail Message from the Menu Bar. A blank message will appear with the return e-mail address already entered in the From blank. If the blank message form is minimized, it can be expanded to full size so that the menu options and buttons at the top of the window are visible.

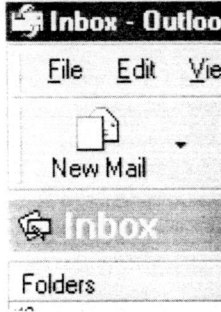

Figure 6-1   New Mail **Button**

To get Outlook Express to accept the message, the **To:** blank must contain a valid e-mail address or a name that is already entered in the address book. If the **Automatically complete e-mail addresses when composing** option was selected previously, typing just the first few characters of an e-mail address that is already in the address book will cause the rest of it to appear. If a name is entered rather than an e-mail address, Outlook Express will search the Address Book for a matching name. If the program finds no matching names, an error message will indicate that the name entered was not found in the Address Book when the computer tries to send the message.

A message can be sent to as many addressees as the ISP allows, which keeps subscribers from sending thousands of spam messages by separating each address with a comma or semicolon. The user can also send copies of messages to more than one correspondent by entering their names or e-mail addresses in the **Cc:** or **Bcc:** fields. **Cc:** stands for *courtesy copy*, or, formerly, *carbon copy*. It indicates to the primary addressee that a copy of the message has been sent to one or more other people and tells them who those people are. This feature is useful if two members of a committee need to keep others informed of their correspondence. **Bcc:** stands for *blind copy*. If the **Bcc:** field is not visible on the message form, click **View/All Headers** on the Menu Bar. The use of the **Bcc:** field prevents the recipients listed in the **To:** and **Cc:** fields from seeing the names of the people in the **Bcc:** field. They will not be aware that other copies were sent.

The subject line of the message should be descriptive of the message contents. Some e-mail users receive hundreds, possibly thousands, of e-mail messages each day. Using subject lines like "**VERY IMPORTANT!**" and "**Stuff**" tells them nothing about the contents. Keep in mind that they, too, may be using message rules, and their e-mail clients may be looking for specific descriptive words in the subject lines.

Clicking in the large space in the lower portion of the message blank will place the cursor in the message area, allowing the user to type a message. It is generally not necessary to begin e-mail messages with a salutation (e.g. "Dear Bob"), although there is not necessarily anything wrong with this, either. The composition of the message itself should follow the rules for a letter of the same nature. Correspondence with a friend allows informal small talk. However, if it is a business message, get to the point quickly.

Remember that e-mail is a very literal medium. A good-natured insult may be fine in a face-to-face conversation; the joke would be understood. In an e-mail message, it is far more likely that the "good-natured" part will not come through. One way to indicate that humor is intended is to follow the critical passage with a *G* in brackets, e.g. **<G>**. This signifies a grin and tips the reader that there is humor intended. Another method is to use a **smiley** or an **emoticon**, which is formed by keyboard characters. For instance, a colon and right parenthesis forms a smiling face, if viewed at a 90-degree angle, e.g. :-)

Signatures can be inserted if desired by clicking on Insert|Signature| Signature Name (meaning the name given to the desired signature block), and that text will be inserted. To routinely insert text into messages, such as a disclaimer or an address change, create a "signature" for this as well, and avoid some typing. A message can contain as many signatures as desired.

Once completed, click on the Send button at the top left of the message window. If spell check was set to run, it will begin. If spell check was not selected, there is the option to do this manually by clicking on the Spelling button at the top of the screen. When this is complete, the message will be moved to the Outbox folder. If the program is set to send messages immediately, it will be sent almost instantly. Otherwise, the message will be sent the next time that a connection is made to the mail server to send and receive messages. Any message can be changed, deleted, or otherwise modified as long as it is in the Outbox, but remember once it is gone, there is no retrieving it.

Sorting and Selecting Messages

E-mail messages accumulate very quickly, and it is very easy to lose track of them. When trying to organize messages for filing into another folder, or even for deletion, it is very tedious go through the list one at a time. The task can be simplified by using the various list sorting and file selection functions within Windows.

At the top of each list of files or messages in a folder, there are some header bars (see Figure 6–2) that note the type of information that falls underneath them. In Outlook Express, the default installation has these as an exclamation point, a paper clip, To, Subject, and Sent, plus some others that may be farther to the right of the display's width.

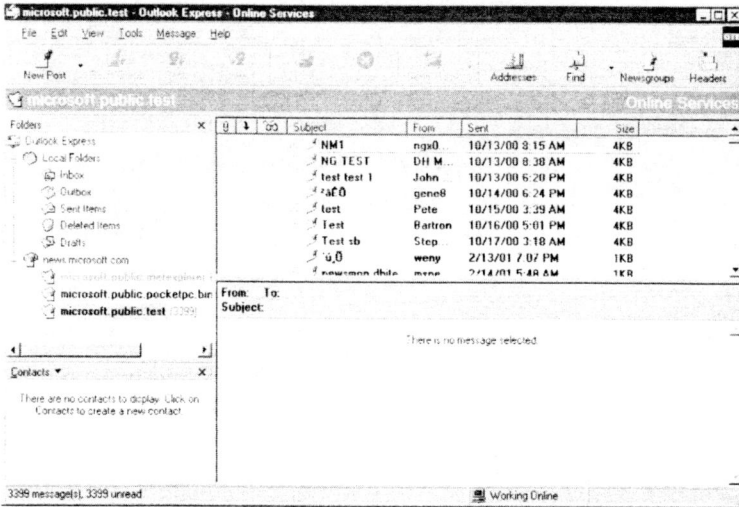

Figure 6-2   Header Bars

What is not readily apparent is that these bars can be used to sort messages. Clicking on one of the header bars will sort the message list on that field. For instance, clicking on the Sent portion of the bar will sort the list in the order that the messages will be sent; clicking again will reverse the order. No change is made to the message file or folder itself, only to the order that messages are displayed.

Multiple messages can be marked at the same time for movement to another folder, deletion, or other action. Clicking on a single message header selects that message. Clicking on another message will deselect the first one. To select both, however, hold down the Control key while clicking the second message; then the first one remains selected along with the second. As many messages as desired can be selected using this technique. In the same way, dragging one to another folder or pressing the Delete key will affect all of the marked messages.

To select a group of messages that happen to be adjacent to one another in a list, which can often be done by sorting them on a common field, such as From or Subject, click on the first or the last one in the list, then hold down the Shift key and click on the message at the opposite end of the list. Both messages and all others in between will be selected.

To select every message or file in the list, hold down the Control key and hit the A key. This is the keyboard shortcut for Select All and works in most Windows applications.

File Attachments

Any file on a computer can be attached to an e-mail message, and that file will be sent along with the message. This is a very useful medium for collaborating on a common project or sending examples of work to a colleague. It also has the potential for misuse and is possibly the easiest way to infect a computer with a virus.

Attaching a file to a message is an easy process. Compose a message: address it, insert a subject line, and type the message body. Then click on Insert|File Attachment from the Menu Bar, or click on the Attach icon, which looks like a paperclip in the Toolbar. (See Figure 6–3).

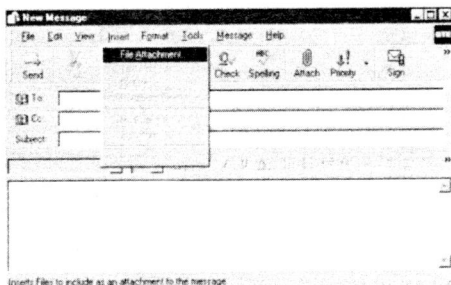

Figure 6-3   Attaching a File to an E-Mail Message

A dialog box will open up and the drive where the file is stored can be selected. Click on the file, then on the Attach button in the dialog box, and an icon for the selected file will appear in the Attach blank, which will not be visible until there are attachments to display. Repeat the process until all necessary files are showing in the Attach blank. Multiple files can be selected at one time using the Shift and Control keys in conjunction with the mouse button, just the same as multiple messages—see the section on Sorting and Selecting Messages.

File attachments can be fun to send along to friends, especially the ones with stunningly clever graphics, cartoons, animation, or sound files. E-mail novices are fond of creating messages to everyone in the Address Book, each bearing attachments with huge file sizes. However, this can quickly annoy many correspondents.

Many people have e-mail accounts furnished by their employers, accessed via a limited bandwidth telephone line or transmitted via a satellite downlink. When the resources necessary to retrieve e-mail are someone else's, limited, or very expensive, sending a big file attachment without asking first if the recipient wants it can create frustration for correspondents. Also, it is important to appreciate that humorous file attachments may not be appropriate for the environment in which the recipient is getting mail, e.g. school or work. Some people have web-based e-mail accounts and get their mail at a public library, where access to the Internet is often furnished for free but at the expense of privacy.

A correspondent will be able to open the file attachment only if the software needed to open that type of file is available. The file extension (the three letters following the period at the end of a file name, e.g. filename.ext) determines the type of application that will be needed. The best way to ensure that a correspondent is able to open a file is to either confirm in advance he or she has the same software and version used to create the file or to use files native to Windows applications.

File Extension	Type of File
.avi	a full-motion, audio-video file
.bat	batch file, a list of **DOS** commands that will run, one at a time, when the batch file is run
.bmp	bitmap graphics file, native to Windows
.cgm	computer graphics metafile, opens with most graphics programs
.com	a program file executable under DOS
.doc	Microsoft Word or Microsoft WordPad file; WordPad is a mini-word processor included with Windows
.exe	executable file, all types of application programs
.fon	font files, native to Windows
.gif	graphics interchange file, opens with most graphics programs and web browsers
.htm, .html	hypertext markup language, opens with most web browsers
.jpg, .jpeg, .jpe	joint photographic experts group file, graphics file, opens with most web browsers and graphics programs

File Extension	Type of File (continued)
.mdb	Microsoft Access database, requires MS Access to open
.mid	MIDI file, a kind of sound file that plays scripted music
.mov	QuickTime movie, a full-motion video and sound file that requires the QuickTime player or a compatible viewer to show
.mp3	audio files used primarily to store and play on a computer music originally recorded on music compact discs
.mpg	MPEG ("emm-peg") file, full motion video
.pcx	paintbrush file, a type of graphics file
.pdf	Adobe Acrobat portable document file, can only be opened with Adobe Acrobat
.png	portable network graphics (pronounced "ping"), a graphics file similar to *.gif
.ppt	Microsoft PowerPoint presentation file
.psd	Adobe Photoshop image, a type of graphics file
.ra, .rm	RealAudio and RealMedia files, sound and full-motion video/sound files viewable with the RealPlayer software
.tga	Targa image, a type of graphics file
.tif	tagged image format, a type of graphics file
.txt	text file, opens with Windows Notepad and most word processors
.wab	Windows Address Book, used by Outlook Express and other applications
.wav	sound file
.wmf	Windows meta file, a type of graphics file
.wpg	WordPerfect Graphics, a type of graphics file
.wri	a type of word processing document that can be created or read with Windows WordPad
.xls, .xlb	Microsoft Excel workbook or spreadsheet, requires Microsoft Excel to open
.zip	a compressed file that contains one or more other files

Before sending a correspondent a large file attachment, first ascertain that he or she really wants it. It is fine to send a document that has been requested; the correspondent will not be too surprised when it comes through attached to a reply message. However, before sending an unsolicited attachment, send a preliminary message explaining the nature of the file and confirm that the other person really wants it. The correspondent may request that the attachment be sent to another person or e-mail account, uploaded to a web site, or placed on a floppy disk and sent by conventional mail.

Some cautious e-mail users will immediately delete any message containing an unexpected file attachment, as well as an attachment from someone that they do not know. This is to avoid infecting their computers with a computer virus or damaging program, and their wariness is well founded. A number of devastating computer viruses have been disseminated through e-mail attachments, some of which have appeared benign. In the early days of computer viruses, the only files that one had to fear might contain a virus were the executable variety, those that had file extensions of *.com and *.exe. More recently, malicious computer code has been hidden in document files and even in long file names. These viruses have resulted in entire networks being disabled and millions or billions of dollars in lost productivity.

Every person who uses a computer, and especially anyone who uses the Internet, should have an autoloading antivirus program as standard equipment on his or her machine. The virus definition files should be updated at least once a month. Some of the more recent antivirus programs will remind the user at preset intervals to check for new virus signature updates and then will auto-install them. Antivirus software should be set to automatically check for malicious code in any file that is sent or received by e-mail. Most do this automatically, but the user should check and make sure.

If there are a number of files to send to a correspondent or the cumulative size of the files is large, it is possible to compress or zip them into a single file with the extension of *.**zip**. The most common software used to accomplish this is WinZip, which is available at a number of shareware download sites. A zipped file consists of one or more uncompressed files that the compression software shrinks to a smaller size. Some file types compress better than others. Document and text files tend to compress substantially, while graphics and sound files shrink very little. Even when there is not much file space saved by compressing files, a zipped file can be easier to handle than a long list of uncompressed files that would need to be sent separately. The WinZip software can also create a selfextracting executable file (one with an *.exe file extension), so that it can be decompressed by someone that does not have the WinZip software loaded on his or her computer and can incorporate a password, keeping anyone without the password from unzipping the file.

When adding files or typing a message, keep in mind that some organizations monitor the e-mail that users on their networks send and receive. Some programs scan all e-mail for sensitive words, including profanity, sexually oriented terms, and words that might tip the employer to unauthorized activities, such as "résumé," "interview," and "salary." Even personal accounts may be seen by family members of the recipient. Use discretion in determining what kind of information, humor, or file attachments are sent to someone's e-mail account. The attachments could cause unexpected problems for them or for the sender.

Reading and Replying to E-Mail

When Outlook Express receives e-mail, the name of the folder containing the unread messages will appear in boldface, with the number of unopened messages in parentheses next to the folder name and icon. The contents of that folder are displayed by clicking on the folder icon and the header lines, which show the name of the sender, subject, as well as date and time received, will also appear in boldface unless some other display option has been set. Clicking once on any message header line will select the message and display the contents of the message in the lower pane of the Outlook Express window. Double-clicking on the message header will open the message in its own window.

Messages with attached files will have a small paper clip icon to the left of the message header in that display window. If the sender of the message marked it as having a different priority than usual, the message may display in a different color or have either an exclamation point or a downward-pointing arrow icon next to it. Messages in any list can be re-sorted by clicking on the control bars at the top of each display column. For instance, clicking on the "attachment" control bar, which has a paper clip as its icon, will sort the messages so that those with file attachments will appear first or last, the order reversing with each click. If no special sorting is done, messages will appear in the order that they were received.

If the message is to be read only and not filed, deleted, forwarded, etc., clicking on the **Next** icon will move to the next message. Individual messages can also be selected in any order by clicking on the message header. To flag a message for special attention later, click on **Message|Flag Message** in the Menu Bar while that message is selected. A tiny red flag will appear in the message list. The messages can be sorted so that the flagged messages appear at the top of the list. The flag can be removed by repeating this process.

To forward the message to someone else, click on the **Forward** icon in the Toolbar. A new message window will open, displaying the message being forwarded. It is usually a good idea to insert text telling the recipient the reason for the correspondence before the original message begins. Insert a name from the Address Book or an e-mail address in the **To**: blank, and then click on the **Send** button.

Probably because it is so easy to forward messages to others, chain letter e-mail messages are extremely popular—and extremely annoying. Most of these messages describe some urban myth or promise that horrible misfortune will befall anyone who neglects to forward the message to their fifty closest and dearest friends. Very few people have any authentic interest in receiving these messages. Moreover, many e-mail clients send forwarded messages as a file attachment, which means that a new file attachment will be created for each forwarding cycle, each containing all of the file attachments that preceded it. Most people find it very annoying to open file attachment after file attachment, only to find that the root of this process is a "friendship ribbon" or a pyramid marketing scheme. Give careful consideration before forwarding any message. If the message contains information that was given in confidence or is not important to the correspondent, it is probably best to send an inquiry to the correspondent first, asking if they want to receive the message.

To reply to the message, then click on the **Reply** or **Reply All** icon. If the message has only one recipient, then both of these icons have the same effect. However, if the original message had multiple addressees (including addressees in the **Cc**: portion), then the reply will be automatically addressed to all of the recipients if **Reply All** is selected.

If the **Send** options have **Include message in reply** set as described previously, the reply will have the original message copied into it, with each line prefaced with an arrow bracket character. The arrow bracket allows the recipient to see which portion of the message is reply and which was from the original message. When this feature is used intelligently, it enhances communication between correspondents. For example, the following original message contains several questions.

How far along are you with this project? When do you think you might be able to meet to discuss our next step? Are there any supplies that you need and have not been able to procure?

When this message is replied to, the reply will start out looking like this.

>How far along are you with this project? When do you think you
>might be able to meet to discuss our next step? Are there
>any supplies that you need and haven't been able to procure?

These questions could be answered in one long narrative, but the answer might be more meaningful if the replies were interspersed with the bracketed text, like so.

> How far along are you with this project?
I think I'm about 40% complete. I'll know more when I hear
back from the other members of my committee.
> When do you think you might be able to meet to discuss our
> next step?
Next Wednesday, the 24th, would be good for me. Unless you
have a conflict, I can come to your office at 1000.
> Are there any supplies that you need and haven't been able to
> procure?
No, I've been able to get everything I need so far, but I may
need to discuss some budget amendments with you for the rest
of this.

Moving around some of the arrow brackets may be necessary, which makes the message and reply much easier to follow.

As the chain of messages and replies propagates, each succeeding message will have a new set of arrow brackets appended to it, so that some lines will look something like this.

> > > > Are there any supplies that you need and haven't been
> > > > able to procure?

Further, the text of the messages at the start of the sequence will append themselves to each succeeding message if they are not deleted, so that messages can become very long, even though the correspondents may not be reading any more than the first few lines at the top. Sending this redundant text wastes bandwidth and results in a lot of wasted paper if someone needs to print a message and does not realize that it goes on for several pages with old content. When replying to messages, it is courteous to delete any extraneous text that may have been copied from the previous message, including any message header or preface that may precede the body of the message, if it is not needed in the reply.

File Attachments in Received Messages

When Outlook Express receives a message with a file attachment, the file attachment is saved in one of Outlook Express' many message folders, most of which are buried deep in the Windows directory structure. It is often tempting to immediately open a file attachment and peruse it, but this is often unwise. Later on the file may be hard to find. If the message that carried the file was moved, it is quite probable that the attachment will be lost entirely.

The best way to resolve this dilemma is to save file attachments to a folder where they can be found later and *then* open them once they have been stored away safely. Where they are saved is not especially important, as long as there is some pattern. It is usually best to save all attached files in a folder under the My Documents structure, since that is the default folder that most Windows applications save to and retrieve from. It might even be reasonable to create a folder called Mail Attachments or something similar for this purpose. Once the file is saved to a folder, it can always be moved later.

To save a file attachment, click on the large paper clip icon in the upper right of the preview message pane (the lower portion of the window where the contents of the selected message appears). As shown in Figure 6–4, two choices will appear: Save attachment and the name of the file itself. Clicking on the file name will open the file directly, but the file will still reside in that deeply buried message folder. Clicking on the Save attachment option will bring up a dialog box asking where the file should be saved (and defaulting to the My Documents folder). Once it is saved, then open it.

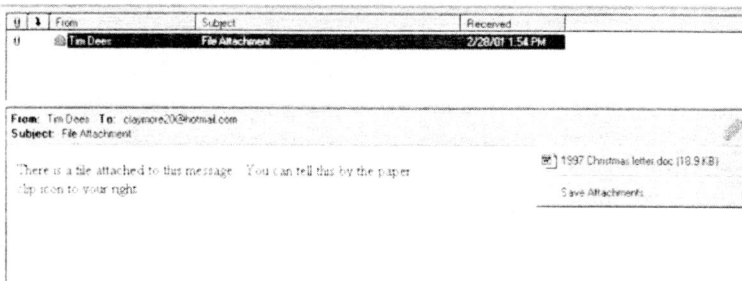

Figure 6-4 Saving File Attachments

Users should *not* open unexpected file attachments or a file attachment from someone he or she does not know and trust. One of the most destructive viruses worked by e-mailing copies of itself to the first fifty people listed in the recipient's address book as soon as the file attachment was opened. Each of those recipients in turn had the virus replicate itself another fifty times by use of their address books, and so on. This crippled e-mail systems around the world by clogging them with traffic and cost millions in lost time. The problem is that the message was passed between people who knew and trusted each other because those people were already in their address books. If in doubt, send an e-mail to the sender of a suspicious message before opening the attachment and ask what it is and why it was sent. When in doubt, just delete it entirely. The correspondent can always resend it.

Encrypting E-Mail Messages

E-mail is a reasonably secure medium, but it is not intrusion-proof. When mail travels from a computer to its ultimate destination, it will probably pass through a number of other computers in between, any one of which can capture the file as it goes past, saving it for later inspection. There will be no way to determine if this occurred, other than learning from someone by word or deed that they did it. E-mail that is received through a network, such as that used in a workplace or educational institution, may be inspected by the network administrators, and many employers routinely monitor the e-mail activities of their employees to prevent unauthorized use of their computer resources. Messages sent from a private e-mail account, such as a Hotmail account that is accessed via an employer's computer or network, can still be monitored once they reach the employer's network server.

The best way to prevent others from intercepting private e-mail messages is to restrict personal activities to a private e-mail account that is not company owned and controlled and is accessible from the home. Even with this method, it is possible that someone could intercept a personal e-mail message or read it from a home computer if he or she gains access to it. For better security, it is possible to encrypt e-mail messages.

File encryption involves scrambling the contents of computer files in an ordered manner, so that they can be descrambled when the appropriate key is applied. This is a highly secure but not totally foolproof method of securing data on a computer. It is not completely foolproof because encryption, like any other security method, can be defeated if the cracker has enough time, knowledge, and determination.

There is nothing new about encryption or coding; this method has been used for a few thousand years. According to Fred Cohen,[3] the Egyptians of 1900 B.C. were the first to use encryption. Even so, the level of sophistication of encryption has taken a quantum leap with the assistance of computers. The

---

[3] Fred Cohen and Associates. *Introductory Information Protection*, n.d. <http://www.all.net/books/ip> (July 10, 2000).

simplest encryption keys are merely substitution schemes, like the old cereal-box Captain Midnight decoder rings used. The letter *a* might be substituted for *b*, *b* for *c*, and so on. Looking for patterns in the encrypted message can often defeat these, and puzzle fans do this regularly for amusement. Computers use encryption keys that vary in complexity by their length, more commonly characterized by the number of bits that they use. A one-bit encryption key would have only two possible combinations: 1 and 0. This would be represented by 2^1 or just 2. A two-bit key would have four combinations: 00, 01, 10, and 11. This number of keys is represented by 2^2, or 4. The number of possible keys is the number 2 raised to the power of the bit length.

When the bit length exponent starts to get into double and triple digits, the number of possible keys is very difficult to crack by the "brute force" method. Had 32- and 128-bit keys been available to Germany in World War II, the Allies would probably not have broken the "Enigma" code that allowed them to read much of Hitler's mail. To be more precise, these keys were available, but they required so much math horsepower that encrypting even one message with them would have required the services of several hundred technicians for a thousand years or so.

In 1973 the National Institute of Standards and Technology adopted 56-bit encryption as sufficiently robust to protect any unclassified U.S. Government documents, and it is still widely used in private industry. A 56-bit key has 72057594037927936 (2^{56}, or about 72 quadrillion) possible combinations, but today it is considered crackable, given enough time and effort. In fact, in the summer of 1998, the Electronic Frontiers Foundation (EFF) won a $10,000 reward from the software firm RSA Data Security for cracking a short message that had been encrypted with a 56-bit key. EFF used a custom-made computer that employed an array of processors capable of trying 2.5 million keys each second. This level of effort is not especially common, but it revealed how vulnerable protected data could be to anyone with the determination to defeat it. More advanced encryption methods use 128- and 256-bit keys. A 128-bit key would tie up the EFF's code-cracker for about 166 quintillion years, trying all of the possible combinations, but advances in computing processing power will eventually bring even that down to a manageable figure.

Using longer keys involves a tradeoff in convenience. If a file is encrypted with a very long key, then it will take that much longer to decrypt it, even when the correct key is known. Long keys are also subject to theft, as they are so long that few users are going to want to commit them to memory. Instead, they will be stored on a disk file someplace, possibly kept on the person of the owner, to be copied onto the computer at the appropriate time. Keys generated by programs such as PGP are of this size and type.

PGP stands for **Pretty Good Privacy** and was designed by a programmer named Phil Zimmerman. Zimmerman is not opposed to law enforcement. He just believes that people should have the right to keep private whatever they deem worthy of being kept private, laws, court orders, and other authoritarian issues notwithstanding. PGP is most often used to encrypt e-mail messages using its public key cryptography method. With public key cryptography, the software generates two keys for each person or entity that wishes to encrypt. There is a public key, which is posted in a common area where anyone can retrieve it, and a private key, kept secret and held only by the owner. If someone wishes to send an e-mail encrypted with PGP, he or she would go to the PGP key server from within the PGP program and retrieve public key of the recipient. The sender then uses the public key to encrypt the message and sends it to the recipient. Upon receipt, the private key is used to decrypt the message. PGP also offers a method of electronically signing messages so that the true senders can be verified.

PGP is available for free to individual users, and the installation process places additional menu items into Outlook Express so that messages can be encrypted, decrypted, or digitally signed with the appropriate key. Many PGP users create signature blocks that include their public keys, which can be quite long. For instance, a public key that the author generated as an example for an article looks like this:

```
------BEGIN PGP PUBLIC KEY BLOCK------
Version: PGPfreeware 6.5.3 for non-commercial use
<http://www.pgp.com>

mQGiBDkrcl0RBADP4/uIyHOidW2ou5j1o2TSWqKJXxVod4rcmsyG
69utd7fm0eR45Tzzjan+Hbus/dlojgJZP23/4c2L6Zr601igWGTeEhOVp
XQ3s4IsMF5J0S0nOkkrIZL1kpIWSvt4LU7nnSXcEQdvJ/ip5GrmLGY
aSM7cKUb5J++zEsBnGMYz/wCg//zj7+qQ6962LLeZ+0073gaqIscD/i
MQtXTL4YsV8Kovfx1beVTP+sZjWzEoWDqXN0ggVg9QHRbrDyfO7
O3gIQkruW/gSTTMGwzCH61eZTOIWMXFPttEg06poFUEV5oWnJI
QrrdJhcS8mI/OabOGMFEj/u9uaTZMq9yGwz5+BVr+aA0IN5YkA8rx
BIEFloLDL3TvYLQkA/4pOM3Sxxaogj51B2HzLeIO2GZOtGmhYg30q
6SHO3M2VMSymTq19cpRcfRN0+rt6yol3gG+3FYHIi48fKL2xVGhp6
ZGKMyL3spaNIoFcN59XDTHh+SyD3scBiMdzuRu3IZWGcqVKhev
HxAxNYozhHMOT+GAttlIDYyhnA9ltZQ6I7QeVGltIERIZXMgPGRIZX
NAY29tcHVzZXXJ2ZS5jb20+iQBOBBARAgAOBQI5K3JdBAsDAgEC
```

GQEACgkQLQ/yoB/cEuNntgCbBRBLYMblaBTflEl+e6iqzTo+f9YAn2
J4Sh5WyKJVGTnjLrAM6doFlF5auQINBDkrclOQCAD2Qle3CH8IF3K
iutapQvMF6PlTETIPtvFuuUs4INoBp1ajFOmPQFXz0AfGy0OplK33TG
SGSfgMg71I6RfUodNQ+PVZX9x2Uk89PY3bzpnhV5JZzf24rnRPxfx2
vIPFRzBhznzJZv8V+bv9kV7HAarTW56NoKVyOtQa8L9GAFgr5fSl/V
hOSdvNILSd5JEHNmszbDgNRROPflizHHxbLY7288kjwEPwpVsYjY6
7VYy4XTjTNP18F1dDox0YbN4zlSy1Kv884bEpQBgRjXyEpwpy1obE
AxnIByl6ypUM2Zafq9AKUJsCRtMlPWakXUGfnHy9iUsiGSa6q6Je
w1XpMgs7AAICCADJU0KuiAvcANdXx+yVPOu1Z1unuhJJHWe/9Q
16gnAGOHe+Z9rOp8oo8S/wskpw+90qlcNc5QCHNlzb2e7wG77zsQ
6KcxWTISisNdrs8G3PFsOnGcQWSxj6a4H0VtEN6ZGTUHw6e6PpX
dX0B6nqn8tn6D5NU9GSMINN99r43sv+YfpPWBx3LAhXCF6ZyrzvG
mA1cxof6jDGwf3KZXpY9fsHJ60IfQVeonvgGx2Gty6CKZpMOK9ogd
7G/2rqUIeJb4TstAqv618cb8wZ3oDzXDNrerl9/Ao9xOXPYUfRzhoqc
BiTvtuWIUo+f3o2VUz57KKCAE6FdxPe+3KXMThJnrPEiQBGBBgR
AgAGBQI5K3JdAAoJEC0P8qAf3BLju3AAn0OeE4zfSuCwjcQ+djG9
kaT+1H+wAJ9FnwXVK7tcb5Bw6iJmrBVPEVryig===ORWW
——-END PGP PUBLIC KEY BLOCK——-[4]

Encrypting and decrypting messages is more of an automatic process than it used to be, but it is still more trouble than it is worth for most e-mail users. There are other encryption/decryption methods that involve purchasing digital certificates that are held by third-party companies and used to authenticate messages and files sent by private and business entities. This, however, is dependent on the integrity of the certificate holder/issuer and on the ability of all correspondents to use the technology.

---

[4] This public key and its associated private key are no longer valid.

Chapter

7

NEWSGROUPS

Electronic mail drove the Internet, and the World Wide Web helped make it popular, but many online junkies live for the traffic contained in newsgroups, known otherwise as **Usenet**.

Usenet arose as a way for people working on similar projects to keep one another current on their mutual progress and ideas. The same thing could have been done by way of an electronic mailing list, but Usenet was more efficient. Usenet discussions consist of any number of newsgroups (there are tens of thousands of newsgroups), each theoretically devoted to a topic. Subscribers to the newsgroups post messages or **articles** (in this context, they are the same thing) under a subject line or header. Each article can be in response to another article already posted in that group of messages, or **message thread**, or can be the start of a new message thread and have its own subject name or header. A message thread might consist of only one article that no one else in the newsgroup felt like responding to, or it can go on for weeks or months.

The newsgroups of Usenet are organized into hierarchies. The names of the hierarchies are divided by periods or dots in the same way that IP addresses and URLs (uniform resource locators) are. The first part of the newsgroup name is its top-level name, indicating the largest division to which it belongs. Some common top-level newsgroup names are shown in the following chart.

114

Top-Level Name	Description
biz	the business world, including newsgroups to discuss particular companies, searching for employment, etc.
comp	computer and engineering topics
misc	miscellaneous groups
rec	hobbies and other nonbusiness pursuits
soc	lifestyle discussions, social life, etc.
alt	alternative lifestyles, discussions, and other groups that defy description

Below these top-level newsgroup domains are subgroups that define the hierarchy. For instance within the alt. domain, there is a group for discussion of food, called rec.food.

Under this subheading are discussions of beverages called rec.food.drink, and within this hierarchy are discussions of specific beverages, as follows: rec.food.drink.coffee; rec.food.drink.tea; and rec.food.drink.beer.

This hierarchy can take any path that its users see fit to use. For instance, beneath the Microsoft top-level newsgroup domain are discussions of each of their software products and services, and beneath those, newsgroups devoted to discussions of particular functions or features of those products. The newsgroups are further subdivided by language, with separate newsgroups for German, Japanese, French, and English (both United Kingdom English and United States English) users.

This is by no means a complete list of top-level domains. Major corporations, especially those like Microsoft that are involved in the computer industry, have their own newsgroups and hierarchies for discussion of issues relating to their products and business. State and local governments may create their own top-level newsgroup domains. Usenet is more of a mechanism for posting these newsgroups than a thing, because the newsgroups are distributed over any number of **news servers**. Some news servers are public, granting access to anyone who wishes it, and others are by subscription only. The subscription servers require an approved user name and password to gain access and are usually restricted to those who pay a fee for their use or who have a business interest in the traffic on the news server. Most major ISPs maintain news servers for the use of their subscribers, who use the same user names and passwords to gain access that they use for e-mail and other access to the ISP's facilities.

Most people who subscribe to newsgroups use **newsreader** software to read and create messages. There are a number of newsreaders available, and which one that anyone uses is largely a matter of personal preference. Microsoft Outlook Express has a newsreader feature, and as was the case in the discussion of electronic mail, will be the software used in this chapter for examples.

There is a **freeware** newsgroup reader called Free Agent that can be found on most downloadable software sites, such as download.com and tucows.com (search for the words *free agent*). Free Agent is designed exclusively for news reading, and many users find it much preferable to Outlook Express. Configuration of this software will not be addressed here, but for someone who plans to spend a lot of time perusing newsgroups, it might be to advantageous to give Free Agent a try.

Newsgroups can also be accessed via the World Wide Web. This method is useful for people who do not have standard ISP accounts and gain access to the Internet through a terminal at a public library or Internet café. Most of the time, users without standard ISP access will use a public news server for Usenet access. Public news servers generally have access to most public newsgroups, either by carrying them on their own servers or by subscribing to a **newsfeed** from other news servers.

Accessing a newsgroup via the WWW is generally less convenient than through newsreader software, as each article or message has to be retrieved individually from the server. Depending on the speed of the Internet connection and the congestion of the net at that time, this can require several seconds, and the wait for each message to appear can quickly become tedious. The people who run the public news servers want their users to spend this time not in composing their replies to posted articles, but in reading the advertisements that appear on the web page that contain the messages. These advertisements pay the bills for the public news servers (as they do for many "free" services offered over the WWW), and it is in the best interests of the public news server that newsgroup messages are not brought up and displayed too quickly.

The Uses of Usenet

Just about every conceivable interest, legitimate and otherwise, is discussed in Usenet. Usenet can be valuable in law enforcement from operational, investigational, and intelligence-gathering perspectives.

Operationally, Usenet can be a great place to get advice on any number of topics, although the information maybe be difficult to find at first. When researching a vehicle problem, for example, a search of the newsgroups for the vehicle make will probably find a group devoted to its discussion. For information about a part of the world that is unfamiliar, there may be a newsgroup that focuses on that area, or if it is a popular destination, a travel-related newsgroup may be a good place to look. For high-tech problems, there are *lots* of newsgroups to choose from, as people who frequent Usenet are usually skilled with computers as well. Most major software and hardware products are likely to have one or more newsgroups filled with subscribers with a variety of problems, as well as a range of skills and abilities that can be helpful.

Usenet can also be valuable in pursuing investigations. The anonymity of Usenet encourages people to be candid, and even brazen, with their activities and information. There are newsgroups devoted to all varieties of illegal ventures. Some of these include discussions of various **warez**, or software that has been copied, for the most part unlawfully, and posted for download. For high-tech cases, these newsgroups can produce investigative leads to follow. Newsgroups such as **alt.drugs.hard** discuss the relative merits of "heroin, cocaine, and friends."[1] Special expertise in interpreting evidence can be had by looking for help in the appropriate newsgroup. In one case where the author was involved, the suspect was claiming extensive military experience in covert operations with the U.S. Army Special Forces and was thought to be grossly exaggerating or even entirely fabricating this. A summary of his military record was obtained, but the author was not sure how to interpret some of the entries listed there. A question posted in **us.military.army** produced a number of responses that helped clarify that, while the suspect had served in the Special Forces, there was nothing to indicate that he had ever been deployed overseas or had been under hostile fire, as he had claimed.

As for intelligence gathering, the possibilities are almost endless. One clear disadvantage that law enforcement personnel have when trying to gather intelligence is that private citizens are reluctant to disclose information to law enforcement, especially if they are either involved in illegal activities themselves or are close to those engaging in crimes. Simply gaining access to the venues where these people gather can be half the battle. By carefully structuring an **identity**, Usenet postings can appear to be coming from a co-conspirator, rather than from a law enforcement official. A famous cartoon from the *New Yorker* magazine showed a family pet, sitting in front of a computer, typing at the keyboard. The caption read, "On the Internet, nobody knows you're a dog."[2]

---

[1] The Complete Reference to Newsgroups, n.d. <http://tile.net/news/altdrugshard.html> (June 2000).

[2] Peter Steiner, "On the Internet, nobody knows you're a dog." *The New Yorker* 69:20 (July 5, 1993): 61.

No one will know if he or she is communicating with a law enforcement officer either, unless the officer reveals the information. Investigators have been using the Internet for intelligence gathering and investigative leads for years because of the veil that this long-distance communication medium provides. In order to use this effectively, the investigator has to set up the news client carefully. Otherwise, the investigator's true e-mail address and possibly his or her identity can be traced by a knowledgeable user. These knowledgeable users are often just the people of whom investigators need to be aware. Unfortunately, they also have the most interest in knowing about law enforcement personnel.

News Servers

Newsgroups are carried on news servers, which work in a way similar to mail servers. When a newsgroup member or subscriber (the terms mean the same thing) posts a news message, it is appended to the appropriate message thread on the server that carries the newsgroup. When subscribers next log on and view the most recent message headers in that newsgroup, the header attached to the new message, along with all of the others posted since the last session, will appear in the list. This process is somewhat more delayed than is the case with e-mail because of the need to disseminate the new message to all of the servers that carry that newsgroup. Thus, it might be a few minutes to a few hours before a message posted to a newsgroup actually appears in the listing of messages provided for all of the newsgroup's subscribers.

Most ISPs provide their subscribers with access to a news server as a part of their service. The news server nomenclature is most commonly something like news.isp.com (assuming an Internet service provider called isp.com). This information should be included in the setup information provided by the ISP when the account is established, but if the information is missing, try that server name.

If an ISP does not offer a news server, a nominal fee can purchase a subscription to a commercial news server. This allows the user to access, read, and post to the newsgroups carried on that server. Because not all servers carry all newsgroups, it is important to check first and make sure that newsgroups of interest will be available. Otherwise, the service will not be satisfactory.

There are also free news servers that can be accessed through a newsreader like Outlook Express, but they tend to be limited to certain subject matter. An example is the news server news.microsoft.com, which carries only newsgroups relating to Microsoft products. The newsgroups there are very useful for those who own or use Microsoft products but probably are not very interesting to others. This is the server that will be used for the examples in this chapter, because it is accessible at no cost to anyone who wants to subscribe.

At this writing, Deja.com offers free, web-based access to newsgroups, but it appears to be the last of a group of companies that offer this service, and even that may go away eventually. Because offering access to a large selection of news-groups means purchasing newsfeeds from multiple newsgroup hosts, running a news server can be an expensive proposition, and it is not difficult to understand why companies that offered the service for free are now charging their users sub-scription fees. Deja.com requires users to register for unrestricted access to their newsfeed and then provides a method where newsgroups can be read and posted to from an e-mail client, such as Outlook Express. This, however, does not work in the same way that a typical newsgroup account does.

Setting Up a Newsgroup Account

Establishing a newsgroup account is very similar to setting up a mail account. From the main Outlook Express window, click on the **Tools|Accounts** selection in the Menu Bar (see Figure 7–1).

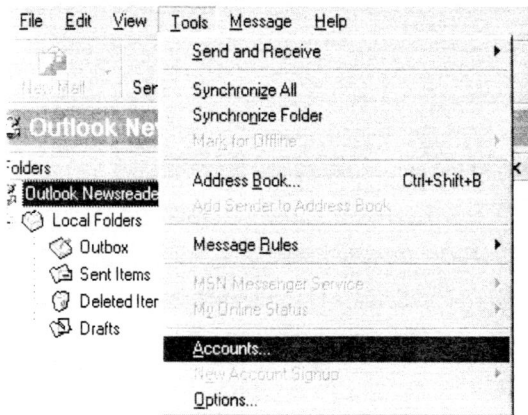

Figure 7-1   Setting Up a Newsgroup Account

When the dialog box appears listing all of the various available services, some of which Outlook Express includes at installation, click on the **Add** button, then on **News** (see Figure 7–2).

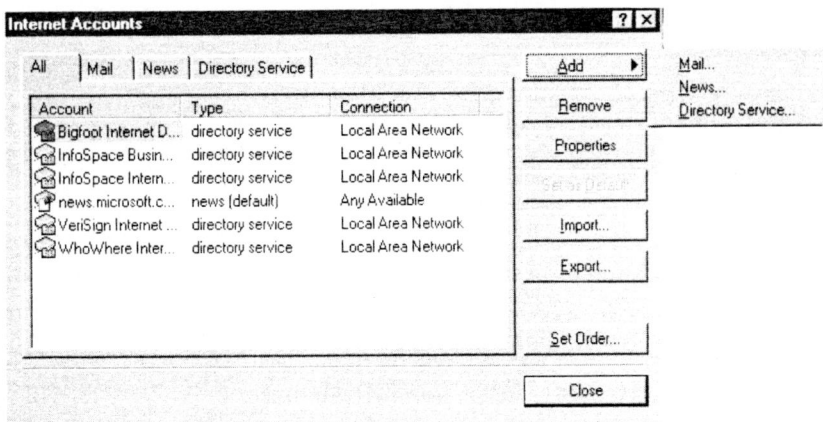

Figure 7-2   Choosing the News Option

This will activate Outlook Express' Internet Connection Wizard, which guides the user through the remainder of the subscription process. The first step is to choose a display name. The most obvious choice here might be one's true name, but there is reason for hesitation. In newsgroup postings, comparatively few users go by their true names. This custom varies, depending on the type of newsgroup. Technically oriented newsgroups, such as those offered at news.microsoft.com, will have more subscribers using their true names, and groups in the alt. hierarchy will have almost none, with their members preferring **screen names** such as *V-Man* and *Rocker.* Whatever display name the user enters in this box will appear next to any posting he or she places on the newsgroup. If the material viewed and responded to is not something controversial, such as seeking technical support with a software problem, then a true name should offer no problems. If, however, a user wishes to conceal his or her identity, an alias can be created now and used as the display name.

The next dialog box in the wizard will ask for the user's e-mail address. This information also appears in any newsgroup posting the user creates. There are two reasons for altering the true e-mail address or using an address from previously created, extra account in addition to a regular mail account. Free e-mail accounts, described in Chapter 6, are useful here.

If a true e-mail address is given, spammers will fill the mailbox with messages describing every get-rich-quick scheme, multilevel marketing ploy, and "adult services" offer on the planet. Spammers troll the news servers with software that filters and captures the e-mail addresses of subscribers and then appends those addresses to distribution lists that they either use themselves or sell to other marketers. If a regular, unaltered e-mail address is part of a newsgroup subscription, there will be a marked increase in traffic to the e-mail account, most of which will be unwanted.

The other reason for not using one's regular e-mail address relates to the display name issue discussed above. When using the newsgroup account for investigations or intelligence gathering, an e-mail address can give away one's true identity. A fellow newsgroup subscriber might recognize the address from some other transaction or activity on the Internet, even though the display name may be different, or just the address itself, especially if it is something like jdoe@AnytownPD.org, may be telltale.

There are two ways to handle this problem. If spam e-mail is the principal concern, then try inserting some spurious characters into the e-mail address. In the example in the preceding paragraph, altering the e-mail address to something like jdoe$$$@AnytownPD.org or jdoeNOSPAM@AnytownPD.org will defeat most of the address-harvesting programs by creating an nonexistent address. A signature line can provide instructions on how to reply to the true e-mail address (e.g. "Remove *$$$* from address to respond by e-mail"). This will allow newsgroup members to respond to the sender personally, if needed.

The other method is to use an e-mail account that has been created specifically for the online persona. Free web-based e-mail accounts, such as those available through Hotmail, are useful here because they can absorb the spam and still provide a method of contact for newsgroup correspondents. It is important to check these accounts frequently, even though most of the messages that will accumulate in them will be spam. There may be an occasional gem in there that can contain better information.

The final dialog box in the Internet Connection Wizard asks for the name of the news server that will be used (see Figure 7–3). In the example here, we will use news.microsoft.com, which does not require its users to log on.

Most news servers will require users to log on and provide a user name and password, just like an e-mail account. This is to keep freeloaders from using subscription servers without paying. When configuring a subscription news server, such as those provided by most ISPs, check this box and provide the user name and password given by the ISP or other news server provider. When using a news server provided by a personal ISP, the user name and password will usually be the same ones used to log on to the ISP or e-mail account.

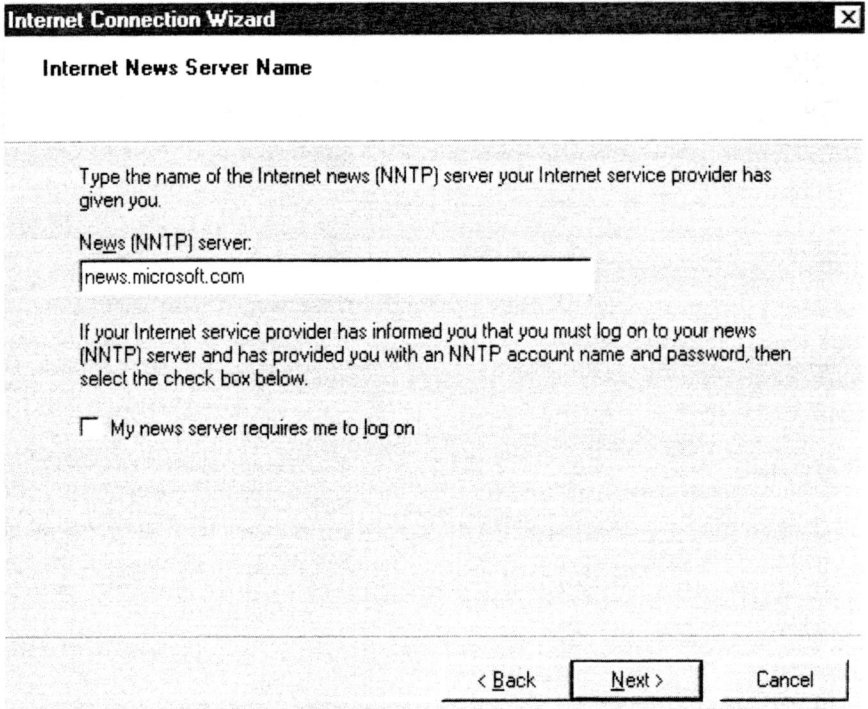

Figure 7-3   Choosing a News Server

If the **My news server requires me to log on** box is left unchecked, then this will be the last dialog box in the Internet Connection Wizard. If a user name and password must be provided, then there will be one more dialog box for that information.

When the Internet Connection Wizard finishes, the user will be asked if he or she wishes to download a list of available newsgroups from the server. If not already connected to the ISP, it may be necessary to manually connect to get the list of newsgroups, depending on how the connection is configured. This is a one-time procedure that may take some time, depending on which news server is being used and the speed of the Internet connection. News servers like news.microsoft.com carry a little over a thousand newsgroups (in the case of Microsoft, all of them pertain to Microsoft products and services), but down-loading the names and brief descriptions of the newsgroups will take only a few seconds, even with a relatively slow dial-up connection.

Getting a list of available newsgroups from subscription-type news servers is going to take appreciably longer than a few seconds. This is because most subscription news servers carry between 30,000 and 50,000 newsgroups, and retrieving just the names and descriptions of these is the equivalent of downloading a large text file. Over a slow dial-up connection, this might take thirty to forty minutes. Once this has been done, however, the only updates necessary will be when new newsgroups are added, and Outlook Express can be configured to notify the user when this has occurred. New newsgroups are frequently created, but it is unlikely that there will be more than a few new additions at a time. Once the list of newsgroups is downloaded, the next step is to retrieve message headers and view some messages.

Navigating Newsgroups

Once there are one or more news servers set up in Outlook Express, each server should appear in the list of folders in the main Outlook Express window. Clicking on one of the news server listings will cause a listing of all the subscribed newsgroups from that server to appear in the right window of the display. If no subscriptions have been made to any newsgroups from that server, clicking on the server name will cause the program to offer a list of available newsgroups, as shown in Figure 7–4.

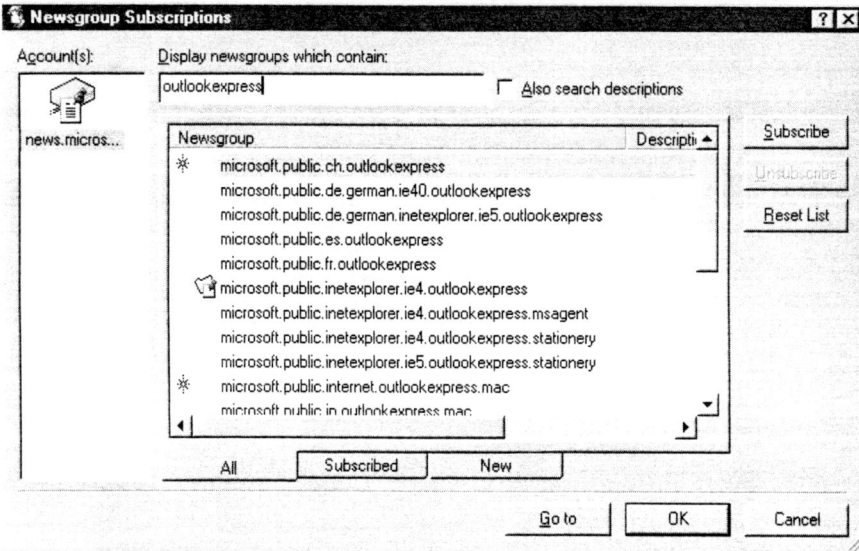

Figure 7–4   Newsgroup Listing

Note that some of the newsgroup names contain a group such as ch, de, or fr. This denotes the language used for most if not all, of the messages in the newsgroup, with the two-letter sequence corresponding to the top-level domain indicating the country where that language is more common, e.g. Switzerland, Germany, or France. Newsgroups without the country indicator are usually American English.

The window at the top of the dialog box is for displaying search terms for filtering the newsgroup listing. Search terms entered in this box are taken literally. Enter *meth*, for example, and any group will appear that has *methamphetamine* in its title, as well as *method, Pat Metheny*, and *amethyst*. To illustrate the incredible diversity of ongoing discussions within Usenet, a search of a subscription news server had newsgroups containing all of these terms. Some newsgroups have descriptions included in their listings. Checking the box to the right of the search window will include the descriptions in the keyword search as well.

In the example in Figure 7–4, the search term *outlookexpress* is used. The words are run together because Usenet does not allow spaces in newsgroup titles, although words are frequently separated by underscores (like_this), periods or dots (like.this), or even dashes (like-this). It can require some experimentation to get a manageable list to choose from, and it is usually best to start with a single word, or even a part of a word, such as *meth*.

After locating a newsgroup of interest, the user should click on the Subscribe button in the upper right of this dialog box to join the newsgroup. A user can subscribe to as many newsgroups as desired without closing the dialog box. Performing a new search will not delete the subscription, even if the subscribed newsgroup does not appear in a subsequent search list. When the search for newsgroups to subscribe to is done, click on the OK button. The subscriptions window can be reopened at any time by clicking on the server listing, then on the Newsgroups button in the right window that will appear.

Because of the massive number of messages posted to newsgroups, most Usenet readers do not download all of the messages themselves. Doing so would take a long time, even with a fast Internet connection, and would take up a lot of hard disk space. Besides, some of the messages will not be of interest anyway. Instead, most users download only the most recent message headers or subject lines and then decide which messages they want to read from scanning the headers. The default is to download the most recent 300 message headers, if there are that many in the newsgroup, when the user clicks on the newsgroup listing. This number can be adjusted by clicking on Tools|Options in the Menu Bar, then on the Read tab in the dialog box that will appear (see Figure 7–5).

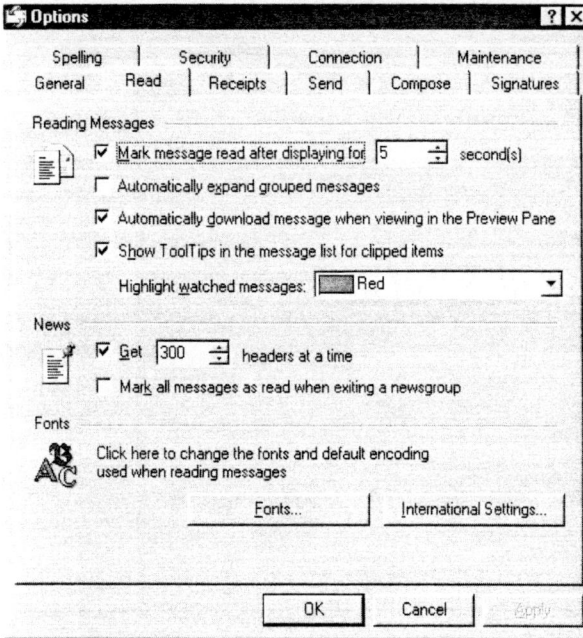

Figure 7-5 Setting Number of Message Headers to Download

Once the message headers are downloaded, the list will appear in the upper portion of the right window, and the selected message will be in the lower right window. A message is selected by clicking on its message header (see Figure 7-6).

Note that some message headers have small boxes to their left, each containing plus or minus signs. These indicate that the message has replies. A plus shows that the message "tree" associated with that header is collapsed, so that only the first message shows, and a minus indicates that the message tree is expanded. The message trees are expanded or collapsed by clicking on the plus or minus boxes. In Figure 7-6, the selected message has had its message tree expanded to show the reply.

Note also that the message header immediately above the selected message (the one with the subject : "Starting newsonly...") no longer appears in boldface font. Once a message has been read or marked as read, its header changes from bold to regular font. However, if a message tree is not expanded, i.e. it still has the plus symbol next to its first entry, and there are one or more unread messages in the message tree that stems from that message, the bold font will remain. When the message tree is expanded, read messages will be in regular font, and unread messages will appear in bold. The purpose of this is so that message threads with new, unread activity are recognizable without having to expand each one of them.

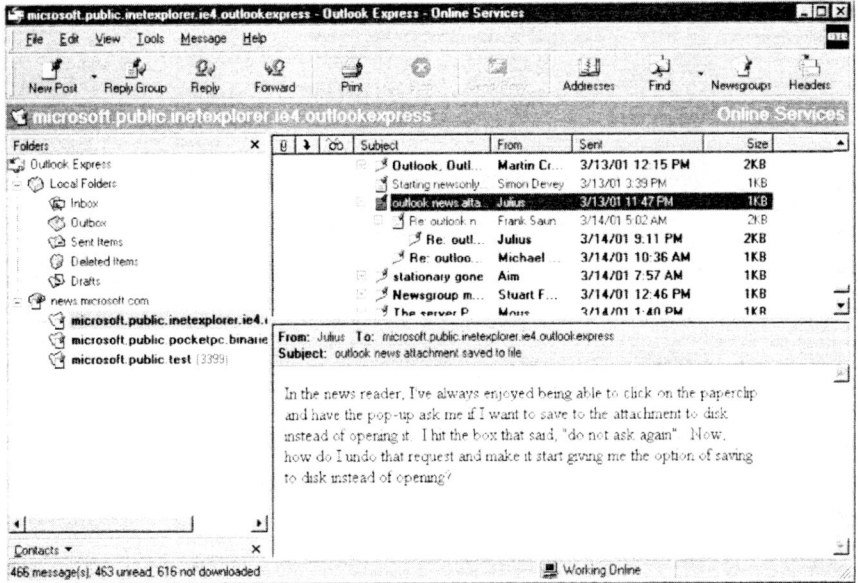

Figure 7-6   Reading Newsgroup Messages

As with other similarly structured lists in Windows applications, the message headers can be sorted by a number of criteria. Note the heading bars above the message header list. In Figure 7–6, they consist first of three icons (a paper clip, a downward-pointing arrow, and a pair of eyeglasses) and the headings **Subject, From,** and **Sent.** Clicking on any of these headings will sort the message header list according to that criterion. For instance, the selected message is listed as being from **Julius.** To sort message headers in order of their authors, clicking on the **From** heading would order them that way, with the list indexed at that message from Julius, and any others that he had posted. Clicking on the heading again would reverse the order of the sort. The default sorting is according to the time that the message was posted on the news server, which may not be the same as the time the message was sent.

The text of each message may not appear in the lower right window as soon as its accompanying header is clicked on, depending on the type of connection to the server. If the server connection is active when the header clicked, Outlook

Express will retrieve that message from the server as soon as it is selected. However, if the user is working offline while browsing through message headers, the program will remember which headers were selected and will retrieve those at the time of the next log on. Users with dial-up connections sometimes like to do their news reading in three sessions: one to get new message headers, one to retrieve the body of messages whose headers they have selected, and one to upload their replies. This reduces the need to tie up a telephone line for an inordinately long time.

Most newsgroups have a list of **Frequently Asked Questions** (known in the online community as a **FAQ**) that serves as a guideline for new users. The FAQ or some other resource file will be posted in most newsgroups at regular intervals, typically about once per month. Another way to read the FAQ for that newsgroup is by posting a short "Where's the FAQ?" message, which may result in a referral to a web page that contains the FAQ. If a new newsgroup user asks a question that is covered in the FAQ, he or she is likely to be **flamed** by another newsgroup member.

Upon getting involved in news discussions or just lurking in the background, users can find message threads that they wish to follow in subsequent sessions. Outlook Express provides some tools to make this easier. The eyeglasses icon in the headings list marks message threads to be watched or ignored. Clicking in the area next to a message header and directly underneath the eyeglasses icon will place an eyeglasses icon next to every message header in that thread and also changes the color of the font, which is user-selectable under Tools|Options|Read. The next time a new set of message headers is downloaded, any new postings within this message thread will show both the title of the newsgroup listing and the message header itself in red boldface, or whatever other color has been configured. The watched message threads can be moved to the top of the list by clicking on the eyeglasses icon in the heading row. Depending on whether the watched messages sort to the bottom or the top of the list on the first click, this may need to be repeated.

Clicking twice in the same space that is used to mark a message thread for watching will change the eyeglasses icon to a circle with a crossbar through it—the "no" symbol—and the software will ignore any future postings in that message thread, not downloading any subsequent headers. These options can be changed at any time.

Figure 7–7 shows a message list similar to that in Figure 7–6, but with one message thread marked for watching, one marked to be ignored, and both sorted to the top of the list.

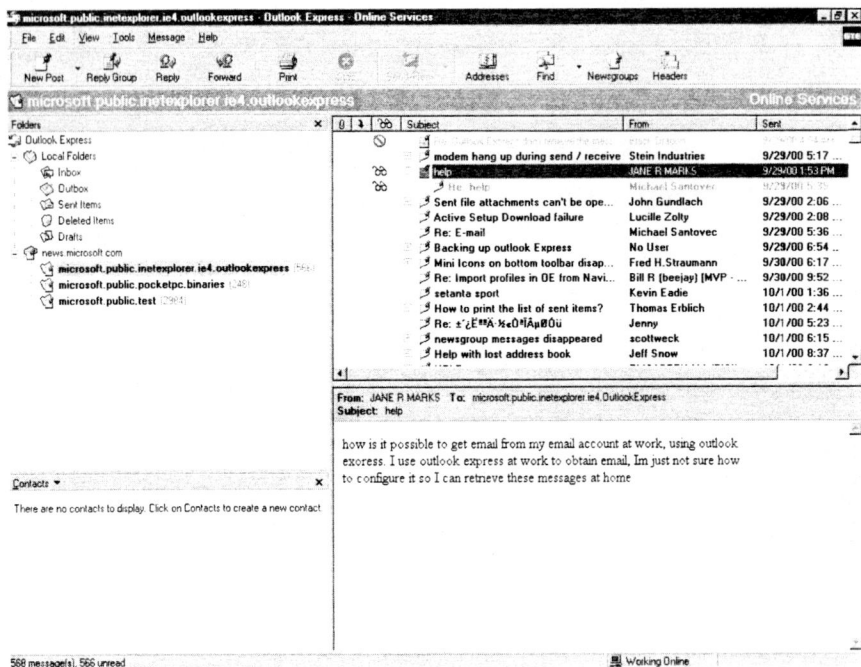

Figure 7-7   Marking Messages as Watched and Ignored

News servers have a finite amount of storage space on their hard drives and cannot retain messages posted to the newsgroups indefinitely. The news server will automatically delete messages based on one of three criteria.

◆ The number of messages held in the newsgroup file
◆ The total size of all messages and attachments in the newsgroup file
◆ The age of the messages

If the news server uses the first method, then a set number of messages will be retained on the server at any one time. When the *n*th + 1 message is received (*n* = the retention limit), the oldest message is deleted. Where the file is limited by file space alone, then the size, not the number, of messages becomes critical. This is common in binary newsgroups, where the size of the file attachments to messages dwarfs the space required for the messages themselves. Finally, the server may be set to delete messages once they are *x* days old. This would be most common in newsgroups that are not especially active.

From the user's perspective, what this means is that clicking on a message header may not download the message because it is no longer available on the server. If a message header sounds interesting enough to read the associated message and it has been deleted, a large news server like deja.com, which archives old newsgroup messages, may be helpful. These archives mean that some news messages almost never go away. A message can be marked in such a way that it will not be archived after it is posted, giving it a limited "shelf life." To do so, insert this as the first line in the message body: x-no-archive: yes. This will prevent deja.com and some other archives from storing the message.

Creating and Responding to Newsgroup Messages

Creating a newsgroup message is very similar to creating an e-mail message. Click on the listing of the newsgroup to select it, then on the New Post button at the top of the screen. Another option is to use the Menu Bar to select File|New|News Message. When creating a news message, there is no need to insert a destination address, as this is already inserted in the message blank. A copy of a newsgroup message can be sent to an e-mail recipient or to other news-groups by placing the appropriate address in the Cc: field. This is called **cross-posting** and is often discouraged.

It is necessary to include a Subject: heading. Using a properly descriptive subject heading is even more important in newsgroups than in e-mail. Most newsgroup readers are confronted with a long list of new news messages every day, and they are only likely to read those that they believe will be of interest to them. In newsgroups where the emphasis is on providing technical assistance, as is the case with those in the Microsoft hierarchy, users look for subject lines that pertain either to a problem similar to the one that they are having or to an area where they might be able to lend their personal expertise. Using a general sub-ject heading like "Help!" or "Outlook problem" is not likely to get as good a response as one that reads something like "Can't send attachments to AOL account." People who give freely of their time and expertise to assist others fre-quent the technical support forums, but one should be respectful and courteous of their efforts and make the job as easy as possible.

The body of the message is formatted in the same way as an e-mail message. Attachments can be included in newsgroup messages, but this is discouraged unless they are posted to a **binary forum**, which will be discussed later.

To reply to a news message already on the server, select that message by clicking on its header, and then click on the Reply to Group button at the top of the screen. An alternative is to click on the Menu Bar for Message|Reply to

Group or use the keyboard shortcut **Control-G**. This will bring up a new message window with the address and subject line already inserted.

Depending on how Outlook Express is configured, the body of the original message may be copied into the reply window with each line prefaced by an angular bracket (>) (see Figure 7–8). This option is configured by checking or unchecking the **Include message in reply** box in the dialog box found by clicking on **Tools|Options|Send**.

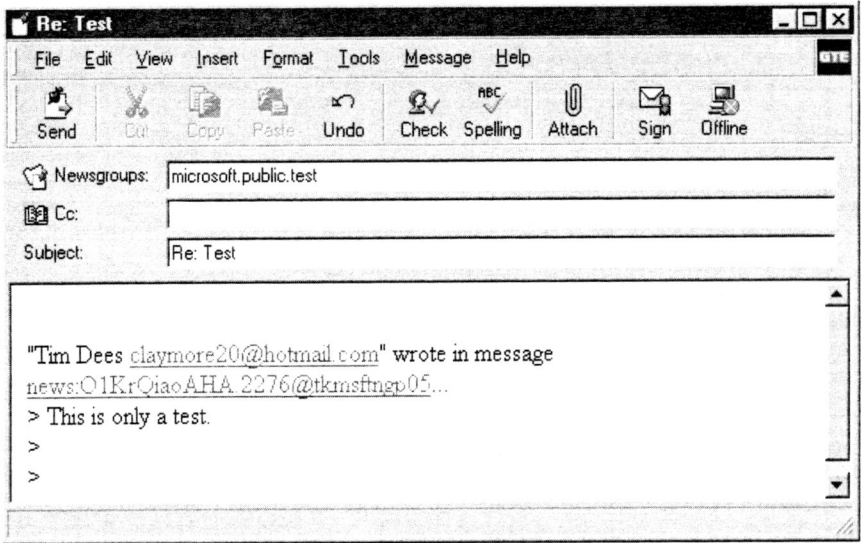

Figure 7-8   **Replying to a News Message**

Inclusion of the parent message in the reply can be useful or bothersome, depending on context. If the parent message is short, then including it might make the reply somewhat more understandable, as the reader will not have to bring up the parent message to see what the reply is about. If the parent message is long and complex, the reply, which will not have the angular brackets (>) characters at the start of each line, can be interspersed with each section of the parent message in order to respond to specific points without having to quote them back. However, a very common etiquette error is to reply to a message, include all of the parent message in it, which may include all or portions of previous messages, and append to the bottom of the message a brief response, like "I agree," "You don't know what you're talking about," or something more colorful.

This requires those reading the messages to scroll down to the bottom of the message to see something that they might not have bothered with had they known a little more about the quality of the content. In short, this can be very annoying.

If the newsreader is set to include the parent message text by default, it can quickly be removed from any reply message by use of the keyboard shortcut **Control-A** (for **Select All**), then using the **Delete** key. Selected portions of the parent message can also be deleted by holding down the mouse button while running the cursor over them and then hitting the **Delete** key. Finally, the response can be posted at the top of the included parent message, rather than at the bottom so that readers will not have to scroll through all of the other stuff. This wastes bandwidth by requiring the newsgroup members to download a lot of redundant text, but it is better than making them scroll through all of that other drivel.

A newsgroup message can be deleted from the server by its author if it is posted in error or if the author has second thoughts after it is sent. To do this, wait until the message appears in the message tree, select it, and click on **Message|Cancel Message** from the Menu Bar. If a message is selected other than one that was posted, this option is grayed out and not available. Deleting a message from the server does not mean that no one will see it. If the message was downloaded by anyone between the time is was posted and when it was deleted, then it is on his or her machine, and nothing can be done about it.

To experiment with the news reader settings and make sure that messages are being posted and retrieved correctly before going live, search the news server for a newsgroup with "test" in the title. These are set up expressly for the purpose of experimentation and are otherwise ignored. If a user posts a test message in a "live" newsgroup, someone will almost certainly flame him or her.

Users can set up a signature line, sometimes called a **sig** or **sigfile**, that is added to the end of any message they send in e-mail or a newsgroup. The signature line is intended to provide brief contact or identifying information, but many newsgroup users have sigfiles that are longer than most of their messages. These sigfiles might contain web page URLs, quotations that represent their personal philosophies, or anything else that the user wants.

Signatures are created and maintained under **Tools|Options** by clicking on the **Signatures** tab. A user can have any number of signatures and set the program to append them automatically to messages or allow them to be added manually. A user with multiple sigfiles can choose which to add for each message (see Figure 7–9).

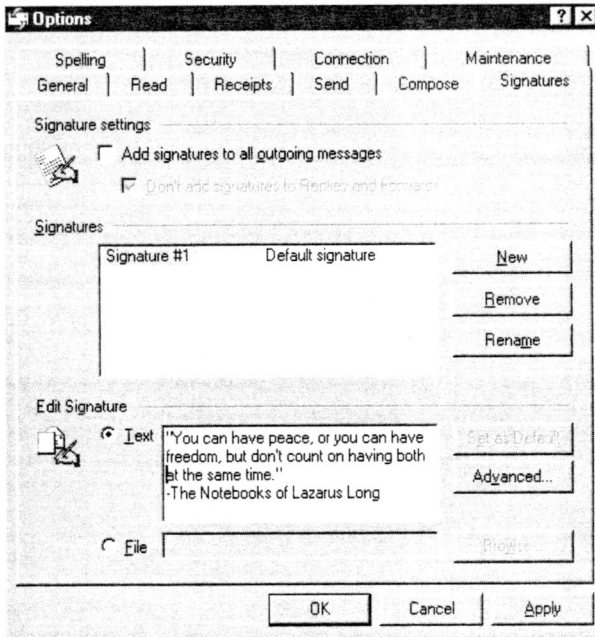

Figure 7-9   Creating a Signature File

If the user has not set the option to add the sigfile to all messages, then he or she can add the sig manually by clicking on Insert|Signature while in the New Message window.

Keep in mind that there may be a significant amount of lag time or latency between the time that a newsgroup messages is posted and when it appears on the server. Newsgroups are far more distributed than e-mail, and the requirement that news servers get newsfeeds from one another to synchronize their lists delays the process. In some cases, it might be a day or more before a new post appears, although this would be unusual.

When finishing a newsgroup session, it may be convenient to have Outlook Express mark all of the message headers that have been reviewed. The ones that were selected and read will have changed from boldface to regular font, but the ones that were not read will still be bolded and will remain that way until they are marked otherwise. To mark all message headers in a newsgroup as read, click on Edit|Mark All Read on the Menu Bar or use the keyboard shortcut Control-Shift-A. This will change all of the headers to regular font. The next time messages headers are downloaded, new, unread message threads and threads that have new messages included in them will be in boldface.

Using Binary Newsgroups

As was mentioned previously, attaching files to newsgroup messages is discouraged, unless the newsgroup is one that includes the word *binaries* in its title. Binary files, as opposed to plain text, tend to be much larger than regular message files, and many users with limited bandwidth or expensive Internet connections do not want to be bothered with the big downloads that come with binary newsgroups.

Binary files can be just about anything that can be stored in a computer file. Most binary files are images, but they can also be programs, system files, documents created in a word processor, sound files, or full-motion video clips.

Unfortunately, the most ubiquitous use of binary files is by users who post pornographic images and other material of questionable taste and arguable redeeming social importance. These are also frequently the areas where law enforcement investigators concentrate their efforts, since some of these images and other files contain material that may be protected by copyright or may violate U.S. Customs or child protection statutes.

Most binary newsgroups are just that—forums for posting of files. There is not much in the way of dialogue, other than an occasional request for a particular file. Subject lines tend to consist of the file name, sometimes the size of the file, a sequence number if the file is split into parts, and possibly the name of the person or entity that is submitting the file. This last piece of information is often intended to draw newsgroup users to the poster's web site where similar files may be viewed or downloaded. If the person posting the file does not have an accompanying web site, he or she may just be looking for the notoriety or self-satisfaction that comes with being the most prolific contributor to a binary newsgroup.

In binary newsgroups where the primary traffic is images, the images will usually be posted as a single file and attached to a single message. Often, the image file will be displayed in the message window when the message header is selected, as is the case in Figure 7–10.

Note that in Figure 7–10 some message headers have a paper clip icon in the column to the left of the subject line. This indicates that there is a file attachment to the message. Until the message is selected and downloaded, there is no way to tell if there is a file attached to the message or not, although the subject line often provides a hint. The same paper clip icon also appears in the upper right corner of the lower right message window. Clicking on this icon will open a small box that gives the user a choice between saving the file attachment or opening it. A file attachment can be opened if the user has the software necessary to run or open the attachment loaded on his or her computer.

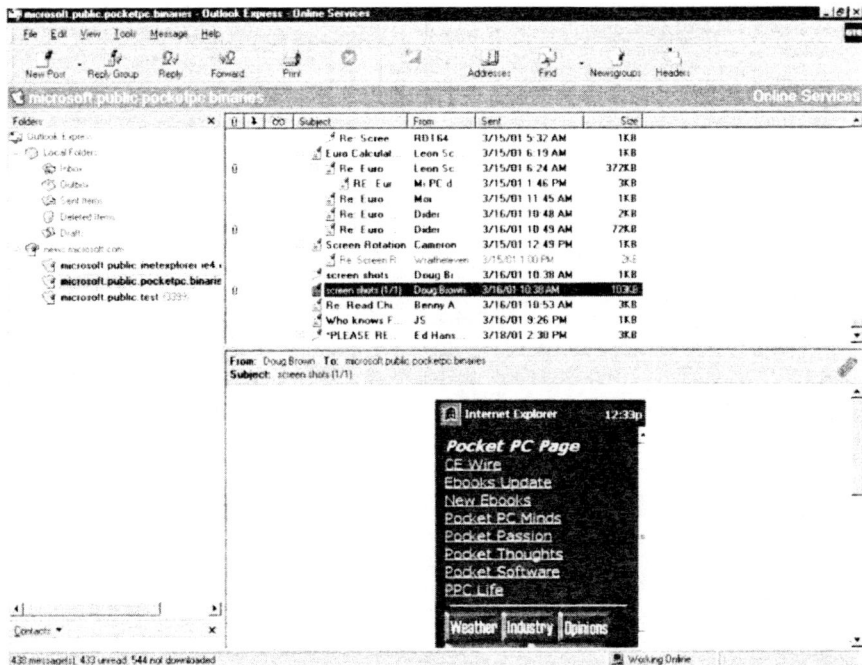

Figure 7-10   Displaying Binary Image Files

With image files, the most common file formats will be *.jpg or *.gif files, both of which can be viewed in a web browser. If a computer has the appropriate software loaded, the file will open automatically. If the necessary software is either missing or not properly installed in the Windows Registry, the computer will ask the user to choose what program he or she wants to use to open the file.

If this problem occurs or to save the file for later use, choose the **Save to disk** option that will appear in the dialog box that appears, similar to Figure 7–11.

Note that this dialog box consists primarily of a warning, which should not go unheeded. Viruses and other malicious codes are frequently disseminated via Usenet, hidden within seemingly harmless files attached to newsgroup messages. Most antivirus software has an option to scan any file attachments and downloads for harmful code and to prompt the user if a file is suspect. Downloading any type of binary file from the Internet without having recently updated antivirus software running is an extremely risky practice.

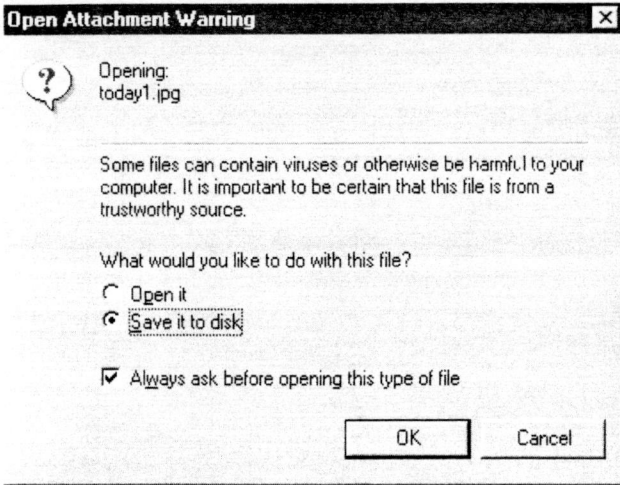

Figure 7-11   Saving a File Attachment

When saving a file by clicking on the button next to that option and then on the OK button, the user will be asked to designate a location for the saved file. It is usually a good practice to create a folder just for this purpose and to save all files there so that they can be easily located later. Folder and file organization strategy is a matter of personal preference, but it pays to be consistent and organized.

Many ISPs will not allow file attachments in excess of a certain size to be downloaded or even uploaded. A common size limit is 1000 K. This is to prevent pranksters from paralyzing a server or a group of accounts by sending e-mail or news messages with huge file attachments. In fact, some ISPs and corporate servers prohibit file attachments for fear that malicious code will be downloaded onto their system, which happens on a regular basis. Usenet users get around this measure by using software that splits large files into smaller component parts, which are themselves coded into plain text, called **Multipurpose Internet Mail Extensions** (**MIME**) coding. A part of a typical MIME-encoded message might look something like this:

```
M!```BA"*RCH6=1R$R704BE`!BLHZ5@%U#/``H/&`H3)=>`SP.L%&\"
#V/\[MPW5A:C#_%2150`!J8.A3"```@\0$B40D)#0#QH0DB`@```5T#
%.+R.AZ]___MB_#K`C/VBSZ+SL:$)(@(```"_Y?```._VH!B\[_5P2);"0
HQX0DB`@```8```#IH00``(U,)#SH0`@``(N/I```(U$$)"A0:B!1C4PD2,:$))
0(```'MZ!L(```"%P'5R:F#HS@<``(/$$$$)"0[P\:$)(@(```(=`Q3B\CHQ?;___
```

A MIME-encoded message would typically be pages and pages of this kind of gibberish, but users do not have to try to read them. Just as there is software that translates binary files into MIME, there is also software that translates the code back again. This feature is built into Outlook Express.

Figure 7–12 shows a portion of an Outlook Express newsreader window listing a number of messages from **alt.binaries.games**, a newsgroup notorious for distribution of copyrighted game software. This is also an excellent place to pick up malicious code that may have been inserted into some of these game programs by "generous" Usenet users anxious to share their games with others.

𝟅	☉☉	Subject		From	▲
		Combat Flight Simulator 2 (ripped version) File 029 of 173 - Rgr CFS 2.r26 (6/9)		Mr. Rogers	
		Combat Flight Simulator 2 (ripped version) File 029 of 173 - Rgr CFS 2.r26 (5/9)		Mr. Rogers	
		Atten: Paine ===> Please repost BAD CRC <=== - WARRIOR2K 001015 - WARSEP...		Crashed Drive !	
		Re: anybody know how to change a CUE file to an ISO file? cdr38a-e.exe [3/3]		Brother Grimm	
		Re: anybody know how to change a CUE file to an ISO file? cdr38a-e.exe [2/3]		Brother Grimm	
		Re: anybody know how to change a CUE file to an ISO file? - winbin.exe (6/6)		JB	
		Re: anybody know how to change a CUE file to an ISO file? - winbin.exe (5/6)		JB	
		Re: anybody know how to change a CUE file to an ISO file? - winbin.exe (4/6)		JB	
		Re: anybody know how to change a CUE file to an ISO file? - winbin.exe (3/6)		JB	
𝟅		Re: anybody know how to change a CUE file to an ISO file? - winbin.exe (2/6)		JB	
		Re: anybody know how to change a CUE file to an ISO file? - winbin.exe (1/6)		JB	
		Re: anybody know how to change a CUE file to an ISO file? - winbin.exe (0/6)		JB	
		(ATTN: Mr. Rogers - Is it possible if you can post all archives up to and not includin...		paul3000@bell...	

From: JB   To: alt.binaries.games
Subject: Re: anybody know how to change a CUE file to an ISO file? - winbin.exe (2/6)

```
M!'''BA"*R.CH6=1R$R704BE`!RLHZ5@%U#H/``H/&`H3)=>`SP.L%&\"#V\[
MPW5A:C#_%2150`1J8.A3""``@\0$B40D)#O#Q0H0DB`@`"`'5T#%%.+R.AZ]__
MB._#K`C/\/BSZ+SL:$)(@("""_Y?''''`._-T!\VH#B\[_5P2)")"0HQX0DB`@`
M`'8'''#IH0H'``(U),#SO0"``G`N\ T`'(`U$U$$$$$@'''''''#&^`^2
MZ!L(`^@%*2P`%G;$`F%M%!@#R&H\_C~_SaH:$)("")0P;\O0[P:$)C~~~XOP
MZP;[S]FHP0VQ`@^~~_%2150""+/HO._Y?'''`._-T!VH!B\[_5P2-3"0\
MQH0DB`@~~+HLP<~`(EL)"C`A`2("''''0''.D#!"``C4PD/ B0!P",]*Y
M,`D''(O8]_&%T@`^$C''`~HP_Q4D54`F#H.`<"(/$($)`2%P,$P,:$)(@(
```

Figure 7-12   MIME-Encoded News Messages

The selected message contains only gibberish **ASCII** characters that are actually representative of the binary file that spawned them when it was translated into MIME. Note the subject line **Re: anybody know how to change a CUE file to an ISO file? winbin.exe (2/6).**

The **Re:** portion indicates that the message is in response to a message whose subject line was **anybody know how to change a CUE file to an ISO file?** This prefix is automatically added to the subject line of any replies to the original message. The **winbin.exe** portion of the subject line is most likely the file that is encoded in the six messages with this similar subject. The numbers in the parentheses **(2/6)** at the end of the subject line indicate the order of this message in the coding sequence, as well as the total number of messages in the entire group of messages that contain the file.

In order to decode the file into something usable, all of the portions of the sequence are required. When these files are large, which is why they are transmitted this way in the first place, it can require many messages to hold all the code, so that sequence numbers like **(x/62)** are not uncommon. What is *very* common is that one or more messages in the sequence fail to reach the news server, which is a continual source of frustration to these software pirates.

To reassemble and decode the file contained in the sequence of news messages, the user must first locate all of the parts of the sequence. In the example shown in Figure 7–12, all parts are visible in the window, and they are even in the correct order and adjacent to one another. This makes the task easier, but even if they were not, this would not be an especially grave problem.

In this example, the user can reassemble the file by selecting either the first or the last message in the sequence by clicking on it and then selecting the message on the opposite end of the sequence by clicking on it as well, but while holding the **Shift** key down at the same time. This will cause the two messages that were originally clicked on, as well as all of those in between, to be selected at once, as shown in Figure 7–13.

θ	∞	Subject	From	▲
		🗐 Combat Flight Simulator 2 (ripped version) File 029 of 173 - Rgr CFS 2.r26 (6/9)	Mr. Rogers	
		🗐 Combat Flight Simulator 2 (ripped version) File 029 of 173 - Rgr CFS 2.r26 (5/9)	Mr. Rogers	
		🗐 Atten: Paine ===> Please repost BAD CRC <=== - WARRIOR2K 001015 - WARSEP...	Crashed Drive !	
		🗐 Re: anybody know how to change a CUE file to an ISO file? cdr38a-e.exe [3/3]	Brother Grimm	
		🗐 Re: anybody know how to change a CUE file to an ISO file? cdr38a-e.exe [2/3]	Brother Grimm	
		🗐 Re: anybody know how to change a CUE file to an ISO file? - winbin.exe (6/6)	JB	
		🗐 Re: anybody know how to change a CUE file to an ISO file? - winbin.exe (5/6)	JB	
		🗐 Re: anybody know how to change a CUE file to an ISO file? - winbin.exe (4/6)	JB	
		🗐 Re: anybody know how to change a CUE file to an ISO file? - winbin.exe (3/6)	JB	
		🗐 Re: anybody know how to change a CUE file to an ISO file? - winbin.exe (2/6)	JB	
θ		🗐 Re: anybody know how to change a CUE file to an ISO file? - winbin.exe (1/6)	JB	
		🗐 Re: anybody know how to change a CUE file to an ISO file? - winbin.exe (0/6)	JB	
		🗐 [ATTN: Mr. Rogers - Is it possible if you can post all archives up to and not includin...	paul3000@bell≡	▼

Figure 7–13   Selecting Multiple Messages

Note that the message with the same subject but bearing sequence number **(0/6)** was not selected. When posting messages in this format, it is customary to include a "zero sequence" message that describes the content in the others. This is so that other users do not have to download the entire file in order to see if it is something that they want. Clicking on the (0/6) message would most likely reveal an explanation that the others contained the parts that would produce winbin.exe, and possibly a short description of what winbin.exe would do when run.

If the messages were not in sequence, that is, if there was an unrelated message somewhere in the list, it could be deselected by holding down the Control key and clicking on it. This method of using the Shift and Control keys to select multiple items in a sequence works consistently through most Windows applications.

Now with the entire sequence of messages selected, move the mouse cursor somewhere over the list of selected messages, and right-click to bring up a context menu. One of the options in the context menu will be Combine and Decode. Click on this option. A dialog box similar to that in Figure 7–14 should appear.

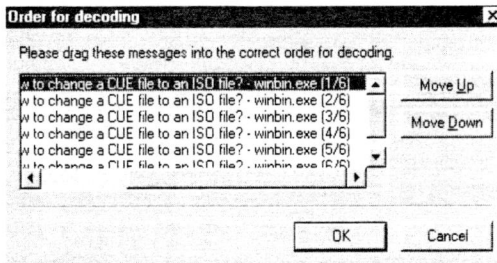

Figure 7-14   Ordering Messages for MIME Decoding

In order to see the sequence numbers in the parentheses, it may be necessary to move the left–right slider in the message list. In this example, the messages are already in the correct order. If one of the messages was out of sequence, e.g. if message (3/6) came before message (2/6), then it would be necessary to click on this message and use the Move Up or Move Down buttons in the dialog box to move it into the correct position. When all messages are in the correct sequence, click on the OK button.

Outlook Express will begin or continue to download the content of all the selected messages. When the process is complete, which can take a considerable amount of time depending on the size of the file, a new message window will open, similar to that in Figure 7–15.

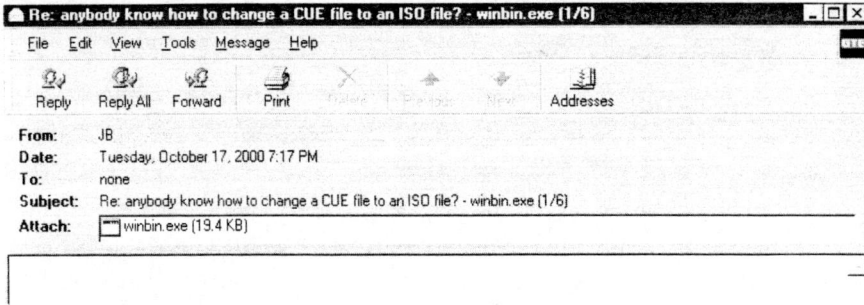

Figure 7-15   Downloaded and Decoded Binary File

There are two options at this point. The first is to double-click on the icon in the **Attach:** window, and the file described there will execute. An image or video file will load into the appropriate viewer and display, and executable files such as the one in the example will begin to run. A user should *never* run an executable file unless he or she is absolutely sure that it is going to do what it is intended to do. The file could be a construct that will wipe out the hard drive or otherwise cause harm to the data on the computer. A safer practice would be to right-click on the file icon and save it to a folder. Then the file can be examined later, possibly on a machine set up for testing, or after taking the appropriate precautions to protect the data on the hard drive.

Getting Along in Newsgroups

One might think that newsgroups would be an excellent place for people of similar interests to communicate, share ideas, assist one another, and generally fraternize. In a perfect world, this would be the case, but the Internet is merely a reflection of the real world, and neither one is perfect. Usenet is fraught with people who seem to have no better purpose in life other than to attempt to make the lives of others as miserable as possible, which in many ways is just like the real world.

For example a search on Usenet for newsgroups that might be of professional interest to law enforcement officers for sharing of information and general communication reveals three likely prospects.

alt.law-enforcement
alt.law-enforcement.traffic
alt.law-enforcement.interpol

One might expect these newsgroups to be frequented by Internet-savvy law enforcement officers with an occasional visitor posing a question or otherwise seeking assistance. In fact, the newsgroups are far better known for criticizing, condemning, and otherwise bashing law enforcement officers. alt.law-enforcement. interpol has very little traffic most of the time, and most messages that are posted there are merely crossposts of other messages whose primary destination was other newsgroups. alt.law-enforcement has a few active law enforcement officers who are regular contributors; however, most of the postings there are from people who are clearly anti–law enforcement and commonly refer to police officers as "pigs," "thugs," and "cowards." alt.law-enforcement.traffic has a similar focus but dwells mainly on people asking questions about how to avoid traffic tickets or "beat" tickets that they have already received.

Are these appropriate activities in newsgroups with such titles? Of course they are. The right of free speech and association is protected in the First Amendment, and while law enforcement officers may be offended at the subject matter in these newsgroups, being offensive is not a prohibited act. The point here is that law enforcement officers who are looking for a warm and fuzzy environment on Usenet are probably going to be unpleasantly surprised by the level of hostility toward them that seems to pervade these forums. There are places on the Internet where law enforcement officers *can* fraternize and communicate in relative safety, and some of these will be discussed in the chapter on the World Wide Web, but they are not likely to find these safe harbors on Usenet.

On Usenet, anyone can act as a self-appointed expert, and people do so with abandon. On the technical support newsgroups, some software manufacturers have created a kind of certification program for knowledgeable customers who frequent the newsgroups and provide good advice to others. On the Microsoft newsgroups, these users carry the title "MVP," or "Most Valuable Professional." These are people recognized by Microsoft for providing assistance to others, and their advice is generally reliable. Advice from others in technical support newsgroups is usually reliable, mainly because any clearly spurious advice will be quickly countered by people who know what they are doing, but it may not be as courteously provided as one might expect. If a Usenet subscriber posts a question or comment that another user regards as foolish or inappropriate, it is unlikely that their perceived faux pas will go unacknowledged for very long. When using the technical support newsgroups for assistance, first look over some of the ongoing message threads to see if the issue in question is already being addressed. If not, then post the question or problem while being as succinct and specific as possible. Be mindful that the people who will be offering advice are doing so for free and that they do not usually work for the companies whose products they are supporting.

In the discussion-oriented newsgroups, such as those in the alt. and soc. hierarchies, it is much more common to throw any shred of civility to the winds. People who can attack others anonymously do not hesitate to do so, and soon it may seem some of these folks have no lives that extend beyond Usenet. The answer is, "Yes, some do not." Some of this animosity comes from simple differences of opinion or perspective, but in some cases it stems from people pretending to be someone they are not and getting called on it. For example, one ongoing and long-standing feud in the us.military.army newsgroup centers on a regular newsgroup member who claims military experience that others maintain he does not have. The insults or flames that pass between the warring parties have no limit. The battle often extends into other newsgroups as well, where these combatants seek each other out and promote their attacks in view of people who probably wonder what all the nastiness is about.

If a newsgroup subscriber who insists on flaming or otherwise being annoying targets another user, the targeted user can prevent the antagonist's posts from being downloaded. Others who do not have that member's messages blocked will see the posts, but the target will not. It is the computer equivalent of turning off a hearing aid during an argument. To do this, click on a message from the offending party to select it, then click on **Message|Block Sender** from the Menu Bar. The computer will request a confirmation to add this address to the Blocked Senders list. Once this option is set, messages from that user will be ignored and left on the server. The list of addresses in the Blocked Senders List can be retrieved by clicking on **Tools|Message Rules|Blocked Senders List** in the Menu Bar. With the Blocked Senders List displayed, someone can be removed from the list, allowing messages from him or her to be downloaded once again, or marked to be included in the list of addresses from which e-mail messages will be refused as well. The Blocked Senders List is sometimes called a **killfile**. Blocking offensive senders removes their primary motive for goading another person. They do not like being ignored, but there is not much they can do about it, so they move on in search of another victim. When adding someone to the Blocked Senders List, a message to that effect is posted in the message thread that contained the sender's address.

Some users just look for opportunities to flame others and post insulting, provocative messages without any apparent motive other than just to annoy. People do this in real life, too, but it is a much safer practice on Usenet. These people are called **trolls**, and while it is always tempting to respond with an equally insulting reply, it is usually better to ignore these folks and let them find another target. They enjoy sucking others into endless arguments that can extend for weeks if allowed to do so.

Some users append very long signature files to all of their messages, usually to reiterate a political position or renew a string of goads with every posting. This is a big waste of bandwidth and is just annoying, which is probably why they do it. Keep signature files short and to the point. In Usenet, it is fine not to use any signature file at all, especially if the user is working in an area where he or she would rather not be identified.

The diversity of Usenet makes it a fascinating and frustrating place. It is a great resource, but it is nothing compared to the World Wide Web.

An Overview of Newsgroup Guidelines

1. Before getting actively involved in a newsgroup, read some of the recent postings and monitor the forum for a few days to get a feel for the atmosphere.

2. Read any FAQs associated with the newsgroup before posting messages.

3. Do not crosspost messages to multiple newsgroups. Try inquiries in one newsgroup at a time.

4. Avoid the use of long signature files.

5. Consider scrambling the **Reply To:** e-mail address by inserting some extra characters in order to minimize being added to spam mailing lists.

6. Be specific with message subject lines. Avoid posting messages with subjects like "Help!" and "Question."

7. Do not feed the trolls. If someone writes an insulting reply, ignore him or her and add the person to the Blocked Senders List.

8. When attempting to give advice, be clear. Experts on the matter at hand should identify themselves; likewise, those speaking from conjecture should also make correspondents aware of that.

9. Do not attach files to messages in nonbinary newsgroups.

10. Do not ask newsgroup members to respond by e-mail. Keep the discussion in the newsgroups and allow others to benefit from it.

11. When testing the newsreader configuration, post any test messages to a newsgroup with **test** in the title.

8

THE WORLD WIDE WEB

Of all of the jewels that the Internet has produced, the World Wide Web may be the one of greatest price. No other development in communications technology has affected as many people as quickly as the web has. Granted, the web would not have gained its current prominence without the underlying computer technologies that support it, but people have been drawn to online computing in huge numbers because of the siren song of the web and all that it offers.

The World Wide Web, hereafter called "the WWW" or "the web" for brevity, has become the great equalizer of publishing. Before the web, anyone who wanted to get his or her message out on a large scale had to have the cooperation of some entity in the communications media to accomplish the goal. Broadcast time had to be arranged and often paid for on a television or radio station, or a publisher had to see sufficient profit or mass interest in the message to devote pages in a book or magazine to the author. Often, giving time to one voice meant that the media provider would be required to give time and space to another under "equal time" laws and customs. If authors had an unpopular point of view or message, then they were often subject to censorship or outright silencing because more powerful voices would overrule them.

The web changed all that, however. Cheap and often free web page editing software, web hosts who would provide space to anyone who asked for the privilege of posting a nonremovable banner advertisement on the page, and increased access to the Internet in homes, schools, and libraries made the web a place where anyone could have an equal voice. Disappointingly, the proliferation of sex-related web sites at a pace that dwarfed other categories made it clear just what people were most interested in.

The commercial value of the web was enhanced by a simultaneous expansion of catalog-based sales in the United States and elsewhere. Shoppers had already become comfortable with the idea of purchasing items that they could not actually examine until after the purchase was made because they could do so without having to travel to the local mall and endure the crowds. When these same items and more became available via the web, the leap from shopping via catalog to shopping via web page was not a great one, and far more merchants were able to get into the game since the cost of constructing a web site was a fraction of the cost of producing and mailing a color catalog, not to mention that there was no limit to how many households they could reach. Customers knew in "real time" if the items they desired were in stock, and delivery services like FedEx and United Parcel Service flourished from the extra business that came their way. The phrase "dot com" went from being arcane jargon to a noun associated with an ambitious business venture.

The web is a communications medium that has tremendously extended the capability of people to communicate with one another and share information. This is not always a good thing, however. Information can be good and bad, true and false, beneficial and harmful; the medium neither knows nor cares of the nature of the information presented over it. Caution is necessary when exploring the World Wide Web, because not everything is what it appears to be.

How the Web Works

In its most basic form, information is transmitted over the World Wide Web via a simple computer language called hypertext markup language, or HTML. HTML contains the text that is displayed on a web page, but more importantly, it contains instructions to the web browser that tell it how to display that text, giving the web page a colorful, graphical appearance and adding all sorts of additional functions, such as animated menus, pictures and diagrams, and wide varieties of color.

It has always been possible to send graphic images over the Internet as e-mail attachments, but graphic images tend to be very large and slow to transmit because of their size. HTML does not send the page image itself, but rather instructions to the browser that tell it how to construct that image and make it appear as the page author intended. Because the instructions (the HTML code) are sent essentially as a fast-loading text document, the page image can be sent and reconstructed on the viewer's computer fairly quickly.

The simple web page in Figure 8–1 contains only a few lines of text, but the text is formatted in two different display fonts and three different colors are used: one for the title, one for the author's name, and one for the background.

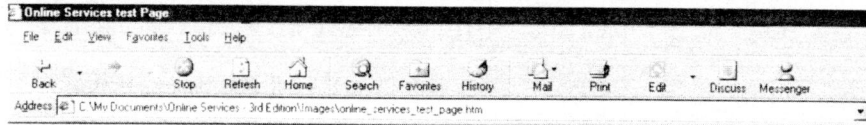

Figure 8-1   Simple Web Page

Simple as this is, the graphic file required to recreate the image pixel by pixel would be fairly large. However, when the instructions to reproduce the page are reduced to HTML, they take up only a few lines of text, as shown below.

```
<html>
<head>
<title>Online Services test Page</title>
</head>
<body bgcolor="#00FFFF" text="#FF0000">
<p align="center"><font face="Saved By Zero" size="7">Online
Services</font>
<font face="Saved By Zero" size="6"> <br> for <br></font>
<font face="Saved By Zero" size="7"> Law
Enforcement</font></p>
```

```
<p align="center"><b><font face="Forgotten Futurist"
color="#0000FF" size="6">
by Tim Dees</font></b></p>
</body>
</html>
```

When this code is loaded into the browser, the image in Figure 8–1 is displayed. If this same image was displayed as a pure graphic file, it would require several hundred kilobytes of code. As HTML, it requires only 436 bytes, or less than half a kilobyte.

This economy is important with sending information over the web because of the limited bandwidth available to most users. Most web surfers will grow impatient if a web page requires more than a few seconds to appear on their screen, and they may just stop the file transfer and look elsewhere. For this reason, most good web designers keep their pages to less than 30 KB per page, although exceptions to this rule abound.

Much of the content of the example web page above is contained in **tags**, set off by arrow brackets, e.g. <html>. Most tags are in pairs, the second or closing tag indicated by a slash as the first character after the arrow bracket, e.g. </html>. These tags provide instructions to the browser on how the content contained between the opening and the closing tags is displayed. For instance, in the example given above, the first line that contains any displayed text is as follows.

```
<p align="center"><font face="Saved By Zero" size="7">Online
Services</font>
```

The <p align="center"> tag tells the browser that this line begins a new paragraph (the *p*), and that it is to be centered on the page. This is followed by a tag that specifies that a font called "Saved by Zero" is to be used to display the text, and that the size of the displayed text is to be 7 on a scale determined by the browser. The text itself, Online Services, comes next, followed by the closing tag (</font>) that tells the browser that the text formatted in this way is finished. This may seem cumbersome, but presenting the formatted text as a graphic image would require considerably more code and bandwidth to transmit.

As web development has progressed, HTML has been supplemented by extensions and adjuncts to the language, such as **DHTML (Dynamic HyperText Markup Language), XML (Extensible Markup Language), Java, Javascript, Flash,** and **Shockwave.** These technologies, most of which are variants of programming languages, allow web pages to display animation, run miniprograms, and interact with the viewer. A web page can contain a game, a calculator, or an e-mail program, thanks to the code generated from these languages.

A user does not need to learn to code or even understand HTML in order to use the web—in fact, most people do not even need to know it is there. This explanation is given only to illustrate why the web is so much more efficient in conveying pseudo-graphic displays than other media on the Internet. However, to see what makes web pages look as they do, select View|Source from the Menu Bar in Internet Explorer or View|Page Source in Netscape Navigator.

Web pages also contain regular graphic images, just like those that can be attached to e-mail messages or sent through newsgroups. These images can range from simple logos to complex photographs, but the more complex the image, the larger the file that is required to contain it. When web pages take a long time to download, it is usually because they contain large graphic images.

Browsers

The interface between the user and the web is called a browser. There are many browsers available, some with special features designed for very small "footprints" (i.e. that take up little disk space) and some that require several megabytes of space. The two most popular browsers are Internet Explorer (IE), which is a Microsoft product, and Navigator, which is made by Netscape. Netscape was purchased by AOL some time ago, so the features of that browser are optimized for AOL users.

Both IE and Navigator are commonly available for free download, although Navigator is technically a shareware program. Users who wish to continue to use the free downloaded version are supposed to register and pay for it, but, unlike many other shareware packages, unregistered versions of Navigator are not crippled in some way, and the software does not stop working after a trial period has expired. Further, Netscape is often shipped as a part of the introductory package of many ISPs and is already configured to use the ISP's web site as its startup page, which will open when the browser is loaded.

IE is part of the same package that includes the e-mail and newsreader client Outlook Express. Microsoft is committed to the idea that Internet Explorer will always be free and available for download from Microsoft's expansive web site. In fact, previous versions of the Windows operating system have included Internet Explorer, automatically installing it on the user's system along with Windows. Because Windows is such a popular operating system, this was labeled as an unfair business practice by Netscape and was a major issue in the lawsuit against Microsoft filed by the U.S. Department of Justice. Because of this, it is uncertain whether or not IE will continue to be closely integrated with the Windows operating system.

The competition for users between IE and Navigator is fierce and has produced some complications for web users. Web pages loaded into IE may appear very different when loaded into Navigator. This is because of the changing standards of HTML and other web page code that both companies try to optimize for their particular browser. It is very common for web page authors to place an icon at the bottom of their pages stating that the page is best viewed with either Netscape or Internet Explorer, depending on what page editing software was used to create the page. Most of the time, the essential features of a page will be visible in either browser, but some of the aesthetic value may be lost by viewing the page in a browser other than the one that was intended for it.

There is nothing to keep users from loading both browsers onto their systems, and if disk space permits, this is often a good solution to ensure that critical features of web pages are available. With each installation, a dialog box will pop up, asking if the user wishes to make *this* browser (the one being installed) the default browser. This means that it will be the one that loads whenever a web-based feature is called by another program. For instance, if an e-mail message contains a "clickable" URL (one that will bring up the associated web page when the user clicks on it), the default browser will be the one that loads and displays that page. These dialog boxes can be very persistent, coming up every time that either browser is loaded, but they usually include a checkbox that will keep the software from asking the user to select a new default browser each time the software is loaded.

For most people, the browser they use does not matter much. The two companies are strongly competitive, and when one comes out with a new browser version, the other is close behind. Occasionally, one company will include technology that allows the user to view special features on a page, such as animations or real-time conversation, but there is usually a **plug-in** available for download that gives the other browser the same capability. Unless there is some desired feature that is unique to one browser, most people simply use the one installed on their system.

Browsers are intended to be easy to use, and they generally are. Typically, the top of the browser window contains an address or location bar that shows the URL of the page currently displayed, a Menu Bar giving access to the other features of the browser, and some icon-like buttons called the **Navigation Toolbar**, which represent the most commonly used features of the browser. Which of these features is on display at any one time can be controlled by options available from the Menu Bar, as is shown in Figure 8–2.

The most commonly used buttons in the features or navigation toolbar are the **Forward** and **Back** buttons. The browser "remembers" which sites have been visited recently and stores some portions of these in a cache file (see the section in this chapter on privacy and security for more detail about this). The purpose of the cache file is to be able to display recently visited pages more quickly by keeping much of their code on the local computer. Therefore the entire page does not have to be retransmitted from the web server if the page is displayed again. Clicking on the Back button will display the page that was loaded immediately previous to the one on screen, and clicking on the Forward button will go back again. If the user has not backtracked to re-view any pages in this session, the Forward button will be disabled.

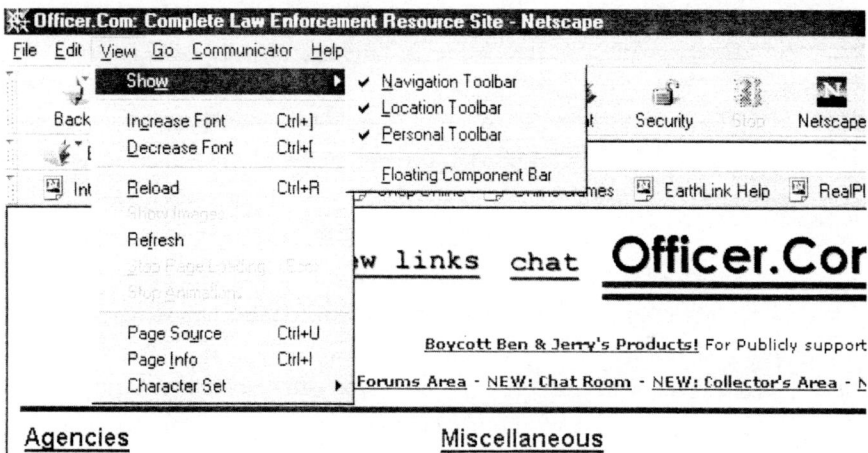

Figure 8-2   Setting Options in Netscape

The Back and Forward buttons also have small, downward-pointing arrows next to them. Clicking on these arrows will display a list of pages previously viewed. If the user wants to jump to a page seen previously but not immediately next in the sequence, clicking on the name of the page in this list will go directly to it, rather than having to press Back or Forward repeatedly to get the same result.

Hyperlinks

One of the most attractive features of the web is that of **hyperlinks**. Hyperlinks are areas of the page that can be clicked on with the mouse to take the viewer to a different site, open a new window, initiate a process, or perform some other function. Hyperlinks make it very easy to navigate between and within web sites because they are so intuitive. Instead of posting instructions like Go to page 85 to learn more about widgets, the word widgets can be hyperlinked to another page that gives the entire history of widgets and what they do.

Hyperlinks are principally of two varieties: text-based and image maps. Text-based hyperlinks are phrases of any length that are usually, though not always, formatted distinctively so that the user can see that the text is hyperlinked. The formatting is most often a different font color, and the hyperlinked text is usually underlined. This formatting can be controlled by the page's author, but it is also possible to format hyperlinks so that they look just like any other text on the page.

Image maps are graphic images that have specific areas within the image designated to activate a hyperlink when that area is clicked on. A single image may contain as many hyperlinks as there are pixels in the image, although it is much more common to make this mapping a little more intuitive. When designing an image map, the page author designates a range of coordinates within the image that are assigned to a particular link. These coordinates usually have a shape corresponding to some distinctive part of the image, such as text within the image, an area of a map, or a component of the image itself. For instance, a page describing equipment carried by a typical uniformed police officer might have a photo of an officer dressed for street duty with image maps tied to his sidearm, his badge, his handcuff case, his baton, etc. Clicking on any of the hyperlinked items would take the user to a description or further detail concerning that item.

Both text-based and image map hyperlinks, even when they are hidden by the page designer, can be identified by the behavior of the mouse cursor when it is over the hyperlink. When the cursor is on a clickable hyperlink, the cursor will change from its usual shape, which is most often an arrow, to a small hand. Further, a status bar at the bottom of the browser window will display the hyperlink under the cursor at that moment. When the cursor is moved off of the hyperlink, the status bar goes blank. A window adjacent to this status bar shows the progress of the loading of a new page, if one is being loaded. As the code for the page is transferred from the web server to the user's browser, a progress bar will expand, showing the relative time to completion.

Because the web is forever changing, **dead links** are very common. A dead link is one that corresponds to a page that is no longer available, and when the link is clicked on, the user gets a generic message indicating that the page is not found or is unavailable. Pages that are not maintained go out of date quickly, and their hyperlinks gradually become invalid. This process is called **link rot**. Sometimes the page is still alive on the web, but the server that contains it is out of service temporarily, or it is overloaded and cannot respond to the browser's request in a reasonable period of time. This happens frequently when web sites have some feature that many users are eager to see or use or when a malicious **hacker** is mounting a denial-of-service attack, where so many requests for information are sent to the server that it is overwhelmed and shuts down. After clicking on a hyperlink and getting a **Page not found** error message, use the **Back** button to get back to the page that held the hyperlink, then click on the link and try to load the page again. If this fails a second time, the page has probably either been taken down or the server is temporarily out of service.

URLs

A unique URL identifies every web page and acts as its address. URLs usually, though not always, start with **http://**. The **http** at the beginning of a URL alerts the computer that the information following is a URL, and that the information should be sent to the default browser. Many word processing programs automatically format any text beginning with http as a hyperlink, so that the text is clickable when viewed onscreen.

A few URLs begin with the letters **https**, which indicates that the page is a secured one. Secured pages reside on special servers that encrypt data sent to and from them, so that the data will be useless if it is intercepted in between. These are routinely used by online merchants for the transmission of credit card information, as well as other business applications, and the data transmitted by this method is probably about as safe from prying eyes as can be reasonably expected. The encryption could be compromised with enough effort, but the costs of doing so generally outweigh the rewards. Secure web pages can be identified in IE and Navigator by the appearance of a locked padlock icon at the bottom of the screen. When the displayed page is a standard, unsecured page, the padlock icon is still visible, but the hasp is shown unlocked.

URLs follow a naming convention similar to e-mail addresses. Consider the following example: **http://www.domainname.com/public/webpage.html**. The **http://** indicates that the phrase begins a URL. The end of this code is denoted by the double slashes. Note that these are *forward* slashes, as opposed to the backslash characters that are used when designating file locations on a storage device (e.g. **C:\My Documents\filename.ext**).

The next portion of the URL denotes the domain name of the web site. This information is contained between the double slashes that follow the **http://** and the next occurrence of a slash in the URL. In the example here, the domain name is **www.domainname.com**. Organizations that register a domain typically use that domain for both their web pages and their e-mail, so an employee of the company that registered this domain might have an e-mail address of something like jdoe@domainname.com.

The last part of this domain name, the .com, indicates that the organization owning it is a commercial venture. This is one of the top-level domains that denote the type of organization that owns it or the country of registration. A more complete discussion of domain names is included in Chapter 4.

Web pages are usually organized into folders, much like those on a disk drive, to keep some order to the arrangement. Two or more web pages can share the same file name (e.g. index.htm) if they reside in separate folders. Folders, in turn, are usually organized according to function or subject matter. For instance, a law enforcement agency's web site might be organized like this.

```
http://www.anytownpd.org
/patrol
      /k9
      /traffic
      /schoolresource
/detectives
      /robbery-homicide
      /burglary
      /sexcrimes
      /autotheft
      /fraud
/communications
/administration
      /training
      /recruiting
      /internalaffairs
      /chief
/images
```

Another way of illustrating this organization is shown in Figure 8–3.

Within these folders would reside web pages that contain increasingly specific information. Each K-9 handler and his dog might have their own page within the http://www.anytownpd.org/patrol/k9 folder, as an example. Proper organization would also require that each folder contain a **home page** with the file name index.html or default.htm (the file extensions of .html and .htm are interchangeable and mean essentially the same thing). This would allow someone accessing the web site to type in something like http://www.

anytownpd.org/detectives/burglary, without knowing the name of a specific page within that folder, and be presented with a home page that included hyperlinks to related pages.

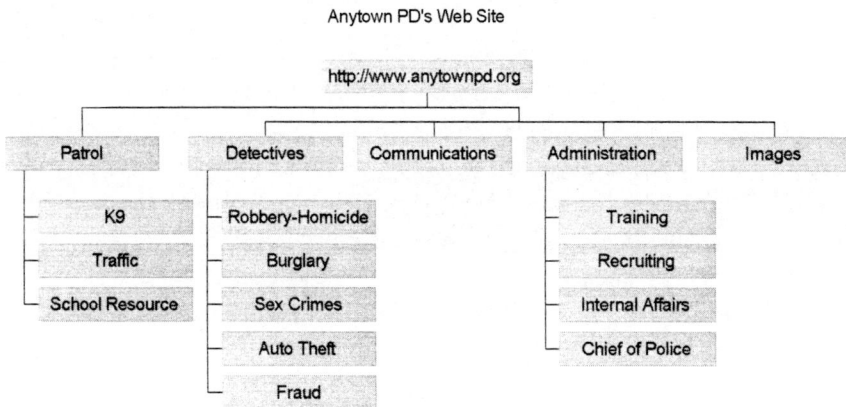

Anytown PD's Web Site

```
                        http://www.anytownpd.org

   ┌──────────┬───────────────┬───────────┬──────────────┬──────────┐
  Patrol    Detectives   Communications  Administration   Images

 ├─ K9        ├─ Robbery-Homicide       ├─ Training
 ├─ Traffic   ├─ Burglary               ├─ Recruiting
 └─ School    ├─ Sex Crimes             ├─ Internal Affairs
    Resource  ├─ Auto Theft             └─ Chief of Police
              └─ Fraud
```

Figure 8-3   Web Site Organization

The inclusion of a storage folder for images is a space-saving measure. In order for web pages on a site to have some continuity, it is common to provide one or more design templates that keep some features consistent, such as a logo, background color, fonts used, and so on. The graphic images used for the web pages in Figure 8–2 are stored in the /images folder, and all pages reference and display them from that folder. Otherwise, it would be necessary to include a separate duplicate image in the same folder as the page resided and waste space on the server. It would also slow the page loading time, as the logo used on one page would likely still be stored in the user's cache folder and could be displayed from there, rather than taking the time to download it again from the server.

Some domain name owners will use a similar method to organize their web sites, placing the name of the subdivision in front of the domain name, instead of in a subfolder. For example, the city of Anytown with the domain name http://www.anytown.org might place its police files into a domain at http://www.police.anytown.org. This is called a **third-level domain**. The subfolder structure would then be arranged similarly to the one in the www.anytownpd.org folder shown above. As long as the user knows where to look for the files he or she wants, the folder arrangement is not especially critical, but it often helps to be aware of how these files are organized.

As noted previously, most web pages will have file extensions of .htm or .html, which indicate less complex web pages. However, some pages contain special code that interacts with the server and the user's machine and have file extensions such as .asp (Active Server Pages), .cgi (Common Gateway Interface), or .pdf (Portable Document File). Of these examples, the first two represent program code that will capture information to search a database, enroll in a marketing program, or display information customized for that user. Some files, such as those in Adobe's proprietary .pdf format, require a special viewer to see the file. Without the viewer, the machine will not be able to open the file, but it is customary to include a link to Adobe's web site where the viewer can be downloaded at no charge. .pdf files are favored for reproducing publications exactly as they appeared in print, maintaining the same layout, fonts, illustrations, and such while keeping the file size manageable. Some web sites will even contain documents created in software such as Microsoft Word or PowerPoint and will require that the parent application be installed on the user's machine in order to view the file.

Viewing and Capturing Files and Images

In most cases, viewing a web page only requires clicking on the hyperlink that is associated with it or typing the URL into the address field of the browser. To save the page for viewing while offline or to capture an image from the page for some other use there are some special measures necessary.

Most web pages are a mix of graphics and text. The computer sees these as independent files and relies on the browser and the instructions in the HTML code to organize and display them in the correct arrangement. The simplest method of saving a web page is to display the page onscreen and then click on File|Save As in the Menu Bar. The simpler Save option is usually not available; the browser needs additional instructions on how to save the page.

The available options, seen by clicking on the downward-pointing arrow in the Save as type: window, are shown in Figure 8–4 and can be described as follows.

♦ Web Page, complete [*.htm, *html]: This will create a file with whatever name the user gives it. This is not limited to the page name that appears in the File name: window—that can be deleted and given any name. It will also create a subfolder in the same folder in which the file is saved, which will contain all of the graphics, sound files, and other nontext elements in the page. The subfolder will have the same name as the file. When the user clicks on the file name to display it later, the browser will retrieve the other page elements from the subfolder. This method preserves all of the formatting and elements of the page, but it also requires the most space.

♦ **Web Archive, single file [*.mht]:** This method will save all of the page elements into a single file, without using a subfolder, but the file will be MIME-encoded and will be somewhat slower to load and display in a browser. This is, however, a good compromise when saving a file to send to someone else as an e-mail attachment, since all of the page elements will be preserved in a single file without subfolders.

♦ **Web Page, HTML only [*.htm, *.html]:** This option saves the HTML code but not the graphics or other elements. When the saved page is displayed offline, there will be gaps where the missing elements used to appear. When the page is called up while online and the missing elements are still available on the servers where they reside, then they will be displayed in the browser.

♦ **Text file [*.txt]:** This saves only the text in the page and removes the most formatting. This method will usually produce the smallest file size and is often more than sufficient for preserving textual information within the page. *.txt files can be read in any word processor or in the Notepad or WordPad applications that are included with all Windows installations.

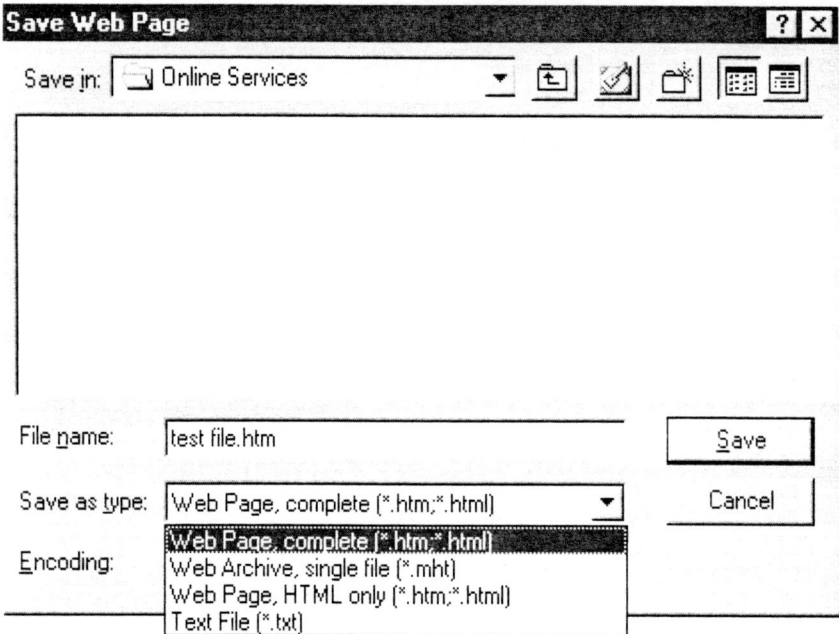

Figure 8-4 Saving a Web Page to Disk

Often, all a user wants to do is save a graphic or a snippet of text from a web page instead of saving the entire page. This is usually easy to do. If the information is in text format, select the desired block of text by dragging the mouse cursor from the start of the selection to the end or vice versa. The selected text will appear in reverse font, as in Figure 8–5.

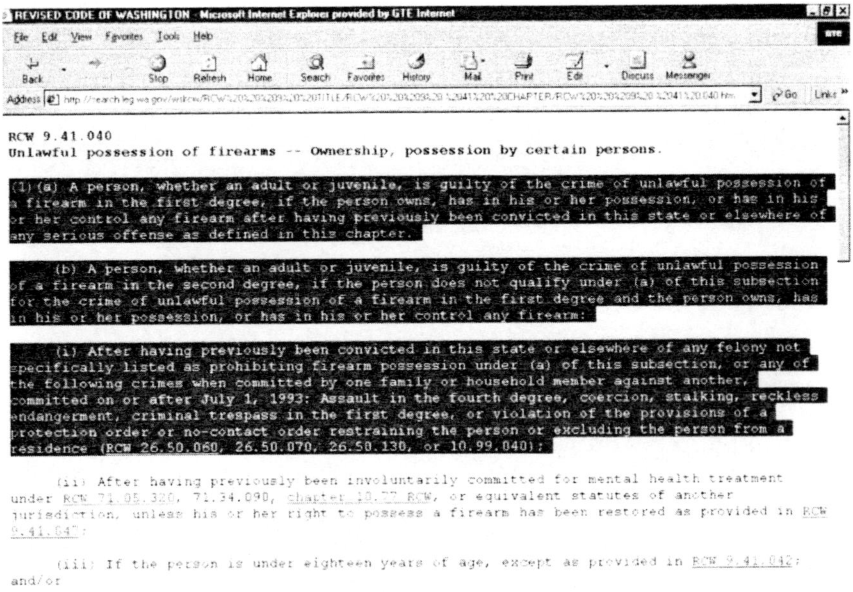

Figure 8-5   Selecting Text in a Web Page

If the text desired spans more than one screen, it can be difficult to scroll through the text and keep the selection active. To select an extended passage, hold down the Shift key, and click on the beginning of the desired passage. Then, use the keyboard (PageUp and PageDown keys or the arrow keys) to scroll through to the end of the desired passage, hold down the Shift key again, and click at that point. The passage between the two Shift-clicks will be selected.

With the desired text selected, right-click on the selection, and select Copy from the context menu that will appear. The selection will then be copied to the Windows Clipboard. Open any word processor and right-click to select Paste, or use the pulldown menu (usually under Edit) to paste the text in. This procedure can be repeated as many times as desired to get multiple selections from a single page or multiple pages. If the user is keeping a file of passages under a common subject, it might be helpful to create a single document file for that topic and then add passages to it as they are found.

Saving graphics can be slightly more complicated, both because of the variation in graphic image types used in web pages and because some web designers purposefully split or fragment their images to keep them from being copied to unauthorized sites. A split image looks the same as an unsplit one when viewed on a web page, but when the image is copied to another application, the user finds that it is divided into multiple parts. An example of this technique can be seen in Figures 8–6 and 8–7, taken from the FBI's home page at http://www.fbi.gov.

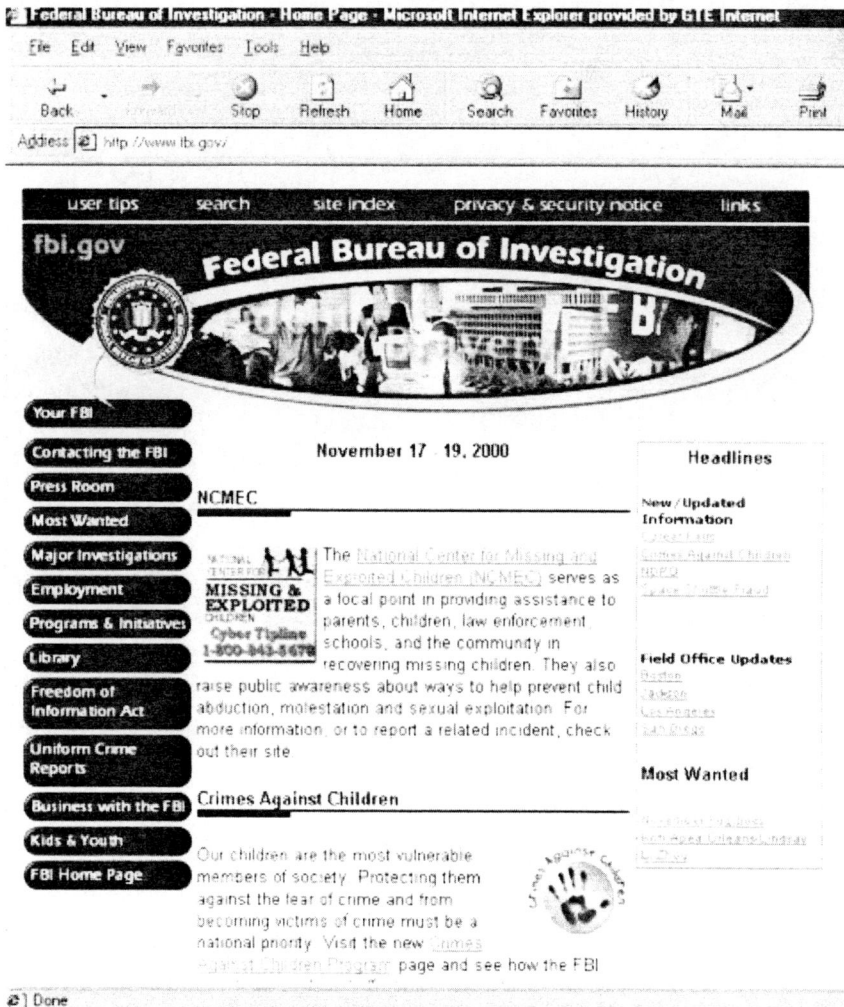

Figure 8-6   The FBI's home page

Figure 8-7   Fragmented FBI Seal

It should be no great surprise that the FBI is concerned about people going to its web site and capturing its official seal for illegitimate and unauthorized use elsewhere. One method used to increase the difficulty of this is to fragment the seal so that an unauthorized user would have to copy two or more portions of the graphic that contain the seal then reassemble them to view the entire seal. This is not impossible to do, but it requires a level of skill above that of the average web site hobbyist/designer. The large, page-width graphic that is seen on the FBI's home page is composed of several smaller components. The graphic components are placed by the use of a table, which fits each graphic image into a grid. The framework of the grid is invisible to the user. The user sees a complex, continuous graphic image, but the image cannot easily be captured with a single command.

Graphics are also split to reduce the time required for them to load. The graphical portions of a web page are usually the largest components of the page. Because HTML files are basically text files, they tend to be small and download fairly quickly. A single small graphic can easily exceed the size of the text file surrounding it by a considerable margin. In the example in Figure 8–5, the HTML code required to display the text and instructions for the entire page takes up 13 KB. The small graphic in Figure 8–7 is 6 KB by itself, and the entire graphic at the top of the page is composed of twenty-six images of similar size. If a user had to download a single large image, it would require a 156 KB (6 KB × 26 images) download, and no portion of the image would appear until the entire file had loaded. Many users with slow dial-up connections will move on before this can be done. By splitting the image up, portions of it appear as they download from the server, and the user knows that the page will soon be complete. The net download time is about the same, but the web designer holds the user's attention for a little longer while the images load.

Images used on the WWW are most commonly in one of two formats: JPEG (pronounced "jay-peg") and GIF (pronounced "jiff" or "giff" with a hard "g") because of their file extensions. JPEG stands for Joint Photographic Experts Group, named for the committee that developed this file standard. JPEG images are most commonly used for color photos and similar images with complex color gradients, and they have file extensions of *.jpg. GIF stands for Graphics Interchange Format and was developed by the CompuServe Information Service (an ISP and content provider now owned by AOL). At one time, the GIF image format was considered to be proprietary by CompuServe, but this format has acquired such widespread use that it is now a standard. GIFs have the file extension of *.gif and are most commonly used for line drawings and other images with relatively few colors. GIF images can usually be converted to JPEGs and vice versa, but they often lose some of their visual appeal or drastically increase in size as a result. Whether an image is shown in JPEG or GIF format is usually a compromise between image quality and file size.

Assuming that an image is not split, as is the case in Figure 8–7, capturing it to a file is a very quick process. With the image displayed on screen, place the cursor over it and right-click. A context menu will appear, with one of the options being **Save Picture As...** as shown in Figure 8–8.

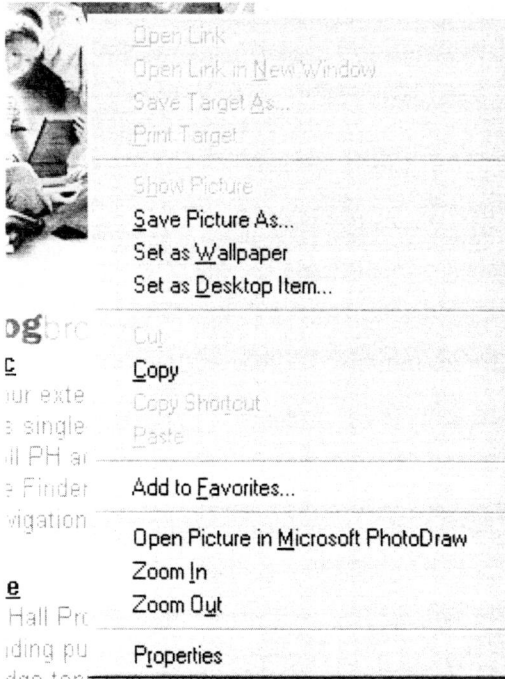

Figure 8-8   Saving a Graphic from the Web

Clicking on this option will open a dialog box with a Windows Explorer-type interface, asking where the file is to be saved. The user can navigate to the folder and give the graphic any name or keep the one that the web designer assigned to it. Be cautious, however, not to change the file extension of the image. It will almost always be in the form *.jpg or *.gif, and changing it will prevent the computer from properly recognizing the file format, which will make the image difficult or impossible to open or display.

Note that other options include **Set as Wallpaper** and **Copy**. If the user chooses the Wallpaper option, the image displayed will be transferred to the Desktop and will reside behind the icons displayed there. It may be necessary to activate Microsoft's Active Desktop feature to enable this. To do this, right-click on an empty portion of the Desktop, and select **Active Desktop** and **View as web page** from the displayed options. Another option is to copy the image to the Windows Clipboard and then paste it into another application, as can be done with any other Windows object.

Running and Saving Files from the Web

Some web pages include files that are intended to be downloaded and run on the user's computer. These include video files in various formats and executable programs that install software or perform other tasks. The user may wish to save these files to a local machine, rather than run them immediately. In fact, depending on the nature of the download, running the file prevents it from being saved, and in order to view it again or rerun the program, it must be downloaded again.

With executable files, it is often more prudent to save files to a local machine before running them. Most antivirus software will filter these files, but it is possible for harmful code to be loaded onto the machine before the antivirus software can catch it, which can harm the computer. Saving the file to the machine before running it gives the antivirus software a better shot at protecting the computer.

Links to downloadable files look like any other hyperlink, but clicking on them will start the file downloading from the server. This may or may not trigger a dialog box asking if the user if he or she wants to save the file to disk or open it. See Figure 8–9.

Note that the file name in the example in Figure 8–9 has a file extension of *.exe, indicating that the file is an executable one. There is the option to **Run this program from its current location**, but this is the most risky option. By selecting

Save this program to disk, the user can designate a folder to save it to then run it later. With software installations, this also permits the user to reinstall the software without having to download it again in the event that a file is corrupted or uninstalled somehow.

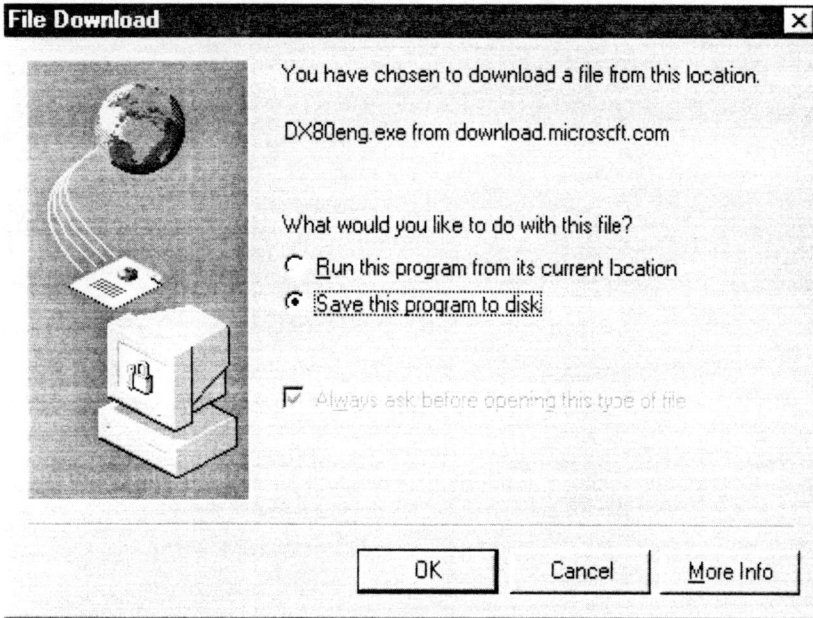

File Download

You have chosen to download a file from this location.

DX80eng.exe from download.microscft.com

What would you like to do with this file?

○ Run this program from its current location

● Save this program to disk

☑ Always ask before opening this type of file

| OK | Cancel | More Info |

Figure 8-9   Downloading an Executable File

A good practice is to create a **Downloads** subfolder within the **My Documents** folder and then create another subfolder for each download (or category of downloads) as they are obtained. Many executable files have cryptic names that are not intuitive as to what they do. For example, the one in Figure 8–8 is a set of drivers for DirectX version 8.0 from Microsoft. DirectX is an application program interface that is used by games and other graphics-intensive programs to allow the computer hardware to display images faster and more efficiently. Thus giving the subfolder a more descriptive name, such as **DirectX 8**, might help with locating the file later.

Subfolders can be created as needed. When saving a file, first navigate to the **Downloads** (or other) folder in which the subfolder will reside, then click on the icon in the top of the dialog box that looks like a folder with a small star in the upper right corner (see Figure 8–10). Type a name for the new folder, otherwise, it will have a name like **New Folder** or **New Folder-1**. Hit **Enter** to save the folder name, then double-click on it to open it. Save the file, and it will be stored in this folder. There is no limit to the number of subfolders, so it makes sense to use this feature to bring some order to one's files.

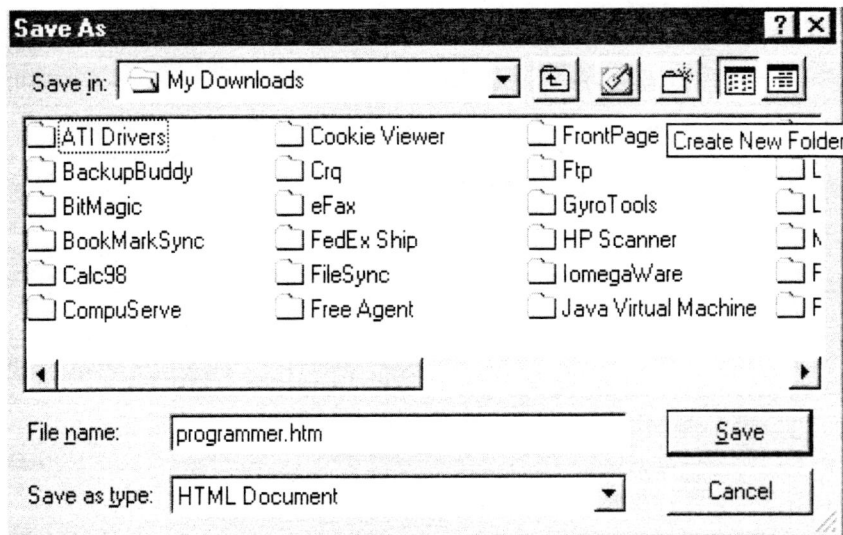

Save As	? ✕
Save in: ☐ My Downloads ▼	

☐ ATI Drivers	☐ Cookie Viewer	☐ FrontPage	Create New Folder
☐ BackupBuddy	☐ Crq	☐ Ftp	☐ L
☐ BitMagic	☐ eFax	☐ GyroTools	☐ L
☐ BookMarkSync	☐ FedEx Ship	☐ HP Scanner	☐ N
☐ Calc98	☐ FileSync	☐ IomegaWare	☐ F
☐ CompuServe	☐ Free Agent	☐ Java Virtual Machine	☐ F

File name:	programmer.htm	Save
Save as type:	HTML Document ▼	Cancel

Figure 8-10   Creating a New Subfolder

Search Engines and Portals

The Internet has been described as the largest library in the world; however, it has no card catalog, and all the books are piled in the middle of the room. The decentralized structure of the Internet makes for something of an anarchist organization with very little order to the millions, possibly billions, of web pages available for viewing. To compound this, something like seven million pages (at this writing) are added every day, and that number will increase substantially before it levels off or recedes.

Fortunately, there are some indexes and services available to assist Internet users in locating the resources that they want. These are called **search engines** and **portals**, terms which have become confusing and are sometimes interchangeable. Search engines record URLs, which are indexed with keywords that describe the content of the pages that they represent. When a user goes to a search engine and types in one or more keywords, the search engine checks its database and then posts a list of URLs that are associated with those keywords, in some order of precedence.

The order of precedence is extremely important to web page authors who wish to attract viewers to their sites. It is not uncommon for a search term to result in a listing of pages that goes well into five figures. Very few users are going to look past the first ten or twenty listings, so the web authors want to get their pages listed as far toward the top of those results as possible to ensure that their sites will be visited at least once. Many web pages are created only to promote an individual, an idea, or someone's hobby, but the money is in advertising. Many commercial web sites display **banner ads** that are created by other commercial vendors of everything from vacation packages to pornography. These vendors post the banner ads with a hyperlink coded with the URL of the page where they are posted. When a user clicks on one of the banner ads, which is called a **click-through**, he or she is taken to the sponsor site of the banner ad, where they will see information about the product or service in greater detail. On the successful, heavily visited sites, advertisers pay just to have visitors see their ads, and the number of times that the ad is displayed is incremented each time a page containing the ad is loaded. Some pages are viewed hundreds of thousands of times every day. When the viewer clicks on the banner, though, the advertiser owes the page owner a substantially greater sum, running from a few cents to several dollars.

Sometimes just choosing one of the listings that result from a keyword search can be profitable to the owner of the search engine. Some web site sponsors pay search engines to ensure that their page will come up toward the top of the list any time certain keywords are entered. One even tells how much it costs them. The search engine http://www.goto.com lists the cost that the advertiser will incur when the user clicks on the link to the advertiser's page. For instance, a search on the term web hosting indicated that the first choice in the results list would be paying GoTo.com $3.00 if someone clicks on their link. Clicking on their link means that someone might use their service to host a new domain name, and it is apparently worth at least that much to get people to look at their list of services.

Search engines make their money through several conduits. The first is by banner advertising, which is often tailored to the user. Typing a search term like Hawaii into a search engine's keyword field might yield a results page that is headed by a banner from a travel agency or an airline offering vacations in the South Pacific. Even the banner on the first page from the search engine's site may be tailored to that search term if the search engine has placed a **cookie** (which will be discussed in the section on Privacy and Security) on the machine. The cookie may have told the web server something about the previous visit, which may include a hint as to what advertising might be most appealing.

Another method that search engines use to make money is to either charge certain web sites a premium if the user does a click-through from that results page or see to it that certain web pages come up higher in the results list than others, even though they may not be as specifically relevant to the request as others are. Search engine providers usually do not make this kind of manipulation especially well known, so it is difficult to determine when the web sites are specific to the request or if their prominent display has been paid for.

Search engines use a number of methods to generate the indexes that they use to produce their results lists. The most common method, which may be combined with others, is to use a **spider**. Spiders are robot programs that "crawl" through the web, recording the text and images on the web pages they find, often using the links embedded in those pages to move to other pages and repeat the process. All this time, they are relaying back to their parent search engines the indexed terms they have found, the relative frequency with which those terms occur, which help determine the focus of a page, and the URLs associated with those terms.

Some spiders look only at the **meta tags** embedded in a page. Meta tags are HTML code that is invisible unless the user looks at the page's source code, and they have no effect on the way that the page is displayed, unlike most other HTML tags. Instead, meta tags contain terms that the page's author wants to have recognized as keywords and other information such as the author's name, the type of HTML editor that was used to create the page, and so on.

Because the frequency of a search term is often the key to getting one's page to the top of a results list, some page authors attempt to stack the deck by repeating search terms numerous times, trying to get the frequency count as high as possible. This tactic is most common on sites with an adult theme (of which there are many), so that an adult site's meta tag might look something like this.

> <META NAME = "keywords" CONTENT="sex nude porn sex nude
> porn sex nude porn sex nude porn sex nude porn sex nude porn
> sex nude porn sex nude porn sex nude porn sex nude porn sex
> nude porn sex nude porn sex nude porn sex nude porn sex nude
> porn sex nude porn sex nude porn sex nude porn sex nude porn
> sex nude porn sex nude porn sex nude porn">, etc.

The other method that search engines use to generate their indexes actually involves people. Some search engines employ professional web surfers to browse the web all day and catalog what they find into a database that is used by the search engine to produce its results lists. Most of these allow users and web authors to suggest a site for review so that it can be placed in the appropriate place in the index. This process usually involves filling out a web-based form, but there is software available that claims to submit one's web page to hundreds of search engines with one operation, saving time and presumptively increasing the number of visitors to the web site.

When looking for a web site based on a single word search term, the task is very straightforward. Go to the search engine's site, type in the word to search on, and hit the Enter key. The search engine will produce a list of sites that relate to that search term, subject to the biases detailed above. In theory, the list of results will be ranked from most relevant to least relevant, so that the sites likely to produce the information desired will be towards the top.

If the search term involves more than one word or if certain associated terms must be excluded from the search, the task is a little more complicated, but it can drastically reduce the time required to locate the desired topic. Most search engines employ some adaptation of **Boolean logic** to express complex search terms, although all do not use it in the same way. Boolean logic is named for nineteenth-century English mathematician George Boole, and it is used widely in the design of computers, as it handily expresses the binary, on or off, yes or no, nature of the way computers work.

As an example, assume that an officer is searching for the text of a speech made by former U.S. Attorney General Janet Reno that addressed gun control. He or she might start by using only the search term *Reno,* but that would likely bring up references not only to Janet Reno, but also to Reno, Nevada, and El Reno, Oklahoma. Further on down in the results list there might be a reference to the Johnny Cash song "Folsom Prison Blues" ("I shot a man in Reno, just to watch him die…"). To narrow the results list without having to cull through it manually, Boolean search terms can be used.

Boolean search terms are linked by **operators**, which tell the search engine what to do with the search term. In this case, we want to see the pages that include the terms *Janet* and *Reno,* but probably not the ones that include *Nevada* and *Oklahoma,* unless the speech happened to be given in Nevada or Oklahoma or one of those states was mentioned in the speech—this is not a perfect system. To include the words in Ms. Reno's name, we would use an operator of *AND,* or possibly the "+" symbol. Different search engines require different operators, but they all have Help pages that explain what is required. So the first term would probably be something like Janet AND Reno or possibly Janet + Reno.

The next step is to rule out the terms that are to be excluded, prefaced by an operator that tells the search engine "Discard any pages that include these terms from the results list." This would look something like this: NOT (Nevada OR Oklahoma).

The use of the *OR* operator further expands the meaning: "Exclude page that includes the word *Nevada* or the word *Oklahoma.*" The parentheses tell the search engine that *NOT* applies to all the terms contained within them. If we were to use an *AND* operator instead of an *OR*, the message to the search engine would be "Exclude any page that includes both the words *Nevada* and *Oklahoma*."

A further refinement might also be to ensure that the resultant pages discuss gun control. Here it is necessary to think a bit more creatively, because *gun* is not the only term that can describe the items of interest, and the search engine is going to literally interpret our search terms. So we might want to include some synonyms for *gun*, like *firearm, rifle,* and *weapon*. So, the next step to the search phase is: AND (gun OR firearm OR rifle OR weapon). The complete search phase looks something like this: Janet AND Reno AND (gun OR firearm OR rifle OR weapon) NOT (Nevada OR Oklahoma).

The order of the search terms can be important. The first operator retrieves a list of pages that contain the words *Janet* and *Reno*. From these, the next operator discards from the list any that lack the terms *gun, rifle, firearm,* or *weapon,* and then further culls from the list any that have the terms *Nevada* or *Oklahoma*.

However, this method will not always find the right pages immediately. Every search engine seems to use Boolean operators in a slightly different way. Some require phrases to be in quotes or use mathematical symbols, so instead of Janet AND Reno, another search engine might want "Janet Reno" or Janet + Reno.

Search engines that use mathematical symbols usually substitute a plus symbol (+) for *AND*, a minus symbol (-) for *NOT*, and a slash (/) for *OR*. Some ignore parentheses, and others use them extensively. With some, any phase in quotes is read literally, so that *Janet Reno* would not locate any page that included only *Reno, Janet* in reference to the former attorney general.

Some search engines have advanced search pages where terms can be placed in blanks and linked with operators in drop-down lists, and others allow searches to be conducted in stages so that a list of terms from one search can be searched again to get only items that contain a separate set of terms. With this method, a search can be done on *Reno,* followed by another search on that list for *Janet.* Then the list can be further reduced by searching for *gun OR firearm,* and so on.

There are many, many search engines to choose from, and users generally have favorites because they are accustomed to the interface. If the search comes up dry, though, do not be afraid to try another engine. No two search engines have the same index, and pages are constantly being added to both the web and to the indexes. Moreover, as few as 3% of the web pages that are accessible to the common web surfer are indexed by search engines, so there may be many pages that will never be found by using a search engine; they simply have to be stumbled upon.

Many search engines have reinvented themselves as portals, serving as a kind of gateway to the Internet. A portal is a web site that offers a variety of services, most, if not all, of which are free. These are intended to attract users back to their site again and again, with the idea that people will see those ad banners and click on one now and again. To ensure that their pages hold appeal for everyone, most have created customized pages for each visitor, usually identified by placing the word *my* in front of the site name, e.g. *MyExcite*, *MyYahoo*, and *MyLycos* (sometimes with and sometimes without the space between the words).

Getting a custom page is easy—if the user is willing to part with some information. Most of the portal sites require that users register in order to get a "my" page, and registration means telling the portal provider the user's name, e-mail address, and often mailing address, phone number, age, year and month of birth, martial status, number of dependents, and income bracket. Of course, there is no way for the site to see if the questions are answered truthfully. An acquaintance of the author has an online profile to the effect that he was born in 1900, makes less than $5 per year, and has no living relatives. His address is usually something like "Refrigerator Box #5, The Bowery." Most people give up their personal data, and the portal sells their names to anyone with the money to buy it.

By registering, the user provides the portal with some extremely valuable information. The personal preferences web page that a new user is asked to create is indicative of his or her personal interests. These pages can display all sorts of information, from sports scores to local TV listings to current stock quotes. If a user indicates interest in Cleveland-based sports teams, and he or she lives in the Southwest, then the web page might display a banner ad for an airline that flies between those two regions. People who want local movie listings might also be interested in home theatre equipment, video rental coupons, or DVD movies. A demographic study could show that people that like to read a quote of the day are literary folks who are also good customers of bookstores.

The personal pages come complete with banner ads, but these have a twist— if a user clicks on them, there is a high likelihood that the company that sponsored the ad will get a message to the effect that "John Doe, who lives at 123 Main St. in Anytown, has an e-mail address of jdoe@isp.com, makes $40,000 per year, is married, has three kids, likes football, was interested enough in your banner ad to click on it. You might consider giving John a call." They will, too. It is easier to get rid of tuberculosis than it is to get off of some of these merchants' mailing lists.

If it is important to have a web page that displays valuable information all in one place, and an increasing quotient of electronic and conventional junk mail, telemarketer calls, and other "consumer opportunities" is not bothersome, then setting up and registering a "My*Page*" will not be a problem. However, if privacy is important, the tactics detailed on pages 171–183 under "Privacy and Security" might be helpful.

One of these personalized pages may also be a personal home page. This is the page that the browser will automatically load by default at start-up if no URL is specified. Virtually any page on the web can be designated as a home page. To do so, navigate to the page to be used, then click on the Tools|Internet Options icon in the menu bar and select Use Current Page from the dialog box under the General tab. In Navigator, the same option is under Edit|Preferences, then click on the Navigator option in the displayed list.

Favorites and Bookmarks

Often, while browsing the web, people come across pages that they would like to be able to return to at some future date for reference or amusement purposes. Unfortunately, URLs are difficult to remember and unforgiving of even the smallest error, so trying to get back by typing the URL in again is often frustrating. Both Internet Explorer and Navigator provide methods to record the URLs of sites to revisit quickly and easily. IE calls this feature Favorites, while Navigator calls it Bookmarks. They have exactly the same function and the terms are interchangeable.

When the browser is installed, it almost certainly comes with a list of bookmarks or favorites installed. This preselected list is going to be heavily stacked in favor of web sites that have paid the browser publisher a fee or some other compensation to be included in this list because most users will not alter the list. In fact, some users will go only to sites listed in their bookmark lists, believing that bringing up other sites is too difficult or even impossible for them.

Using the bookmark list is extremely easy. Open the browser, click on the Communicator|Bookmarks or Favorites item in the menu bar, and select a site or category of interest. Categories, which look like file folders, hold subcategories, or sites relevant to those categories. Upon locating an interesting site listing, click on it, and the browser will go to that page, providing that it is still available. IE users can access their Favorites list right from the Start menu. Click on the Start button, then on Favorites, and select the desired page. IE will open to that page.

However, the most useful feature of Favorites and Bookmarks is the ability to create personal bookmark lists. In the simplest method, a page can be added the bookmark list by pressing Control + D on the keyboard while that page is displayed in the browser. This method works for both IE and Navigator. After a while, though, bookmark lists become long and difficult to navigate and will even contain some duplicates if the user has forgotten which pages have been added to them. That is when it pays to organize the bookmarks.

In IE, click the **Favorites** option on the menu bar, then on **Organize Favorites**. A dialog box will appear similar to that in Figure 8–11. First, create new folders that describe the type of web sites listed. Click on the **Create Folder** button, then give the folder a descriptive name. Hit the **Enter** key, and the folder will appear in the list in the dialog box, although it may be at the bottom of the list. Repeat this task as many times as necessary to get the folders that are necessary, then start putting the favorites into their folders. Do this by clicking on a favorite to select it, then on the **Move to Folder...** button. A list of only folders will open, and clicking on the folder in which the favorite is to reside will move it there and off the root list. Favorites can also be moved by drag and drop, clicking on the favorite to be moved and dragging it to the appropriate folder. This works best if both the folder and the favorite are visible in the display window, which is not always the case.

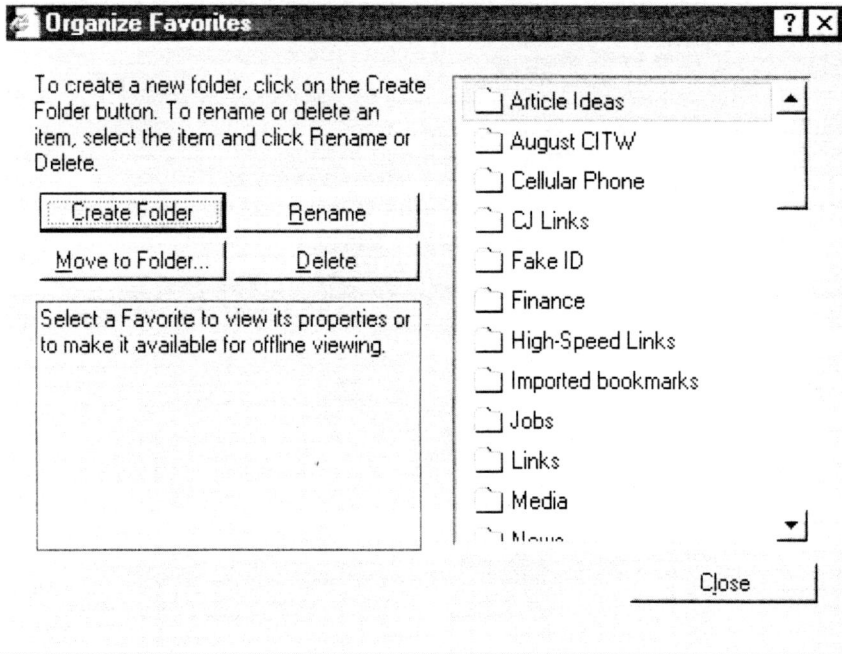

Figure 8-11   Organizing Favorites in Internet Explorer

To get rid of the favorites that came with the browser installation, just click on the favorite or its folder and then on the **Delete** button. Selected favorites can be moved out of the to-be-discarded folders to other folders that will be kept or to the root list, and the rest can be discarded.

The user is not tied to the name of the page that the web designer used, although this is the one that will default to the favorites list. If a page has a long name like **Great Things That We Want You to Know About Acme Handcuffs** and needs to be simplified, just right-click on that item in the favorites list, and select **Rename** from the context menu (see Figure 8–12). Enter the new name (**Acme Handcuffs**), and hit **Enter**.

When Favorites is organized, click on the **Close** button to close the dialog box. Now the Favorites list will not be in alphabetical order. To re-alphabetize, click on the **Favorites** option in the Menu Bar, then right-click on the list. The context menu that will appear will include an option for **Sort by Name** (see Figure 8–12). Click on that, and the entire list will alphabetize itself. This same trick works for items in the **Start** menu as well.

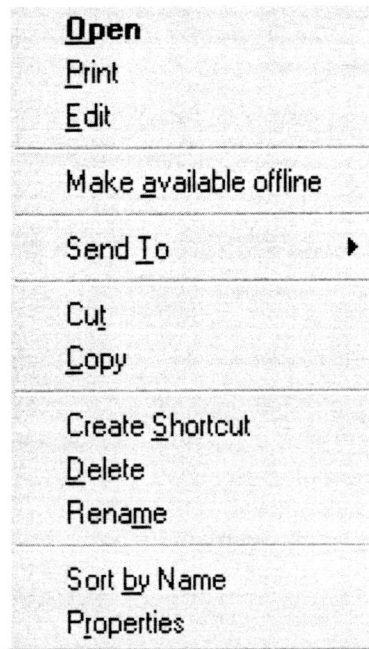

Figure 8-12   Sorting the Favorites List

Privacy and Security

Everyone should be concerned about threats to personal privacy and security on the Internet, and there is a growing consciousness of this issue among the general public. What is not well understood is the nature of the threat and what aspects of the privacy of individuals are threatened.

While it is technically possible for someone to crack a computer via the Internet and delve into the files stored there, this does not happen very often. This is even more rare in cases where users have dial-up connections. This is because dial-up connections use dynamic IP addressing, which assigns a new IP address each time the connection is made. The IP address is analogous to the computer's "telephone number" on the Internet, and in order to connect with the computer, a cracker has to either know the IP address or stumble onto it. Because dial-up connections are of relatively short duration, the window of opportunity that a cracker has to do this over a dial-up connection is very small.

Users with always-on connections, such as those via cable modem and DSL, have a different situation. Some DSL and cable modem connections assign a static IP address that is always the same, and others assign IP addresses dynamically, establishing a new one every time a connection is made to the Internet. Static IP addresses are more vulnerable because they do not change. However, even dynamic IP addresses via DSL and cable modem are more vulnerable to cracking because these connections are usually valid for the duration of that computing session, e.g. until the connection is broken manually or the computer is turned off. Some users leave their machines on continuously, so they have what amounts to a static IP address for security purposes.

Protecting a computer from crackers via the Internet is fairly easy by installing and keeping current antivirus software and using a firewall. There are a number of products that are available for this purpose, and which one that to choose is largely a matter of price and user preference. However, online computing without these safeguards is needlessly risky and threatens not only the user's privacy, but also the integrity of the files on his or her computer.

Although the entertainment industry regularly portrays teenagers who can dial into any computer and invade it, this is rarely done with desktop machines. The reason for this is that few people have their modems set to answer the phone when it rings. If the computer will not pick up a call, then there is no way for anyone to dial in. Desktop and laptop computers become more vulnerable to this kind of attack if they are running some kind of telephone answering or fax software that causes it to connect to incoming calls. There is also software that allows users to connect to their home or office computers by dialing them up and using a password scheme. These utilities can be useful, but they do provide a path whereby a malicious caller can access a computer. Keeping the machine set to ignore incoming calls on that line, which is the default setting for most modems, is far safer. Answering machines are not expensive, and there are incoming fax numbers via the Internet for free. If it is necessary to install remote-access software to access files when away from home base, be very cautious about setting passwords, and use the highest level of security setting that the software allows for.

The explosion of online shopping, or e-commerce, has been hindered by a common perception that sending one's credit card number to a merchant via the Internet is inherently risky and opens one to misuse of the credit card account. In truth, it is probably no more risky to use a credit card to pay for a meal in a restaurant. In the typical restaurant setting, the server brings the bill, and the diner gives him or her the credit card. The server takes the card, runs it through a terminal, and gets a receipt for the diner to sign. Because this transaction usually takes place out of view of the customer, it is impossible to know how many times the server ran the card through the terminal or if he or she recorded the credit card number, name, and expiration date on a pad for later use elsewhere. The customer trusts the restaurant to treat the card with care and good business practices. The vast majority of the time, that is exactly what they do.

Sending a credit card number to an online merchant is not much different. Most web pages that accept ordering information use **Secure Sockets Layer (SSL)** encryption, which encodes the information between the sender and intended recipient. If an interloper does intercept the data packets that contain this information, they will be encrypted and useless to him. The risks in buying online are the same that one assumes when dealing with any other catalog merchant, online or otherwise. Will the product be substantially the same as advertised? Will it be delivered on time and in good condition? Can it be returned? There is seldom a great deal of risk when dealing with well-established businesses; they would not be well-established if they had not treated their customers fairly. When dealing with less well-known merchants, more caution is appropriate.

The real danger in having credit card information captured fraudulently lies in the security, or, more accurately, the lack of security, of the merchant. Crackers will occasionally invade a company's system and retrieve the database of its customers and their credit card numbers, which will usually number into the thousands. These numbers get posted on newsgroups or web pages, or are sold or otherwise exploited by the cracker. They do not remain valuable for very long, because as soon as the merchant notices the break-in, the customers are notified using the same database and are cautioned to obtain new account numbers. Because virtually all merchants use computer databases to track their customers and their credit card accounts, online merchants are only slightly more vulnerable to this kind of invasion that are the traditional brick-and-mortar businesses. Most large merchants have an online presence of some type, so the difference between the two is blurring more and more all the time.

Many sites, whether they deal in e-commerce or not, will ask their users to register in order to get access to an enhanced set of services. These can range from online games to discount coupons to newsletters, and most of them are free. The reason the they can provide this service at no cost is because they use the information that the user gives them to produce narrowly targeted prospect lists for other businesses, as was mentioned previously. The site is also very likely placing a cookie on each user's computer, so that it can recognize individuals as a registered users or previous visitors the next time that they stop in. Cookies are small text files that contain information about the user, including what he or she did the last time the site was visited and what sort of things he or she might be interested in. The information is usually not in plain text form, but rather in a coded form that the web server can interpret. The cookie will more than likely contain the person's name, whatever user name was chosen for that site, and possibly a password, which it will pass to the web server as soon as the page is loaded, making it unnecessary for the user to reestablish his or her identity, plus a coded string that might look something like **16819193499954357075**.

That string of numbers was taken from a cookie on the hard drive of the author's computer. It might tell the web server, "This person has made a purchase from us previously, in the $50–$100 range. He lives in the Pacific Northwest. He likes new electronic gadgets, has a cell phone, and visits the web site about once a month. He is on our mailing list for both e-mail offers and catalogs, and we sold his name to other merchants nine times as of his last visit." It is not possible to tell what the code string says about someone. However, all of that information and more could be extracted or inferred from monitoring a user's habits while on a web site and would be valuable to marketing people. The buying and selling of prospect lists has become such a big business that many online merchants take a loss on their advertised merchandise, getting the bulk of their profits from the marketing of their customer lists. Of course, many of these businesses also fail, which explains at least part of the high mortality rates of the dot-com businesses that have come and gone in recent years.

Some cookies can be even more insidious. One Internet marketing company that is responsible for the placement of many web sites' banner advertisements was found to be gathering information in their cookies not just from the banner ad, but also by tracking the browsing habits of the cookies' users after they had left that site. The next time that the user came into contact with a banner or web site that could access that cookie, the information contained in it was retrieved. This was, in turn, cross-indexed with customer profiles that they had purchased from other marketers or compiled themselves and sold to still more firms.

The implications of this can be frightening. Imagine a fictitious Internet marketing company called market.com. Officer Linda Smith visits a web site that sells dog training supplies, and the site contains an ad from market.com, which she clicks on, causing a cookie from market.com to be placed on her hard drive. In fact, it might not even require that she click on the banner ad, depending on how the page is coded. The market.com cookie records what merchandise she looks at and/or orders, as well as her name and shipping address. Unfortunately, the cookie's activities do not end there. The cookie continues to be active, recording selected information about other web sites that she visits, even is she is careful not to leave her name or address. The next time that the cookie communicates with its home server, which happens when Linda goes back to the same dog training site or some other site that holds a cookie from market.com, it updates her file in their database, indicating what sort of activities she has participated in on the web. This information is combined with mailing list data already in their files, and she starts to receive all sorts of unwanted mail, having no idea how these companies got her name.

Cookies are not inherently evil things. They can make web surfing much more convenient and tailor the pages to fit user preferences. The customized "My*Site*" portal pages explained previously use cookies to retrieve from their web servers the information that a given user is most interested in, although they may be selling names, too. Web sites from banks, insurance companies, and investment firms that display personal account information use cookies to save the trouble of typing in a name and a password every time a user logs in. Of course, if more than one person has access to the computer, then it is best to log into these sites manually, because otherwise anyone who browses a Favorites/Bookmarks list or just knows the primary user's bank can log into those same sites and view the account information. If the site permits the transfer of funds from those accounts, another person can do that, too.

Someone who has been surfing the web already may not be aware of how often cookies are loaded onto his or her machine. They are present in many commercial web pages and are also embedded in HTML-formatted e-mail messages. The user can control how the e-mail and web browser clients handle cookies. They can be set to accept or reject all cookies or to prompt the user for consent before any cookie is accepted. Internet security software also often includes an option where the transfer of cookies can be regulated.

The simplest method of regulating cookie transfer is to set the appropriate option in the web browser. If Internet Explorer is used for web browsing and Outlook Express for e-mail, setting this option will affect both clients, because IE and OE are bundled applications that use the same user preferences. In IE, the settings for cookie transfer are under the Tools|Internet Options menu. When this dialog box is open, click on the tab that reads Security, and then on the Custom Options button. A list of options will appear that looks similar to Figure 8–13. The settings for cookies are about a third of the way down the scrollable list.

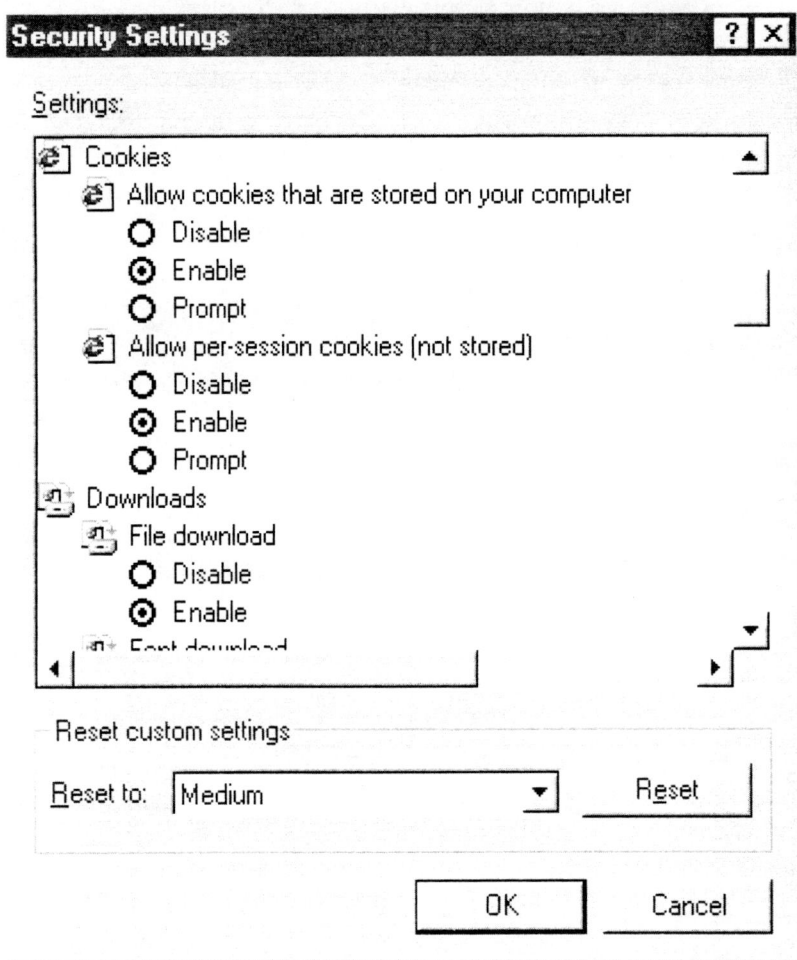

Figure 8–13   Setting Security Options

In Figure 8–13, the indicated settings are at the least-secure level, which is how most people have them set. With these settings, cookies will be transferred to the user's computer whenever they are embedded in a web page, and the user will not be aware of it. Selecting the **Disable** option will reject any cookies without further issue, but this will also limit the options that many web sites can offer. For instance, customized web portal pages will not be an option, and a password protected site will require a manual log-in.

Note that the Security Settings list differentiates between **cookies that are stored on the computer** and **per-session cookies. Per-session cookies** are deleted as soon as the browser is closed. They are used for activities like web-based games, where the server needs to keep track of the user's score and movements, since most people probably are not the only ones playing the game at that moment. When the browser is closed, that information is automatically erased. **Cookies that are stored on the computer** are otherwise called "persistent cookies" and carry with them an expiration date. In most cases, the expiration dates are years away, so the persistent cookies are essentially permanent, unless they are manually deleted. For the most part, the persistent cookies are the ones that are cause for concern, although per-session cookies can carry away confidential information, as well.

When the **Prompt** option is selected, a dialog box like the one in Figure 8–14 will pop up every time a cookie is offered to the computer and will ask for the user's consent to receive the cookie. If this option is selected, the number of times this request appears may be surprising. Some web sites have cookies that number into double digits, and before the web page loads completely, the user will be asked to approve every one. Most people grow weary of this task.

In Figure 8–14, the **More Info** button was clicked to show the data contained in the cookie. In this case, the cookie was sent from the web portal site msn.com, and the cookie, if accepted, will reside on this computer until the year 2020, at which time the computer will probably be in a landfill. The data field shown in the dialog box is coded, with the code's meaning known only to the msn.com server. One might expect that this code reflects whatever preferences the user has already defined to msn.com for the customized page that is presented to him or her.

In this case, clicking on the **Yes** button will accept the cookie, and the **No** button will reject it. If the user clicks the box that reads **In the future, do not show this warning**, then the option to accept persistent cookies without a prompt will be reset in the browser's security options list, even though the user may have set it manually to reject or prompt for cookies. Keep in mind that anyone else who has access to the computer can reset the security options merely by checking this box while browsing.

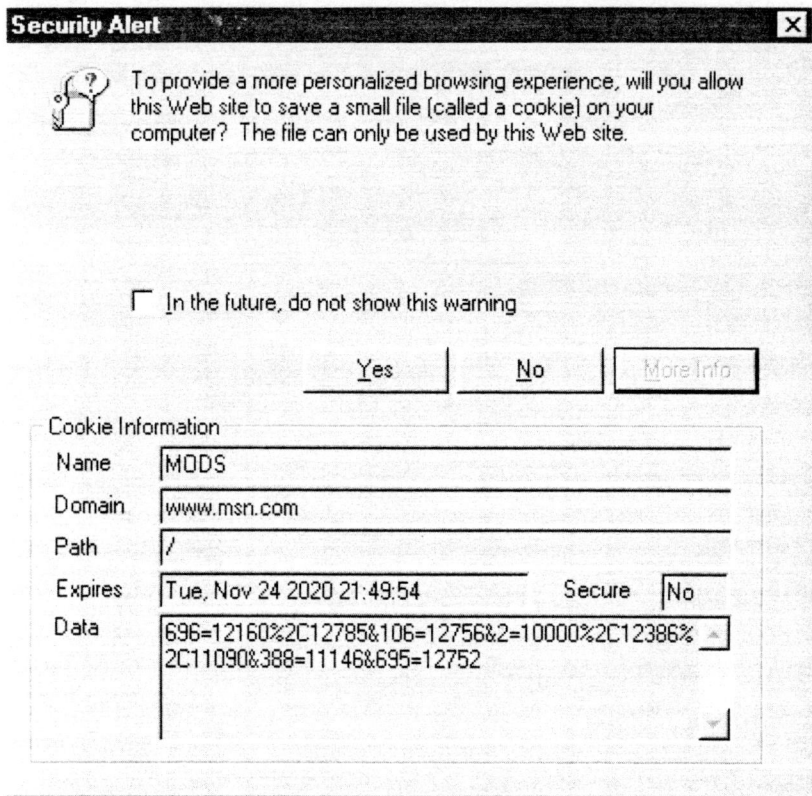

Figure 8-14   Accepting or Rejecting Cookies

There are commercial, freeware, and shareware programs that scan the hard drive for cookies and delete them, show their contents one by one, or selectively filter cookies from predesignated sites. For those who are concerned that someone might be snooping on their online activities, it might be prudent to acquire and use one of these packages.

In the same listing of security options that includes the settings for cookies, there are some options for **ActiveX** and Microsoft **VM** (**Virtual Machine**). Active X and VM are related to types of small programs that are contained in many web pages and provide animation, interactive features, and other innovative options.

ActiveX controls usually relate to the way that sounds, animations, and other multimedia elements appear on a web page. ActiveX is a considerably complex technology on which several books have been written. For purposes of security, ActiveX controls can conceivably be instrumental in invading privacy or causing harm to data because they are, in essence, miniprograms that are downloaded from the Internet. For this reason, downloaded ActiveX controls are usually "signed" by the authors or owners, meaning that they carry a digital certificate telling who created or sent them. If the authors/owners are trustworthy, then it stands to reason that the controls are as well. The security options list includes settings where the user can immediately accept or reject ActiveX controls or be prompted before both signed and unsigned ActiveX controls are downloaded to the system. Most ActiveX controls are going to be harmless miniprograms that may or may not add to the enjoyment of the web site, but a malicious programmer could try to sneak one by that does some harm. It stands to reason that most malicious programmers would not digitally sign their work to avoid it being traced back to them, so the security options differentiate between signed and unsigned controls. However, a control signed by a vandal from maliciouspunks.com might still be harmful. Further, even an otherwise reputable company might have a renegade on staff who surreptitiously placed a harmful ActiveX control. The safest setting is to reject all ActiveX controls or at least to have the browser prompt the user before they are downloaded. If the latter alternative is chosen, however, the user will have to answer a lot of prompts. A more practical, although more risky, option is to accept signed ActiveX controls and to prompt for unsigned controls. When a dialog box appears requesting permission to download a control, consider the nature of the site that is trying to send it before agreeing.

Virtual machine settings are not as controversial because virtual machines are those that run within the computer, isolated from the operating system and other applications. The virtual machine is created on the fly and generally runs small programs called **applets** that are written in Java. The applets perform any number of functions, but they are usually very small so that they can be downloaded quickly on demand and are designed to be very specific for the task at hand. There has been some experimentation with Java applets that would replace large, installed applications, like word processors, by downloading to the user's machine only the components that were needed at that moment. While typing a document, there might be one applet, but as soon as spell-check or a special formatting feature was engaged, another applet would be downloaded for that purpose. The advantage is that the storage capacity on the user's machine would need to be far smaller than what is presently the case, and the applications would always be the most current version, since they could be updated more or less continuously on the provider's server. The downside is that the user would have to be connected to the Internet or at least to a server that was capable of downloading the applications whenever he or she was working. Computers that are limited to this kind of processing are called **network computers** or **thin-client** machines. They have the advantage of being relatively inexpensive to produce, since they do not require a lot of processing power or storage resources; that portion would be held on their parent servers. They are not very useful, however, when there is no network connection; there is not much in the way of stand-alone resources on the user's machine. Most personal computers in common use today are **thick-client** machines, meaning that they contain their own data and applications and are relatively independent of a network.

Virtual machine applications are somewhat safer than other downloaded applications because they run independently of the operating system and other installed applications. The disadvantage is that this isolation usually makes them incapable of interacting with the parent machine's applications and data, and the resources contained there are unavailable to the applet. This notwithstanding, someone is undoubtedly producing or has already produced a Java applet that can not only interact with its parent computer, but can do harm to it. Thus, even Java applets are not entirely safe, which is why there is a security setting to keep the browser from downloading them. Most of the time, they are safe to download, but the very cautious web surfer will set his or her security settings to prompt before a Java applet is downloaded, just to make sure.

Java, by the way, should not be confused with the similar-sounding Javascript, which is a scripting language developed independently from Java. Javascript is widely used to format web pages and provide some interactive features, but it is not as powerful or potentially harmful as Java.

For some people, the greatest threat of invasion of privacy comes not from the parties that sponsor web sites, but from people in their own homes and offices who have access to the same computer and may be looking to see what they have been doing. A few precautions will keep all but the most determined snoops from looking into personal online activities. These concern two features of the browser: the temporary Internet files folders and the history folder.

When the browser downloads a web page, it stores the various components of the page (graphics, HTML code, sounds, etc.) in a cache folder, also called the Temporary Internet files folder. The cache file continues to fill until its preset size limit has been reached, at which time the oldest files are deleted. If the user returns to a web page that has been viewed previously, the browser looks in the cache first to see if any of the components of the page are stored there, and if it finds them, it retrieves those from the cache, rather than from the web server. Many pages on the same site will use the same components (graphics, logos, etc.) on more than one page, and this speeds the time required for the page to load. The browser can be ordered to retrieve all new files from the web server by clicking on the **Refresh** or **Reload** button. This is occasionally necessary when viewing a page that has data that changes frequently, as might be the case with news headlines or stock quotes.

When a web session ends, the contents of the cache file remain and can be viewed by anyone with access to the computer. The cache file is disorganized and will contain a lot of fairly meaningless garbage, but viewing of the various graphics and other files there will give strong evidence as to the recent browsing activities of the computer's user(s). With Internet Explorer, the cache is usually stored at C:\Windows\Temporary Internet Files. However, the cache can be viewed, controlled and even cleaned out from within Internet Explorer. See Figure 8–15.

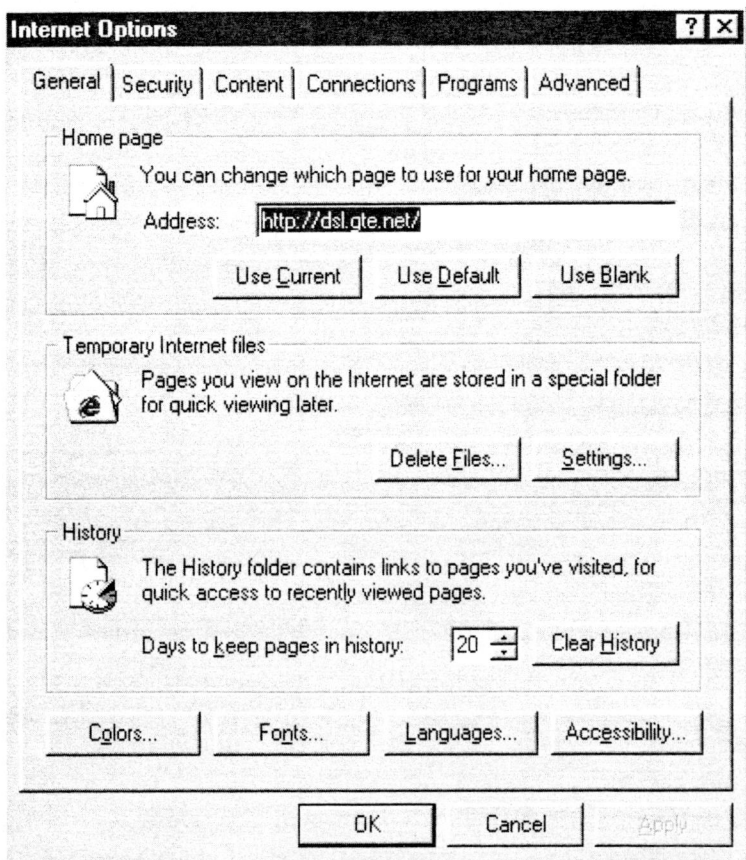

Figure 8-15   Cache and History Files

The dialog box in Figure 8–15 is accessed by clicking on Tools|Internet Options from Internet Explorer, then on the General tab. The topmost box contains the URL for the web page that will automatically load whenever the browser is started and no other URL is preselected. This URL can be set to any that the user prefers. The middle portion of the dialog box controls the settings for the browser's cache. Clicking on the Settings ... button will bring up another dialog box, similar to that shown in Figure 8–16.

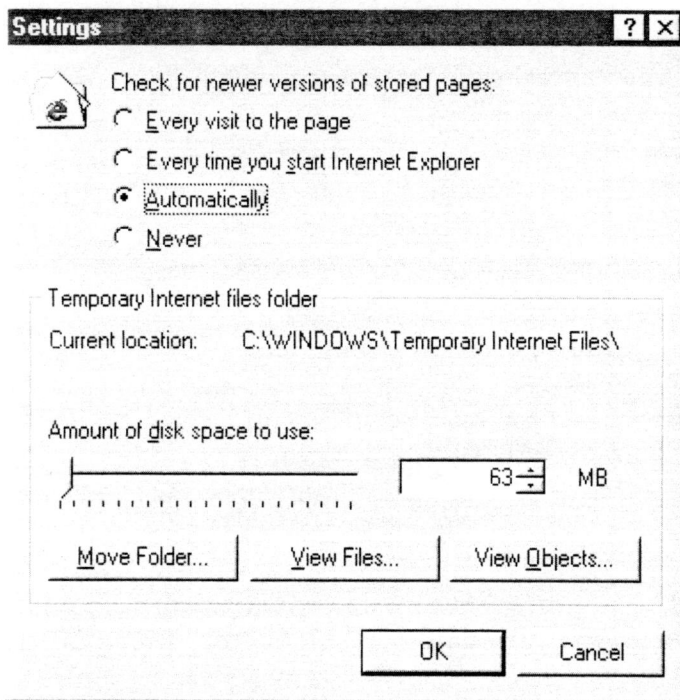

Figure 8–16 Setting Cache Folder Options

The Check for newer versions of stored pages options list tells the browser when to look to the web server for updated files. Most users set this option to Automatically. If it is set to Every visit to the page or Every time you start Internet Explorer, the time required for the program to load and start to retrieve pages will increase dramatically. If it is set to Never, the browser will retrieve new files from the web server only when the Refresh command is given or when the URL is typed into the address bar or a hyperlink to the page is clicked.

The lower portion of the window controls where the cache will be located and how much space it will occupy on the hard drive. It also offers the option to view the contents of the folder. The size of the folder is whatever the user wants it to be. In most cases, this size is based more on the available hard disk capacity than anything else. A smaller cache size will cause the browser to have to retrieve files from the web server more frequently, and a larger cache size will require this less frequently. **View Files** . . . opens the folder in a window similar to one in Windows Explorer so that the contents can be viewed and edited manually. This is also where the cookie files are stored. **View Objects** . . . allows the user to see what miniprograms, mainly plugins that allow viewing of specialized web applications, have been installed.

To move the cache file to another location, perhaps one that is not so easily accessed, click on the **Move Folder** . . . button. However, interested parties can always see where the cache is by accessing this same dialog box.

Getting back to the **Internet Options|General** dialog box in Figure 8–15, this is where users can delete or "dump" the cache, making it more difficult to monitor the user's activities by browsing the cache. Clicking on the **Delete Files** . . . button will bring up a dialog box to confirm this action and clean the cache file. Remember that most, if not all, of these files will be sent to the Windows Recycle Bin, where they can be restored if the bin is not emptied. A complete cache dump requires that both the cache and the Recycle Bin emptied.

The History folder is the other major telltale for prying eyes. The History folder maintains a list of every URL visited by the browser within the range set in this dialog box (Figure 8–15). This feature is useful for those who remember that they saw something on a web page they went to on Wednesday, for instance, but cannot remember the URL. To clear the current History folder, click on the **Clear History** button, and the contents of the folder are deleted. To keep the browser from accumulating additional history data, set the **Days to keep pages in history** option to "0."

The simplest technique for protecting privacy is to not tell people who or where one is. The use of online personas was discussed in the chapter on newsgroups, and the techniques apply similarly here. When filling out web-based forms, consider using an alias or changing some personal data, such as a middle initial, to determine if a site has taken personal information and disseminated it elsewhere. Unless there is a need to receive conventional mail from a site sponsor, provide a fictitious address or route mail to a post office box. Set up an e-mail account with a free service and use that account for online registrations and enrollments. Hotmail is the most popular, but some web pages will reject Hotmail addresses just because so many people have availed themselves of this option. Set up a free Internet fax account and provide that number if asked for a fax destination. When entering contests or subscribing to free or discounted offers, deception may disqualify users from their benefits; it is expected that people use true information for those activities.

These security precautions may seem complicated, but most of them need to be set only once, and then the browser's software will filter the potentially harmful applications and manage the telltale settings. Law enforcement personnel need to remember that the same privacy techniques described here are also used by the criminal sector, which has as much or more incentive to keep their activities from being discovered. Because computers are involved to same degree in so many different types of investigations, these techniques should be a part of every officer's tool kit, even if the officer is not directly involved in typically high-tech cases.

Protecting Your Privacy

1. Consider requiring a password to start the computer. This option is usually available under the Setup screen that is referenced at start up (e.g. **Press F1 for Setup.**)

2. Establish a free web-based e-mail account to use for online registrations.

3. Acquire an Internet-based fax number for online activities.

4. When registering or providing one's name on web sites, change some aspect of the spelling or use an entirely different alias.

5. Have mail sent to a post office box.

6. Dump the contents of the Temporary Internet Files folder after every browsing session.

7. Set the History folder to retain the URLs of visited pages for zero days.

8. When ordering online, use the same credit card account for all transactions and consider establishing an account for online activities *only*. If the account is compromised, other accounts will not have to be cancelled.

9. Never conduct controversial or politically sensitive web activities on a computer used at work, unless it is required as part of the job. These activities should be confined to a private account at home.

10. Remember that almost any online activity can be monitored or traced if the person doing the monitoring wants to go to enough trouble to do it.

Creating a Web Page

After looking at some of the millions of web pages posted by individuals who wanted to showcase themselves, their hobbies, their causes, or their employers, some users decide to create their own for others to see. Some web sites are purely narcissistic and probably go unseen by anyone other than their creator and maybe a few interested colleagues. That is not necessarily a bad thing. The egalitarian nature of the web is such that anyone can post a web page on any topic, at any time, and it is just as accessible as a page from the richest or most prominent person on Earth. So if a user wants a web page to express him- or herself, there is no reason not to have one.

In order to have a **web site**, which is a collection of web pages, the first step is to decide on a **web host**. Browsing through the back pages of most computer magazines or searching the web using keywords like web host or domain host will reveal thousands of companies anxious to get web-hosting business. These companies are intended mostly for persons or companies with their own domain name, but many of the services will assist customers in obtaining a domain name. Any domain name not already claimed by someone is available for an annual fee of about $30 per year. Once a domain name is registered, the owner can re-register it and retain claim to it as long as he or she keeps paying the annual fees. The entire process of registering a domain name seldom requires more than a few minutes online and a valid credit card.

A commercial web hosting service will typically charge anywhere between $8 and $25 per month for basic hosting services. This will typically include 5 to 50 MB of space for files on their servers and a range of other optional technical services. Of all these technical services, the most critical is technical support. If the user cannot get access to edit, delete, or post web pages as needed, the site is worse than useless. Before committing to a service contract with a web hosting service, it is wise to get their technical support contact information and make a test inquiry or two to assess the quality of the support given and the time required for a response.

Most private individuals who want to post web sites are not interested in the project enough to register a domain name, however. Most of the time, web sites from private individuals are projects where having a unique domain name is not critical, and as long as the web site creator can provide a URL to point others to his or her work, the creator is happy. Fortunately, there are a number of venues where amateur web designers can post their pages without incurring any additional costs, although most of them come with some collateral obligations.

The first place a user should look for a host for web pages is his or her ISP. Many ISPs, both the big international varieties and the small Mom-and-Pop operations, will offer space on their web servers to their subscribers, free of additional charges. Some even provide wizards, which are automated programs that will help the user design the web site and create the page, all without having to know anything about HTML coding. If this method is chosen, the web page will have an address like http://www.myisp.com/members/customername.html. This might not be especially easy to remember, but the price is right. AOL members, for example, can post pages under the third-level domain http://members.aol.com, and CompuServe members have pages under the domain http://ourworld.compuserve.com.

If the ISP does not offer this service, then check out any of the many web portals and other services that offer free hosting of web pages. The drawback of these services is that most of them come with a separate browser window that will pop up whenever the page is loaded, which will contain advertising that supports the service. These windows can usually be closed, but they will pop up again every time a page on the site is loaded; they can be maddeningly persistent. Some free web hosts place banner advertisements onto their customers' pages, and there is usually no choice as to what is advertised, since revenues from the advertising go to the web host. Viewers of a user's web page may associate him or her with the advertiser, and if the subject matter of the advertisement is controversial or in poor taste, then the user can be judged negatively. For some web page topics, this is not an issue of concern, but it is clearly something to be aware of.

After identifying where to post the web site, then it must be designed. As mentioned previously, many web hosts offer some kind of automated assistance with the creation of web pages, where a number of templates, backgrounds, clip art images, and fonts can be combined into a finished page. Unfortunately, these pages tend to have a very similar cookie-cutter appearance, and most people want to have something more original and unique. For that, there are web page editors.

One of the most popular web page editors comes with a full download of Internet Explorer. It is called FrontPage Express and is a miniversion of Microsoft's commercial web page editor, FrontPage. Another editor, called Netscape Composer, is included with an installation of the Netscape Communicator package, which includes the browser Navigator. There are other commercial and shareware HTML/web page editors that can be obtained from one or more of the many shareware download sites on the web.

Because HTML code is, in its most basic form, nothing more than a text file, it is possible to hand code a web page in any text editor or word processor, and that is exactly how most early web authors did it. This is also a great way to learn about HTML code and have a full understanding and control of the look and construction of a web page. However, for most people, this is a lot more trouble than it is worth. An apt analogy might be one of pizza from a pizzeria versus homemade pizza. Anyone can make his or her own dough, knead it, and let it rise; prepare or buy pizza sauce; sprinkle on cheese and toppings; and so on, but most of us would rather spend the extra money and have Domino's or Pizza Hut do it for us, even if the store-bought product is not *exactly* the way we like it. It is close enough, and it is a lot less trouble. If the user wants to do his or her HTML coding, there is nothing wrong with that, but it is a lot of trial-and-error work.

Big and expensive commercial web page editors like FrontPage, GoLive, and DreamWeaver can produce just about any web page design or effect that is technically possible; the free editors are not as sophisticated and are geared towards most homegrown page designs. When planning a complex web site with many pages, **CGI (Common Gateway Interface)** scripts, plug-in applications, and other fancy features, one of the more upscale editors will probably be necessary.

The content of the web page is up to the designer, but the host of the page will have some say in the matter as well. If a page contains copyrighted material, advocates any unlawful practice, contains images or words that might be unsuitable for younger people, or is objectionable in some other way, it can be removed from the server without recourse to its designer. Each web hosting service has a **Terms Of Service (TOS)** agreement that the designer must agree to before they will allow files to be posted. Agree to, in this context, usually means clicking on a hyperlink that says something like, I have read the terms of service for the XYZ Web Hosting Service and agree to them without reservation. Most people never bother to read the terms of service since it is not necessary to do so in order to agree to them. If the user's web site has any potentially controversial content, it might be wise to read the terms of service in advance. If the site is taken down by the web host, users will come up blank when they enter the URL, and it will be difficult to advise them of the new URL. This problem is avoided by registering a domain name.

Web sites are excellent and inexpensive ways for law enforcement agencies to reach out to their service populations. If a free hosting service is used, the cost of putting up an agency web site is free, except for the time and labor involved. It is certainly preferable to have an easy-to-remember URL like anytownpd.org, but a web site at www.angelfire.com/anytownpd/, which is a popular free web hosting service run by the Lycos web portal service, is better than no web site at all. So many agencies have developed web sites, some of which are very high in quality, that *Law and Order* magazine now has an annual law enforcement web site competition.

A law enforcement web site does not have to feature every operation of a department. It can focus on an individual neighborhood, an ongoing project, or the accomplishments of a special team or an individual officer. With the addition of simple e-mail forms, a web site can provide a conduit for communications between citizens and officers, one that can be accessed anonymously, if desired. This is a communications medium that has yet to be fully exploited by police agencies, mostly because it is not well understood by them. Once an agency establishes a web presence, they find out very quickly how many of their customers are already active online.

The web is the best-known and possibly the most versatile component of the Internet. There are a number of services that use the Internet that can save departments money and make them more versatile. Several of these technologies are also used in online and conventional investigations. These are discussed in the next chapter.

Dos and Don'ts of Web Page Design

1. Consider what the page will look like when it first loads. Like the front page of a newspaper, have the most interesting topics linked to text or features that are "above the fold," i.e. visible toward the top of the page.

2. Use consistent design features, such as colors, arrangements of text and graphics, and other styles throughout the web site to give the pages a uniform appearance.

3. Do not overload the pages with graphics. Graphics require a lot of time to load, and some users with slow Internet connections may get tired of waiting for graphic images to appear.

4. Make sure that good grammar has been used and that all the text throughout the site has been spell-checked.

5. Avoid using background music files that play when the pages load. These are cute once, but they get annoying very quickly—especially when there is no way to shut them off.

6. Test the site by viewing it in as many browsers and at as many screen resolutions as possible. Web pages that look great on one computer look very different on another.

7. Try to keep every page to under 30 KB, including any graphics on the page. Split long pages into smaller components.

8. Provide a navigation menu on every page so that users can go directly from any page to the root/home page or to the principal page of another section of the site.

9. Make sure that contact information appears on every page in case someone viewing the page has questions or comments.

10. Update the content of the site frequently. People will not visit a site regularly unless they know that there will be something new to see.

MISCELLANEOUS SERVICES

In previous chapters, we have looked at some of the Internet's crown jewels: e-mail, the web, newsgroups, etc. There are also a number of services with less universal appeal, but they are nevertheless very useful. Every one of the utilities described in this chapter could be the basis for a book of its own, and most of them have been, but there is just enough information here to allow the reader to decide if one or more of these services are something to explore further.

Audio and Video

Most people can remember the days before cable television, when television reception was limited to the number of channels that could be pulled in with the rabbit-ear antenna on top of the set or maybe from a rooftop antenna. Some might even remember when there was no television, and broadcast entertainment was limited to the radio—and in mono, at that.

Today, entertainment and information multimedia are coming at us from every direction—direct broadcast, coaxial or fiber-optic cable, overhead satellite through either a large or pizza-size dish antenna, and telephone lines. Only the broadest-bandwidth conduits can normally handle the volume of information that audio and video **streaming** requires, but through a combination of engineering and some compromises of image and sound quality, it is possible to receive real-time audio and video broadcasts through an Internet connection.

Given the brief discussion of the effect of graphic-laden web pages on download times in the previous chapter, it is not hard to illustrate why some tweaking is necessary to achieve the same quality in an Internet feed that is expected from cable or satellite television. Standard broadcast video consists of about thirty frames or images per second, each, in essence, an individual still picture. A full-screen JPEG image may vary from a few hundred to several thousand KB (several MB) in size. For a conservative example, suppose that it will take up 1 MB of bandwidth, and in order to achieve the same standard of quality, thirty images must be loaded every second. That translates to a bandwidth requirement of 30 MB per second (1 MB per second = 8 Mbps, because bandwidth is measured in bits, not bytes, per second), which is about the capacity of the expensive T3 lines. This is not a fair comparison, though, because a full-screen JPEG image would be of much higher quality than a typical television image. However, the bandwidth required for the sound that goes with the picture has not been considered yet. But the main idea is that streaming audio and video requires a lot of bandwidth.

Streaming audio and video refers to programs that appear to play on demand and without interruption. A user might go to a news web site and view the videotape associated with a news story by clicking on an icon and then seeing the sequence play on his or her monitor. It might also be possible to view, in nearly real time, a **webcast** of an ongoing event, such as an athletic match or entertainment program. These programs are not broadcast in real time in the same way that a television program would be. The throughput of television broadcasting is sufficiently broad that, unless there is an intentional delay in the program, which is often done, someone watching the actual event and a televised version at the same time would see in essence the same actions at the same moment. With webcasting, the video and audio stream must first be digitized, then broken into data **packets** small enough to be transmitted by the network. These packets are sent to their intended destination(s), but each can conceivably take a different path, and they may not arrive in the order that they were sent. Because each packet contains not only its destination address, but also sequencing information, the client on the receiving end can reassemble the packets into a meaningful order and then display the images and sound.

In nonstreaming applications, the multimedia files are downloaded completely, stored on the destination machine, and then played back from the storage device (the hard drive, in most cases) on the destination machine. An apt analogy might be renting a video tape from the local store and then playing it on a VCR. The entire program is on this storage device, and it can be played when desired. Streaming applications allow the program to be played while the packets that complete it are still coming in. This is usually done by using a **buffering** scheme, where data is sent ahead, stored temporarily, and then played back while the packets for data further in the program are still being received. This is why most streaming audio and video requires a delay of several seconds to several minutes before playback starts while the destination client assembles enough packets of data to sustain the process. Even so, congestion on the Internet, slowdowns at any point in the transmission chain, and other technical issues make streaming audio and video an unreliable proposition. If the local movie theatre interrupted a film showing as often as most streaming multimedia sites did, people would be looking to get their money back. But in the case of Internet-based streaming audio and video, the price is usually right—as in free—so complaints are reduced.

Purveyors of streaming audio and video achieve greater throughput of the entire program by degrading the quality of the transmitted image. There are a number of techniques for doing this, but most involve some combination of reducing the image size, cutting back on the number of frames shown per second, and compressing the data during transmission for re-expansion at the destination. It is highly unlikely that a television-quality, full-screen image will be transmitted over an Internet connection. Most of the time, the image will occupy only a small fraction of the full display and will still appear choppy from the reduced number of frames shown. For instance, by transmitting only every third frame in a presentation, a standard television image can be reduced from about thirty frames per second to only ten, a much more manageable number.

Sound is transmitted via a similar method, but here the reduction in size is achieved by narrowing the range of frequencies sent down the pipe. The human ear is capable of hearing sounds that vary in frequency from about 20 to 20,000 cycles per second, but the range of frequencies in a normal speaking voice is far narrower, from around 100 to 1000 cycles per second. By narrowing the range of frequencies that are transmitted, a tremendous reduction in the amount of digital data necessary to produce those sounds is achieved, and less bandwidth is required to send it.

The technology used in creating MP3 files is similar in this regard. The trading and distribution of MP3 files, most over a quasi-network called Napster, has received a great deal of attention in recent years. Most of the controversy concerning this technology is centered on the copyright issues associated with creating MP3 files from commercial compact discs, since the artists and producers of these CDs receive no royalties from the copies once the original is sold. Compact discs contain all-digital information, and they are capable of reproducing sounds considerably beyond the range of most human ears. Audiophiles believe that the audible harmonics and residual remnants of these sounds give greater depth and realism to the recording, and this is why CDs are generally thought to be superior to vinyl phonograph records, which store analog information, for reproducing music. When an MP3 file is created from a track on a CD, the digital information is not copied verbatim, as that would require a file size of 60 MB or so, depending on the length of the recording, which would be too large to be handled and transmitted easily. Instead, the frequencies in the recording are deleted in the extreme upper and lower ranges, making for a lower-fidelity recording, but dramatically reducing the file size to typically 1 to 3 MB. Because MP3 files are usually played back on relatively low-fidelity equipment, such as pocket MP3 players and computer speakers, the difference is not readily detectable. Besides, the user most often gets the recording for nothing, which makes some sacrifice in quality much more tolerable.

There are several methods for transmitting streaming audio and video via the Internet, the most common being a format called RealVideo and/or RealAudio, both of which are products of RealNetworks, Inc. In order to view or hear RealVideo/RealAudio files, the user must have RealNetwork's proprietary software installed, called RealPlayer. RealNetworks has, throughout its corporate history, made available a free version of RealPlayer that anyone can download, although it comes with a built-in commercial to persuade the user to purchase their "Plus" version that offers better quality video and audio and is also downloadable—but for a price.

RealPlayer will not only play RealAudio/RealVideo files that are found on the Internet, but it also has a built-in directory of sites where the user can obtain streaming audio and video content of news stories, sports events, movie reviews, comedy routines, and others, not unlike the selection on a cable television account. Most of this content will be a few minutes long and will play in a window about 1/4 the size of the display, with fairly low fidelity and occasionally choppy video. However, it is all coming over the Internet, generally costs nothing, and the fact that it works at all is pretty impressive.

There are also a number of radio stations and other audio-only information streams that one can receive using RealPlayer or Microsoft's software, called

Windows Media Player, which is downloadable at no cost from Microsoft's web site. Some of these are regular commercial radio stations that pipe their output onto the Internet so that anyone with a connection can hear it, and others are homegrown amateurs with a driving ambition to be disk jockeys or talk show hosts. Internet radio has the same faults as other streaming media, in that it is low fidelity, and the audio stream is occasionally interrupted because the data packets necessary to sustain it do not arrive quickly enough. However, it can be a great way to hear programming that cannot be received in a given location or is not available anywhere else.

Internet audio and video are also useful for monitoring and day-to-day communications. It is now possible to have a video-audio connection to another user, in real time, over the Internet, and at no cost, other than the online connection. The audio quality will be fair, and the video image will be small and probably only a few frames per second, but the person on the other end can be seen and even share files and run applications via this connection.

There are several methods of accomplishing this, but the most widely used is via a free Microsoft application called NetMeeting, which is automatically installed with many versions of Internet Explorer. This program can be downloaded from Microsoft if it is not already installed on the computer. NetMeeting requires the use of a NetMeeting server, of which there are several. To connect with another user, open NetMeeting, connect to the server where the other party is logged on, locate him or her in a list of users, and "ring" his or her computer, requesting to connect. Obviously, this requires some prior planning, but some regular NetMeeting users log on to a NetMeeting server when they boot up their machines in the morning and accept NetMeeting calls in the same way that they accept phone calls. These are very useful for situations where a face-to-face interaction is important or where there is a need to share images, files, or some other computer resource.

NetMeeting works with Outlook Express in the sense that the user can enter the NetMeeting server information on a special form in the Contacts list and then attempt to establish a NetMeeting connection with him or her by right-clicking on the appropriate entry and selecting Call Using NetMeeting from the context menu that appears.

NetMeeting is a popular medium for voyeurs and sexual content peddlers who establish a presence on a NetMeeting server and include in their profile (a text file that describes what business they engage in on the server) their sexual preference and/or expectations. In fact, browsing the users on the server may reveal more of this type of user than regular business users. It is not rare to receive random requests from users on the NetMeeting server for calls or chats and find that they are looking for sexually-oriented content. The settings in NetMeeting allow the user to reject call requests from anyone except for those on a preapproved list to avoid this kind of unwanted interruption.

Users with a need to remotely observe distant locations can also make use of Internet-based audio and video. There are several applications now available that allow users to set up cameras that transmit their output to a web page or to a specific user's machine on demand and in real time. The frame rates of these images are fairly slow, at typically one to five frames per second, but this is usually more than sufficient to be able to determine what is going on at the location. Business owners are using this technology to monitor their employees' activities at any time they choose without having to travel to the business site, and the output can be recorded either continuously or when a particular event, such as a robbery alarm, is triggered. Using this technology, it might be possible to conduct a round-the-clock surveillance of a location without ever leaving one's desk.

The cameras that connect to the computer are not expensive (typically, less than $50), and this is borne out by the number of webcams on the Internet. A search for *webcam* in any search engine will turn up hundreds of sites where people have webcams trained on their pets, the freeway onramp outside their home, the company coffee pot, or anything else that they think someone might want to look at, with the image from the webcam refreshed anywhere from every few seconds to every half hour or so. This is not intended to be full-motion video, but rather a pictorial representation of what is going on at that location, more or less at that moment. Most of these are more fun than functional, but it might be important to someone to know if the snow is still on the ground on the quad at the University of Nevada, Reno (http://www.unr.edu/quadcam.html).

Instant Messaging

Electronic mail might be close to being "instant messaging," but the time when a correspondent actually receives a message is dependent on a number of factors: whether he or she is at a computer, whether the e-mail client is open and active, and if he or she reads messages as soon as they arrive. Many e-mail users handle their electronic mail the way that they do their postal mail, setting aside a time during the day to read and respond to correspondence. It might be necessary to ask a quick question or send a reminder to someone about a meeting that is to take place in five minutes, but the sender is dependent on that person reading the e-mail message immediately. For that kind of communication, there is **instant messaging** (**IM**).

Instant messaging requires that users have their instant messaging client application installed and running on their computer, and that the computer be connected to the Internet. It is best suited for computers with an always-on connection, such as those on a network or that have a DSL or cable modem connection, but it will work with a dial-up connection as long as the connection is active.

When the IM client is installed on a user's machine, he or she is required to create a user name and is usually assigned a unique identifier, such as a serial number. The user may also be asked to provide information on their interests, languages spoken, part of the country where he or she resides, etc., and will be asked if he or she wants to keep this information confidential or make it available for other users browsing the IM service. When the program is activated on a computer with a live Internet connection, the client automatically logs into the IM server with its unique identifier, which the server will associate with the record created at installation. Now, if another user of that IM service is also logged on and has the first user's identifier in their "watch list" of people with whom they regularly converse, both will see the other's user name in the window displayed by the IM client. This tells each of them that the other is available. If one user wants to communicate with the other, all he or she need do is click on the correspondent's name and type a message. The other user will receive an audible alert and will see the message displayed on his or her screen. Responding involves a similar, and simple, action.

IM users can also browse the IM server to see other users who are using the same IM client and have consented to have their information posted. These lists are frequently indexed on not only names, but also on interests, e-mail addresses, zip codes, and other keys, so those who are just looking for someone to chat with can locate a kindred spirit. While chatting, and depending on the IM client in use, users can transfer files between themselves, and some even allow transmission of video images from a connected camera.

If there were only one IM client, then this might be a truly wonderful system, but that is not the case. There are at least three IM clients in popular use. The most widely-used IM software is arguably **ICQ** ("I Seek You"), which is produced by a company called Mirabilis. The other two are MSN Messenger, from Microsoft, and AOL Instant Messenger. In 1998, AOL acquired Mirabilis, and many features of ICQ and AOL's Instant Messenger are similar and compatible. CompuServe had an IM client, but since AOL has acquired Compuserve, the two clients are essentially the same.

What makes these IM services imperfect is that they operate independently, and in some cases they even conflict with one another. ICQ users cannot send messages to MSN Messenger users, (unless those users are also using another IM client), and vice versa. At one time, installation of MSN Messenger on a computer that had AOL Instant Messenger already installed disabled the AOL software, and AOL's installation program did the same thing to MSN users. These conflicts have been mostly resolved, but there is still no universal IM client or system with which users can be sure that they can reach out to everyone with IM interests.

IM is of interest to law enforcement because of its practical communications applications and also because some predatory types use IM clients to troll for victims. Because the user can create any profile for him/herself that he/she chooses, there is no way of knowing if a person is really who or what he or she claims, unless the person is an acquaintance. Many IM users have friends all over the globe, most of whom they have never met. When these people get together, they can have a wonderful get-acquainted session—or be victimized by a predator. Even if law enforcement officers do not use IM technology themselves, they need to understand it to do investigations and communicate the potential dangers to the people they serve.

Chat Services

Chat services or chat rooms are similar to IM services, but they introduce one more level of distancing oneself from the other participants. All of the participants in a chat room have to join the chat in order to participate; they are not contacted by someone who sees their name or identifier on a list and then sends them an instant message, inviting them to chat. Chat participants are generally drawn to a chat room by the posted subject matter of the chat room, and there are many chat rooms to choose from.

Chats, like instant messaging, occur more or less in real time. A participant uses some type of chat client, which can be anything from an independent software application, like **mIRC**, to a specially designed web page, and then joins the channel, or conversation, of his or her choice. Channels are generally designated by topic and can vary from fans of a certain soap opera to persons employed in law enforcement. As the participants on a chat channel type messages, they are displayed in a window that everyone on the channel sees, prefaced by that participant's screen name, as seen in Figure 9–1. Participants can usually make their conversation private, so that only selected participants can see it and take part. An analogy to this might be meeting someone at the bar of a lounge and then moving the conversation to a table to talk more privately.

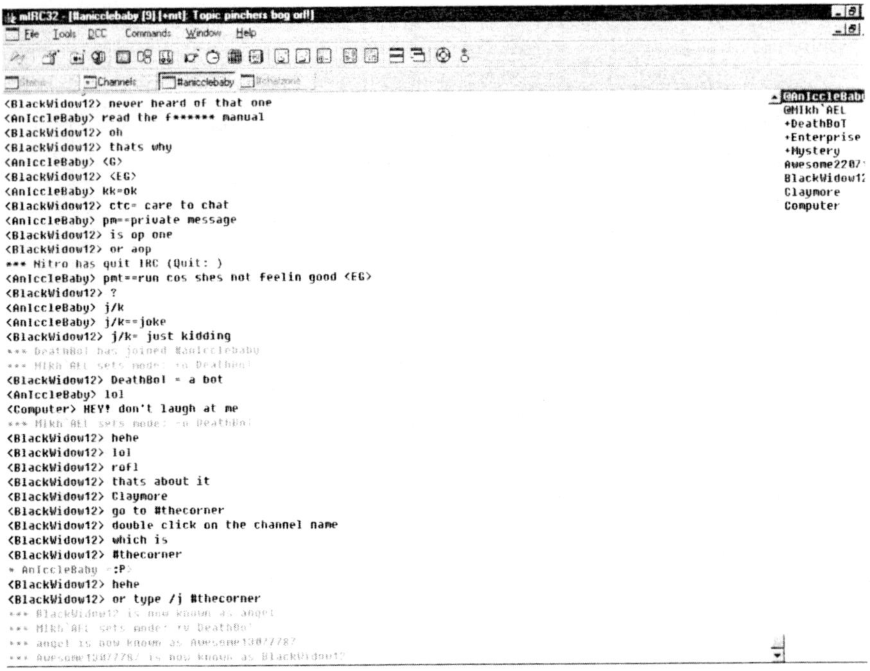

Figure 9-1   An Active Chat Window in mIRC

Users can also "squelch" or filter out the output of selected participants so that messages from them do not appear on their display. Depending on the type of chat client and the server in use, participants can send files to one another, use shortcut commands to type in longer messages with only a few keystrokes, and even participate in several ongoing chats simultaneously.

Some users have found chats to be addictive and will log onto chat rooms for hours at a time. The ability to reach out and connect with someone at any moment, coupled with the ability to remain anonymous and faceless, is very attractive to people who are homebound or have poor social skills. This has led to many chat room participants assuming other personas that are very different from whom they really are. Some chat rooms are intended for young people, and predatory "chickenhawks" will log onto these conversations, pretending to be another youth. They usually try to elicit sexually-oriented conversation from the other participants and may send them pornographic images as file attachments to gauge their reactions. The most dangerous of these will attempt to arrange face-to-face meetings with their correspondents and may then try to abduct a victim or entice him or her into a lewd act.

These schemes have been known to backfire for a couple of reasons. The predators will occasionally encounter one another online, and when the meeting comes to fruition, they find that they have fooled each other. Also, law enforcement officers have played along, masquerading online as innocent teens, and have arranged meetings with the predators that were actually stings, resulting in arrests. These cases can be difficult to make because of jurisdictional issues. It may be difficult to establish that an offender committed a lewd or otherwise prohibited act within a particular jurisdiction, and the use of federal statutes is favored in many cases for this reason.

Finding a particular chat room can be challenging unless the user knows both the server or service where it is carried and also the official name of the chat room. Most of the web portals have chat services, as do the major ISP/content providers. Even some web sites have their own chat services that run independently of the portals and ISPs. Many chat users are not technically sophisticated, knowing only the keystrokes and mouse clicks necessary to get into their favorite chat sites. If they are asked the name of the server or channel where their chat room is located, they may not be able to respond. When the objective is to monitor a particular chat room for activity or the presence of an individual as part of an investigation, it may be helpful to allow the witness/victim to log into the site, while the investigator takes notes on the user's actions and records them so that he or she can get into the same site again.

Finding a particular user can also be frustrating because chat users seldom follow a set schedule. They may log on at a regular time every day, but more often they troll the net, checking in at one chat room or another, often changing their **handles** or screen names to shake off people trying to track their activities. In most cases, users have to log onto the chat servers with some kind of established account, and that information can often be subpoenaed, if necessary. Sometimes this is the only way to run down a predatory user.

Chat users are fond of using abbreviations to save keystrokes and express themselves in ways that would not translate well over the chat medium. Some of these abbreviations, also known as smileys or emoticons, are formed of keyboard characters that resemble faces when viewed at a 90-degree angle. Other abbreviations are just letters that represent phrases or single words. Some examples follow.

brb	be right back	wb	welcome back
bbl	be back later	wtf	what the f***
np	no problem	rtfm	read the f***ing manual
ttfn	ta ta for now	rotfl	rolling on the floor, laughing
bbiaf	be back in a flash	\<G\>	grinning
imho	in my humble opinion	wth	what the hell
lol	laughing out loud	iae	in any event
jk	just kidding	iac	in any case
re	hi again, as in "re hi"	wthk	who the hell knows

Many of these terms have also found their way into use in e-mail and other online communications, but their roots were in chat rooms.

Chat rooms can also be useful to network with other law enforcement officers in real time, but one should be cautious about his or her choice of venues. Some services check the credentials of their members better than others, and it is difficult to be certain that a person in the chat room is a bona fide law enforcement officer, even though he or she might say so. Before sharing any sensitive information, it is wise to confirm the identity of a correspondent, or, better yet, arrange to share information through a medium that is more secure, such as encrypted e-mail or the telephone.

Internet Telephony

Data sent via the Internet passes over a network of transmission lines that are also used for telephone calls, so it should be possible to make telephone calls over the Internet. The fact is that it is possible, although it requires the use of a different methodology than a regular telephone call. When one makes a telephone call, a circuit or "pipe" is created between the person and the party he or she is calling. This circuit is continuous throughout the duration of the call. Even if there is no information (sound) being transmitted at any given moment, the pipe remains open—and the connect charges continue to build. This is the essence of an analog transmission, where the communication is in a more or less continuous form.

Information is transmitted across the Internet in digital packets, and the various servers and nodes through which any data packet might pass are more like loading docks than pipes. They are delivered from one node to another, each getting closer to its destination IP address, until they arrive at their intended destination. The transmission is usually close to instantaneous, but there can be delays because of congestion on the network.

For Internet-carried telephone conversations to be possible, the sounds made by each caller's voice must first be converted from analog to digital format, then broken into data packets for transmission. These data packets are sent to the device on the other end of the conversation, recombined into a phrase or sentence, converted back to analog mode, and are heard as analog sound by the other party. This requires a considerable amount of computing horsepower to be possible at all, and in fact it was not possible until a relatively short time ago, since most desktop computers did not have the capacity to process all this data quickly enough.

One can always converse with another party through NetMeeting or some similar technology, but that requires that both parties be logged onto a NetMeeting server, so spur-of-the-moment calls are not possible. Internet telephony generally uses one of three methods: software to software, hardware to hardware, or software to POTS. All three of these methods and their combinations are called **VoIP**, or **Voice over Internet Protocol**.

The software-to-software method is actually a lot like NetMeeting. The two parties in the conversation must be using the same software, which logs onto a server when the Internet connection is made and the software is loaded. When one user desires to place a call, he or she queries the server that stores the names and IP addresses of all those online at that moment, and if the other party is up and running, places the call. Digital voice packets are passed between the two parties for as long as they wish to speak. The only cost to either party is the cost of their Internet connect time, and, of course, the cost of the software that they needed to buy in the first place.

In a hardware-to-hardware scheme, both parties in the conversation purchase special telephones that are capable of establishing a voice conversation over an Internet connection. These are not really telephones, but rather telephone-like terminals that dial into an ISP (often one owned or leased by the hardware manufacturer), look up the IP address of the party to be called, and signal their "telephone" that a call is pending. This is not a bad way to go if there is another party whom a user wishes to call on a regular basis without incurring long distance charges, but it is still inconvenient because of the special hardware requirements.

The third method is the one that shows the most promise. Software-to-POTS Internet telephony uses the Internet to make the caller's voice sound as if he or she were using a regular telephone (close enough to make the toll charges tolerable, anyway), then uses the conventional telephone network to complete the connection. The person initiating the call dials the other party's phone number into a software application or a web site, and the application places the call to that telephone number, using the regular telephone system. The voices on the call are transported partially across the Internet through VoIP and partially via POTS.

VoIP, despite its cost savings, sacrifices considerably in the quality of the voice transmission. At best, VoIP is as clear as a medium-quality analog cellular phone call. There is often a delay between the time that a party speaks and the time his or her voice is heard on the other end of the conversation, voices are occasionally broken up as data packets are dropped or lost, and callers sometimes hear echoes on the line. International calls are not always possible because of differences in the telephone systems between countries or the absence of close, cost-effective transmission nodes in the foreign country. On the plus side, one can usually make oneself understood if persistent, and if the Internet connection is already paid for, the call is free.

One of the most popular applications of this technology uses a web site-based Java application to transmit the call across the Internet. Callers need to have a headset with earphones and microphone to make this effective; a standard microphone and speakers will often produce feedback and make the conversation difficult to understand. If loss of quality in the clarity of the voice traffic and repeating things now and again will not be issues, VoIP can be a great tool.

Internet-Based Fax Services

Before there was the Internet, there were fax machines. Facsimile technology was the only way to instantly transmit an exact copy of a document from one point to another, and it was not long before every business listed both its regular telephone and its fax number. Those who got the two mixed up were greeted with a screeching fax answering tone when they called. The problems with fax machines are that they are dependent on a large piece of relatively expensive equipment, they tie up a telephone line, and they have only one function. Fax machines are limited to sending and receiving faxes, and when they do, there is noticeable degradation in the quality of the image, especially if the "original" is also a faxed copy.

We have already shown how virtually any file that can be created or stored on a computer can be attached to an electronic mail message and delivered over the Internet. If the correspondents on both end of the communication have e-mail accounts and software capable of reading the file attachment, this is a preferable method of sending information; there is no degradation in quality due to the transmission. The digital copy that is received will be exactly the same as the digital copy that was sent. This same technology can be used for both sending and receiving faxes, and the finished copy is generally superior in quality to one sent by a conventional fax.

Sending a fax to a conventional fax machine can be done with a computer without using the Internet. Microsoft includes Microsoft Fax as a component in its Windows operating system, and there are other software packages, such as WinFax Pro, that accomplish the same thing, sometimes with more bells and whistles.

When using a fax utility of this type, the computer connects to the fax machine in the same way that it would connect to a dial-up ISP. The user sending the fax "prints" the document, but the printer designated for this task is actually the fax utility, a kind of "virtual printer." Instead of sending the document to a hardware printer, it formats it to be sent as a fax, and the utility asks for a destination fax number. The user types this in, and the computer dials the destination fax machine, using its installed modem. When the fax machine on the receiving end answers and sends the telltale fax tone, the modem hears this, goes through a "handshaking" protocol similar to that used when connecting with another modem and sends the document down the phone wire in a form that is recognized by the fax machine. The fax machine on the receiving end produces what is usually a fax superior in quality to one that would be sent by an conventional fax machine.

If the user is willing to allow the computer to answer the telephone, the fax software can even be set to answer with a fax tone and receive incoming faxes. They are stored as graphic images, which can then be viewed onscreen or printed on whatever printer is attached to that computer. These utilities often work very well for low-volume offices, because the fax software can be programmed to run unattended, send faxes late at night, or "broadcast" faxes to multiple numbers without any human intervention. However, given the advent of Internet fax services, these utilities are falling into disuse.

When sending a fax via the Internet, the document to be faxed is attached to an e-mail message, which is sent to a fax server operated by the fax service. The server then places a conventional telephone call to the destination fax machine and transmits the file as it would to any other fax. If multiple destinations are specified in the outgoing fax message, then the server handles all of the multiple calls. The sender transmits only a single message. Charges associated with the service are billed to an account established by the sender and are usually charged monthly to a credit card.

Receiving faxes via the Internet requires setting up a telephone access number through an Internet fax company. Internet fax services typically reserve a block of numbers in areas where telephone service is not in high demand, such as in rural states. This conserves costs for them. The subscriber sets up an account and is assigned one of these numbers from the block. The subscriber then gives the number to anyone that might want to send him or her a fax. Senders transmit their faxes to that number in the usual fashion and hear the number answered by a fax tone—but it is not really a fax machine. Instead, the number is answered by the fax server, which receives the file, stores it in digital form, and then sends it to the subscriber as an e-mail attachment. The subscriber uses special software supplied by the Internet fax company to open and examine the document, after which he or she can store it, delete it, print it, or attach it to another e-mail as he or she pleases.

This kind of service has two real advantages to it. One is that the subscriber's faxes can be retrieved from anywhere he or she can pick up e-mail. If the subscriber is traveling, there is no need to have faxes sent to a hotel, which can incur a charge of up to $2.00 per page, and the receiver has no way of knowing who else has read the fax. Instead, the subscriber logs onto his or her e-mail account, picks up the e-mail and its attachment, and opens it at his or her leisure. This works as well across town as it does across the country. The other big advantage is that this incoming fax service is usually free. The Internet fax companies are hoping to upgrade users to more feature-laden "plus" services that operate for a fee, and they also manage to insert advertisements into the viewing window of the fax translation software; they know that users are going to see those ads every time they get a fax. But for the basic incoming service, there is usually no charge. Outgoing fax service does incur a charge for the cost of the telephone call, but it is far less than the cost of maintaining a separate phone line for a fax machine.

On the downside, the fax number may be many miles from the user's residence, so that locals who want to send a fax have to dial a long distance call, and others just wonder why the telephone number is in California and the fax machine is in Ohio. Most of the Internet fax companies have available phone number blocks in parts of the country that are not so isolated, but they may charge for this service.

To transmit a document that was not created on a computer, like a poster or a contract, the document must still be converted to digital format. This can be done with a scanner. These were once expensive, but they can now be had for well under

$100. Most scanners have software included that will scan documents directly to the fax software, and the fax software will likewise link with the scanner utilities.

Computer-based fax software can be used to annotate documents, drawing circles or boxes to highlight areas, placing text boxes to include captions or insert phrases, and other fairly simple modifications. It is often easier to use this software to place comments on a document than it is to print the document, draw notes on it, and then rescan or refax it to include the notations.

Because of the low cost of Internet-based fax, it is both possible and cost-effective to give every division, or even every officer, in a department his or her own fax number, rather than use a central fax machine with little or no security.

Thin-Client Applications

There has been something of a cyclic method in the way that personal computers have been used since their introduction in the early 1980s. The earliest PCs were very slow as compared to today's machines, and they had very little storage space. They had no CD-ROM drives, and few of them even had hard drives. In order to take advantage of the information store that was available via a computer, users had to rely on online services like The Source and CompuServe, which were essentially mainframe computers that used the PCs as terminals. People played games, read stock market reports, and sent messages to each other by retrieving a small amount of information from the mainframe, reading it or processing it, and then either sending it back or disposing of it to make way for the next item. As PCs became more powerful and had more room to store files, users would keep very large files or databases on their local machines or networks, and the online services and the Internet were used mainly as conduits to transfer this information from one PC to another. PCs that keep most, if not all, of their applications, data, and processing power on the local machine are called, in this context, thick clients.

There is an emerging trend to return to a form of the old method of computing by keeping the bulk of the software on a remote server and downloading only the code needed at any given moment to a user's machine, which is not much more than a terminal. The computer/terminal in this scenario is called a thin client. This is now possible because of the tremendous increase in throughput brought on by broadband technologies, something that was not available in the 1980s. This also addresses the problem inherent in increasingly complex software applications, where the code that creates the applications is millions of lines long and is virtually impossible to create without introducing multiple errors or bugs, any one of which can bring down the entire machine.

People who are responsible for administering networks and providing technical support for computer users in an organization know this problem best. Suppose that the Anytown Police Department decides to adopt (the hypothetical) SoftWonder Office Suite for use by all of its officers and employees. The suite includes a word processor, e-mail program, personal information manager, group schedules, and presentation package, and everyone in the 500-person agency is trained to use it on laptops and desktop computers. Six months into the deployment of this software, SoftWonder notifies the MIS manager at Anytown PD that they have released a service pack which includes a number of bug fixes reported by their users, and that it is imperative that the service pack be installed on all of the computers with SoftWonder Office installed on them, lest the data on those machines be exposed to malicious hackers and/or even file corruption. The MIS manager is faced with having to find a way to install this service pack on 500 different machines, which are in use at different times in different locations. More often than not, by the time that the MIS manager gets all the computers updated, SoftWonder will announce Service Pack II, starting the process all over again.

In a thin-client environment, all of the application software resides in a single repository on a server, as does much of the data. Users log into the network and download to their thin-client machines only as much software as needed to perform the task they are working on at that moment. Their data, personal settings, passwords, and other information all reside on the server. They do not have to consciously download any software to get their work done, as this is done automatically as they update their calendars, compose and read e-mail, or create documents.

Users may have some basic software residing on the local machine for times that they are disconnected from the network. For instance, an officer with a laptop computer in the field may be able to collect information at a crime scene sufficient to create a basic report without being connected to the network, but when he goes back to his patrol car and plugs in the laptop, the data is integrated into a report template via a wireless interface.

Thin-client computers are also less expensive than thick-client-capable machines, because they do not need the processing power, memory, and storage capacity of a thick-client machine. Fewer resources on board often mean fewer things to break or malfunction, so reliability can be enhanced as well.

There is a trend in the software industry to aggressively market thin-client software applications. For consumer software, this would mean having the software reside not on the department's network server, but rather on the manufacturer's server, accessible via the Internet. The user would not purchase the software, but rather pay a use fee for the time period needed to use the software. In exchange for this, the user would always have access to the latest version and most recent bug fix of the software and would be able to use it from any Internet connection. The companies that supply these network-based applications are called **Application Service Providers**, or **ASPs**, and they include most of the big players in software production.

This kind of arrangement makes many people uneasy. The idea that they could lose the ability to complete their work because the Internet was not working properly is frightening. However, this is already becoming a reality. Consider how many day-to-day services rely on a steady flow of data from somewhere else, much of it piped partially or entirely via the Internet, and it becomes apparent how reliant we are on this infrastructure now. There will always be traditional, thick-client applications where network connections are too expensive or unreliable, but expect thin-client scenarios to become increasingly common.

Software Download Sites

A trip to any computer retailer or even most office supply stores will illustrate that there are thousands of computer software applications available for purchase. Most common modern business operations center on one or more office "suites" such as Microsoft Office, WordPerfect Office, or Lotus SmartSuite, which typically include modules for word processing, spreadsheet construction, presentations, personal information management, and database management. These applications generally have links to one another that allow them to share information between the modules, e.g. a customer database can be imported into a word processor to create business form letters. Many desktop and laptop computers come equipped with one of these integrated packages, and they have achieved widespread acceptance.

However, there are many computer-based tasks that do not require these large packages, and in fact the large office suites may just get in the way for some processes. The following scenarios provide some examples.

- ◆ An officer keeps a floppy disk or Zip disk in his briefcase to keep backup copies of files that otherwise reside on his desktop machine. From time to time, he needs to ensure that both the Zip disk and the desktop machine have the most current versions of those files, but going through the list and comparing each file date and time stamp is tedious and time-consuming. A small shareware application called FileSync will compare the two lists and copy the newest files onto the opposite list.

♦ If applications are routinely installed for testing or evaluation and then removed from the system, they always seem to leave behind some residual files that take up space and clog the application menus. There are several utilities that will monitor the state of a computer before and after a program's installation and will return it to the configuration it had before the last software install.

♦ If there is a phrase or paragraph that a user routinely types several times a day or a complex keystroke sequence that he or she needs to complete a process, there are keystroke and macro recorders that will store these sequences and then play them back on command of a couple of shortcut keys.

♦ Some people occasionally need a simple timer to clock the number of minutes that they spend on the telephone or meeting with a client or colleague. There are a number of clock and timer applications that can be loaded into the taskbar, ready to pop up with a single mouse click.

Many of these applications are called shareware. They are developed by programmers with small or side businesses who distribute them on an honors system, allowing users to "try before they buy." If a user likes the program and decides to keep using it, he or she is supposed to register the software by sending the programmer a small registration fee, usually less than $20. Some programmers include "incentives" to encourage the user to pay the registration fee. These include **nag screens**, which pop up each time the software loads and require the user to click or press a key to clear the screen (one clever variation caused the time that the nag screen took to clear to increase slightly every time that the software was used), and "crippled" software that will not allow the use of certain functions unless the proper registration code is entered. Others function only for a preset trial period and then refuse to work again until they are registered. Some shareware, however, works exactly the same in the trial version as in the paid-for version.

Some shareware is entirely free. Computer magazines will produce small applications for promotional purposes, or a hobbyist programmer will develop an application for his or her own use and then put it out for free distribution. These software authors usually do not want to go to the trouble necessary to track registrants and process their fees, or they use the shareware application as a kind of business card to entice potential customers to contract them to produce other custom applications.

Shareware often lacks the polish of commercial software applications. The graphics are not as sharp and snazzy, and the user interfaces are not quite as refined. This does not mean that they are inferior applications. Many shareware applications are as good or better than the big, expensive software tools that they are intended to supplement or replace. Some popular commercial software applications started life as shareware.

There are a number of web sites that are put up solely for the purpose of distributing shareware applications. Most of these are heavily ad-laden, which is how they are financed, but the software that is downloaded from these sites is free, at least in the trial/shareware form. Most of these sites categorize the applications by function, name, author, etc., to make locating application easier. Most of these sites also scan the software for viruses and other harmful code before they make it available to their users, so downloading applications from these sites is generally safe.

Conclusion

The Internet has changed all of our lives, and the changes are not yet complete. This medium is still unexploited in many ways, and law enforcement officers need to be aware of the developments in order to provide adequate protection and service to their communities. This book has only begun to introduce the capabilities of online technology, but hopefully it has provided the reader with a starting point.

The appendices that follow include a glossary of terms used throughout the book and an index of web sites and other online resources that may be of interest to law enforcement personnel.

See you online.

WEB RESOURCES

At the outset of the project of writing this book, I had intended to include a comprehensive index of Internet resources that were of interest to law enforcement. Looking at a previous edition where I had located and reviewed over 500 of these sites, I found that most of them had disappeared. The web is a highly transient place, and web sites and other entities come and go continuously. There are a number of excellent listings of police resources, many of which do a much better job of keeping their online listings current than I could do with a paper listing that will be obsolete before it is published. There are also many search engines that can be used to locate resources on the Internet. In the listing that follows, I have tried to provide a starting point. I have undoubtedly overlooked a great many deserving sites and resources, and for that I apologize.

I also had difficulty categorizing some of these listings. Should the listing for the American Correctional Association be under "Associations" or "Corrections?" I just took a stab at getting it right, and I hope I have not made it too confusing in so doing. Where page formatting has required that URLs be broken up or wrapped onto more than one line, they should still be entered as one long line, with no spaces or line breaks.

First, here is a list of some resources that were addressed in the various chapters of the book.

Chapter Four-Internet Service Providers

4Anything Network
http://4internetservice.4anything.com/
> A guide to Internet service providers of all types

DirecPC
http://www.direcpc.com/
> Internet access by satellite disk

DirecPC Fair Access Policy
http://www.direcpc.com/consumer/cost/describe_fap.html
> DirecPC's Fair Access Policy (FAP) that seems to be the source of so many complaints

DSL Reports
http://www.dslreports.com/
> Ratings of DSL service nationwide

Freedom List
http://www.freedomlist.com/
> A guide to free ISP service

Gilat Satellite Networks
http://www.gilat.com/gilat/
> A two-way, completely wireless Internet connection

Juno
http://www.juno.com/index.shtml
> Free Internet access

The List
http://www.thelist.com/
> The most complete directory of ISPs on the web

NetZero
http://www.netzero.com/
> Free Internet access

Visual Networks
http://www.inversenet.com/products/ims/ratings/
> Ratings of ISP services across the country, including downtime rates

Chapter Six-Electronic Mail

CoolMail
http://www.codemail.com/
> Access your e-mail from any phone or from the web.

Distribution Center for PGP
http://web.mit.edu/network/pgp.html
> Free download of Pretty Good Privacy software

File Extension Search Engine
http://extsearch.com/
> If you come upon a file and can't figure out where it came from or what it does, try looking it up here.

Free E-Mail Providers Guide
http://www.fepg.net/
> A list of free providers

SpamCop
http://spamcop.net/
> An organization that will assist you in getting rid of all that junk e-mail

Chapter Seven-Newsgroups

Anonymous Mail2News
http://www.m2n.org/
> Assistance for protecting your identity on Usenet

Deja News
http://groups.google.com/googlegroups/deja_announcement.html
> Access to newsgroups, as well as a search function for current and old newsgroup articles

Forte, Inc.
http://www.forteinc.com/
> Source for Free Agent newsgroup client software

Chapter Eight-The World Wide Web

About
http://www.about.com/
> Good for simple searches. For complex ones, go elsewhere.

All-in-One Search Page
http://www.allonesearch.com/
> Over 500 of the Internet's best search engines, databases, indexes, and directories in one single site.

AltaVista
http://www.altavista.com/
> Choice of different web search firms, portal features

America Online
http://www.aol.com/
> Lots of features on its search page, but not the greatest results

Ask Jeeves
http://www.ask.com/
> Allows plain-language questions, like "How many people were on the Titanic?" The URLs generated are very lengthy and difficult to paste into another document.

Direct Hit
http://www.directhit.com/
> Rates web sites by popularity, so those that get the most traffic will be at the top of the results lists

Excite
http://www.excite.com/
> User-configurable pages, portal features, "precision search" tool

FAST Search
http://www.alltheweb.com/
> Simple design. Uses plus and minus characters instead of typical Boolean operators.

Go.com
http://www.go.com/
> Frequently updated search "home" page

Google
http://www.google.com/
> A very simple search page that produces very well-focused, to-the-point results lists. Try the "I'm feeling lucky" button.

GoTo
http://www.goto.com/
> Results lists will favor those who pay the most to GoTo for click-throughs. You get to see exactly how much your clicks are going to cost the destination web site.

Hotbot
http://www.hotbot.com/
> Their advanced search page makes it very easy to construct complex Boolean searches without knowing a lot of Boolean operators.

Internet Explorer
http://www.microsoft.com/windows/ie/download/ie5.htm
> The latest (as this is written) version of Microsoft's Internet Explorer

iWon.com
http://www.iwon.com/
> Offers daily, monthly, and annual cash prizes for those who use the site, but the results aren't that great—unless you happen to win.

Learn the Net
http://www.learnthenet.com/english/index.html
> An Internet tutorial

LookSmart
http://www.looksmart.com/
> Good results, except that you can't exclude terms from a search

Lycos
http://www.lycos.com/
> Portal site with lots of extra features

MSN

http://www.msn.com/

> Headquarters for a major portal and ISP. Results lists favor those sites patronized by MSN.

NBCi

http://www.nbci.com/

> This site is good for entertainment-related questions, but not so hot for highly technical issues.

Netscape 6

http://home.netscape.com/browsers/6/index.html?cp=hop12p4

> At this writing, the most recent version of the Netscape browser package

Northern Light

http://www.northernlight.com/

> A very good search engine for specific requests. Portions out the results list into folders, grouped by subject.

Raging Search

http://www.raging.com/

> Uses the same index as AltaVista, but tends to provide more specific results

Yahoo

http://www.yahoo.com/

> One of the first search engines, now a major portal. More of a directory than a search engine.

Chapter Nine–Miscellaneous Services

911_er

http://911_er.homestead.com/

> Web-based chat room dedicated to emergency services personnel

AOL Instant Messenger

http://www.aol.com/aim/home.html

> Source for download of AOL Messenger software

DialPad

http://www.dialpad.com/
> Make free telephone calls from your PC to any phone in the United States.

Download.com

http://download.cnet.com/
> Another free software download site

eFax

http://www.efax.com/
> Get your own fax line at no cost.

ICQ Software Download

http://www.icq.com/products/
> Source for ICQ download

Internet Telephony

http://www.cs.columbia.edu/~hgs/internet/internet-telephony.html
> A technical guide to Internet telephony issues

Microsoft NetMeeting Download

http://www.microsoft.com/downloads/release.asp?ReleaseID=10494
> Source for NetMeeting software

mIRC

http://www.mirc.com/
> Source and help files for mIRC—Internet Relay Chat access software

MSN Messenger Service

http://messenger.msn.com/
> Source for download of MSN Messenger software

Police Chat

http://home1.gte.net/joking/police.htm
> Web-based chat room for cops

Real.com

http://www.real.com/
> Source for RealPlayer software downloads

A Short IRC Primer
http://www.irchelp.org/irchelp/ircprimer.html
> Actually a long file with much information on Internet Relay Chat

TheCops.net
http://www.thecops.net/
> References and chat rooms for law enforcement

Tucows
http://www.tucows.com/
> Free software downloads

Windows Media Player
http://www.microsoft.com/windows/windowsmedia/en/download/default.asp
> Source for download of Windows Media Player

Academic Sites

California Criminalistics Institute
http://www.ns.net/cci
> Sponsored by the California Department of Justice. Good forensic science material.

California Lutheran University Criminal Justice Department
http://www.clu.edu/
> Programs, faculty, and courses

California State University at Stanislaus Criminal Justice Department
http://cjwww.csustan.edu/cj/cjhome.html
> Faculty, criminal justice clubs, online surveys

Cambridge Institute of Criminology
http://www.law.cam.ac.uk/crim/index.htm
> From Cambridge University in the United Kingdom

Indiana University at South Bend Criminal Justice Association
http://www.iusb.edu/~crimjust/
> A criminal justice student organization

Jacksonville (AL) State University Criminal Justice Department
http://www.jsu.edu/depart/criminal/criminal_justice.html
> Classes, faculty, student organizations, and a link to the police academy

Kent State University Department of Justice Studies
http://dept.kent.edu/cjst/
> Faculty, staff, course listings

Lambda Alpha Epsilon - The American Criminal Justice Association
http://www.vcu.edu/safweb/soweb/acdacj/laemain.htm
> For students and academics in criminal justice

Temple University Department of Criminal Justice
http://nimbus.temple.edu/~blawton/cj/
> Courses, calendar, faculty listings

The University of Alabama Criminal Justice Department
http://ua1vm.ua.edu/~bamacj/
> Guidelines on graduate and undergraduate programs, including their popular distance-learning Practitioner's Plan

Professional Associations

Airborne Law Enforcement Association
http://www.alea.org/
> For officers involved in aviation operations or those who want to be

American Bar Association
http://www.abanet.org/
> Access to various legal resources

American Board of Forensic Entomology
http://web.missouri.edu/cafnr/entomology/index.html
> Bugs can be your friends.

American Civil Liberties Union
http://www.aclu.org/
> Perspectives on civil rights of many general and special groups

American Correctional Association

http://www.corrections.com/aca/index.html

> Representing all levels of professionals in corrections and criminal justice

American Jail Association

http://www.corrections.com/aja/index.html

> For professionals involved in the administration of jails

American Polygraph Association

http://www.polygraph.org/

> Everything you want to know about lie detectors

American Special Operations Sniper Association

http://www.cros.net/asosa/

> An association for professional snipers

Americans for Effective Law Enforcement

http://www.aele.org/

> Providing assistance to law enforcement

Anti-Defamation League of B'nai B'rith

http://www.adl.org/

> Information on anti-Semitism and hate crimes

Association for Crime Scene Reconstruction

http://www.acsr.com/

> Professional forensics association

Association for Retarded Citizens Access to Justice Initiative

http://thearc.org/ada/crim.html

> Information for all persons who deal with developmentally disabled citizens

Association of Public-Safety Communications Officials International

http://apcointl.org/

> The association is very active in allocation of radio frequencies throughout the United States.

CivilRights.org

http://www.civilrights.org/

> Authoritative civil rights site

International Association for Identification
http://www.theiai.org/index.html
> One of the leading professional associations for criminalists

International Association for Property and Evidence
http://www.iape.org/
> For officers in charge of property and evidence functions

International Association of Arson Investigators, Inc.
http://www.fire-investigators.org/
> Health, safety, and technology references, and information on their certified fire investigator program

International Association of Asian Crime Investigators
http://www.iaaci.com/
> Seeks to reduce crime in the Asian community

International Association of Auto Theft Investigators
http://www.iaati.org/
> Professional association of investigators assigned to auto theft; training and networking benefits

International Association of Chiefs of Police
http://www.theiacp.org/
> The largest organization of police executives

International Association of Crime Analysts
http://www.iaca.net/
> Organized to improve analysis of crime

International Association of Directors of Law Enforcement Standards and Training
http://www.iadlest.org/
> Dedicated to improving public safety and EMS personnel

International Association of Financial Crimes Investigators
http://www.iafci.org/start.html
> Seeks to end financial fraud on both national and international levels

International Association of Law Enforcement Firearms Instructors
http://www.ialefi.com/
> Focuses on improving techniques used in firearm education

International Association of Law Enforcement Intelligence Analysts
http://www.ialeia.org/
> Site dedicated to exchange of ideas about law enforcement intelligence

International Association of Marine Investigators
http://www.iamimarine.org/
> Information on marine crime and investigation

International Association of Undercover Officers
http://www.undercovercops.org/
> Geared to needs of undercover officers

International Crime Scene Investigators Association
http://www.icisa.com/
> Law enforcement personnel who are involved in the processing of crime scenes

International Narcotics Interdiction Association
http://www.inia.org/
> Provides interdiction training to law enforcement officers

International Police Mountain Bike Association
http://ipmba.org/
> For bicycle officers

International Society of Crime Prevention Practitioners
http://www.crimeprevent.com/iscpp.htm
> A network of crime prevention officers

Law Enforcement Alliance of America
http://www.leaa.org/
> An association of police officers and citizens allied against crime

Law Enforcement Bicycle Association
http://www.leba.org/
> Training and networking for bike officers

Law Enforcement Bloodhound Association
http://www.leba98.com/
> Seeks to expand the use of bloodhounds in law enforcement work

Law Enforcement Emergency Services Video Association
http://www.leva.org/
> Information on the use of video documentation in law enforcement

Law Enforcement Executive Development Association
http://www.leedafbi.org/
> Seeks to improve police management and administration

Law Enforcement Thermographers' Association
http://www.leta.org/
> For users of thermographic surveillance in law enforcement

Marine Patrol Association
http://www.marinepatrolassoc.org/
> Officers involved in waterborne law enforcement

National Association of Drug Diversion Investigators
http://www.naddi.org/
> Focuses on the abuse of prescribed drugs

National Association of Field Training Officers
http://www.nafto.org/index.htm
> Dedicated to the training of police apprentices

National Association of Property Recovery Investigators
http://www.napri.org/
> Professionals in pursuit of stolen property

National Association of School Resource Officers
http://www.nasro.org/
> Law enforcement personnel dedicated to the safety of America's children

National Information Officers Association
http://www.nioa.org/
> Focuses on the advancement of professional information officers

National Police Canine Association
http://www.npca.net/
> Advocates the work of police service dogs

National Rifle Association
http://www.nra.org/
> Gun control issues and firearms training for police and private citizens

National Sheriffs Association
http://www.sheriffs.org/
> For elected law enforcement administrators

National Tactical Officers Association
http://www.ntoa.org/
> Officers involved in tactical operations at all levels

North American Police Work Dog Association
http://www.napwda.com/
> Promotes and provides training for dogs involved in police work

Peace Officers Research Association of California
http://www.porac.org/
> A federation of police associations in California. This is one of the largest organizations of its kind.

Police Executive Research Forum
http://www.policeforum.org/
> Research into law enforcement issues of all types

Prosecutors Bar Association
http://www.ipba.net/
> An organization for attorneys involved in prosecuting crimes

World EOD Foundation
http://www.eod.org/
> For officers involved in explosives ordinance disposal

Careers

Cop Spot
http://www.cop-spot.com/employment/
> Job listings in law enforcement

Cops2Be.com
http://www.cops2be.com/
> Guides for people aspiring to law enforcement careers

GovtJobs.com
http://govtjobs.com/safe/index.html
> Listings of career opportunities in the public sector

Ira Wilsker's Job Listings
http://www.ih2000.net/ira/ira2.htm#jobs
> Direct links to active law enforcement job announcements

Jobs4Police.com
http://www.jobs4police.com/
> Job listings and hints on doing better on tests

LawEnforcementJob.com
http://www.lawenforcementjob.com/
> Job listings in law enforcement

Public Safety Executive Association
http://www.policechief.com/
> A job search board for law enforcement

Corrections

American Correctional Association
http://www.corrections.com/aca/
> Conferences, training, publications, and membership information

Corrections Connection
http://www.corrections.com/
> Corrections information of all types

Corrections USA
http://www.cusa.org/
> A national voice for corrections officers

Dead Man Talkin'
http://monkey.hooked.net/m/hut/deadman/deadman.html
> Web site produced by an inmate on death row at San Quentin State Prison in California

Death Penalty on Trial
http://courttv.com/news/death_penalty/
> Discussions on capital punishment

National Center on Institutions and Alternatives

http://www.ncianet.org/ncia/home.html

> Seeks to improve care in institutions and correctional facilities

The Other Side of the Wall

http://www.prisonwall.org/

> Corrections from the perspective of inmates and their families

Penal Lexicon

http://www.penlex.org.uk/pages/index.html

> Information on the correctional system in the United Kingdom

Prison Activist Resource Center

http://www.prisonactivist.org/

> Advocates the abolition of institutional rehabilitation

Prison Art Gallery

http://www.prisonzone.com/prisonart/index2.html

> Artwork produced by Anthony Papa while he was an inmate in New York's Sing Sing Prison

PrisonGuard.com

http://www.prisonguard.com/

> News and links for corrections officers

Religion Behind Bars

http://www.fac.org/publicat/prison/table.htm

> A guide to the religious rights of prisoners and the limits placed on them

Stop Prisoner Rape

http://www.igc.apc.org/spr/

> Dedicated to ending sexual assault in prison

Courts

Communities Against Violence Network

http://thearc.org/ada/crim.html

> Advocates for victims of violence, domestic and otherwise

Court Related Web Sites

http://www.ncsc.dni.us/court/sites/courts.htm

> A listing of court web sites at federal, state, and local levels

Judicial Watch
http://www.judicialwatch.org/
> A watchdog service on the courts.

Federal Agencies

Bureau of Alcohol, Tobacco, and Firearms
http://www.atf.treas.gov/
> Their various missions, photos, most wanted lists, and available jobs

Bureau of Justice Assistance
http://www.ojp.usdoj.gov/BJA/
> Training and grant information

Central Intelligence Agency
http://www.odci.gov/
> Descriptions of their mission and functions as well as job listings

Community Oriented Policing Services
http://www.usdoj.gov/cops/gpa/grant_prog/default.htm
> Grants, programs, and activities

Consumer Information Center
http://www.pueblo.gsa.gov/
> All sorts of consumer information, plus information on ongoing scams and frauds

Federal Bureau of Investigation
http://www.fbi.gov/
> Their ten most wanted list, publications, uniform crime reports, and guides to FBI careers

Federal Bureau of Prisons
http://www.bop.gov/rframe.html
> How to get inmate information, including a phone list for every state corrections department

Federal Judiciary
http://www.uscourts.gov/
> Frequently asked questions, publications, news releases, job opportunities

Financial Crimes Enforcement Network

http://www.ustreas.gov/fincen/

> Ongoing programs, assistance to local law enforcement, publications

Government Agencies Directory

http://www.lib.lsu.edu/gov/fedgov.html

> An index to federal web sites from Louisiana State University

Government Printing Office

http://www.gpo.gov/

> If there is a government publication that you want, you can probably get it here.

Internal Revenue Service

http://www.irs.ustreas.gov/

> Their web site is not what you might expect. There are job listings and downloadable tax forms of every description.

National Criminal Justice Reference Service–Grants and Funding

http://www.ncjrs.org/fedgrant.html

> Funding opportunities from the federal government

National Security Agency

http://www.nsa.gov/

> They have the reputation for being so secretive that some say that NSA is supposed to stand for "No Such Agency." Here's where you can find out what they do.

Office for Victims of Crime

http://www.ojp.usdoj.gov/ovc/

> Guides to proposed and ongoing programs, as well as training and technical assistance information

U.S. Census Bureau

http://www.census.gov/

> Maps, statistics, and demographic information on all portions of the United States

U.S. Customs Service

http://www.customs.treas.gov/

> Guides for travelers, import and export information, enforcement activities, and career opportunities

U.S. Department of Justice
http://www.usdoj.gov/
Publications and documents, press releases, fugitive information

U.S. Drug Enforcement Administration
http://www.usdoj.gov/dea/
A link to their museum, demand-reduction programs, statistics, fugitives, traffickers, and job listings

U.S. House of Representatives
http://www.house.gov/
A directory of House members, bills passed and in process, committee rosters, records of roll call votes

U.S. Postal Inspection Service
http://www.framed.usps.com/postalinspectors/
Crimes investigated by the service and information on mail fraud

U.S. Senate
http://www.senate.gov/
Schedules of hearings, senatorial rosters, roll call records, guides to art in the Senate

United States Secret Service
http://www.treas.gov/usss/index.htm?home.htm&1
How to detect counterfeit money, careers, most wanted list, and how they protect the President

General Interest

911Audio
http://911audio.com/
Downloadable recordings of various incidents, humorous and otherwise

Actual Bizarre Police Photos
http://www.geocities.com/Heartland/Estates/8944/istrange.html
Photos of every description, some of them quite graphic

Amnesty International
http://rights.amnesty.org/rightsforall/police/index.html
> Amnesty International's view on police use of force in America

Badges Law Enforcement Discussion Group
http://www.mylist.net/tsi/badges/
> An ongoing discussion for law enforcement

Blueheart
http://www.blueheart.org/
> A central forum for law enforcement, survivors of violent crime, and Second Amendment issues

Calibre Press
http://www.calibrepress.com/
> Great resource for active duty officers. Access to the best portions of the site is via a password. Instructions on how to gain access are on the site.

Code Officer
http://www.codeofficer.cc/
> For code enforcement officers across the United States

Commission on Accreditation of Law Enforcement Agencies
http://www.calea.org/
> Information on getting and staying accredited

Cop Car
http://www.copcar.com/
> Everything you want to know about police vehicles

Cop Talk
http://www.geocities.com/CapitolHill/3945/
> Features stories from the law enforcement field

CopCrimes
http://www.copcrimes.com/
> Links to stories about police misconduct nationwide. Not a pro-police site.

Cops Who Care
http://www.copswhocare.org/
> A charitable organization of police officers to benefit the needy

Copswatch Report
http://www.culturejam.com/copswatch/copswatchreport.htm
> Link to a webcast that features explanations of police procedure based on the *COPS* TV show.

Crime Guide
http://crazygourmet.com/crime.htm
> An interesting collection of police-related sites

Draw the Law
http://www.drawthelaw.com/
> "Roll Call" police cartoon

EmergencyNet
http://www.emergency.com/
> Focuses on all aspects of disasters and emergencies

Funny Police Photos
http://www.geocities.com/Heartland/Estates/8944/ifunny.html
> Funny pictures taken of and by police officers

IACP Use of Force Database Project
http://www.theiacp.org/profassist/useofforce.htm
> Collecting information on use of force issues in law enforcement

Intercept Northwest
http://www.northwestradio.com/
> Police frequencies throughout the NW United States and British Columbia

International Criminal Justice Resource Center
http://www.internationaljustice.org/
> Dedicated to assisting institutions that combat crimes against humanity

International Web Police
http://www.web-police.org/
> Apparently self-appointed Internet police force

Internet Police Service
http://internet-police.tripod.com/
> Another apparently self-appointed law enforcement organization on the Internet

Law Enforcement Firearm Survey

http://www.geocities.com/CapitolHill/Senate/1703/lefs.htm
> Data on firearms

Law Enforcement Internet Directory

http://www.bgpd-wa.com/lepages/
> Links to other sites, broken out by category

Law Enforcement JPG, GIF, and WAV Resource Page

http://www.geocities.com/heartland/prairie/7696/
> If you're looking for clip art or sounds to spruce up a web page or presentation, you might find something here.

Metro Tactical Bulletin Board

http://www.metrotactical.com/wwwboard/
> A bulletin-board interface for posting messages concerning law enforcement

National Public Safety Information Bureau

http://www.safetysource.com/
> One of the largest collections of individual department web sites

The New Blue Line

http://www.pilotonline.com/special/blueline/
> The perspective of one police officer

New York City Police Museum

http://www.nycpolicemuseum.org/
> The official museum of the NYPD

Officer.com

http://www.officer.com/
> One of the most complete listings of law enforcement-related sites anywhere. If you can't find it here, it probably doesn't exist.

Police Complaint Center

http://www.policeabuse.com/
> Dedicated to helping citizens who are victimized by police

Police Farce Page

http://dogsnob.webhostme.com/
> Anecdotes and stories by and about police officers

Police Stress Links
http://www.policeworld.net/user/links/
> List of other web sites with information on stress in law enforcement

Police Stressline
http://www.geocities.com/~halbrown/
> Focuses on stress related to police work

PoliceScanner.com
http://www.policescanner.com/police.stm
> Real-time police broadcasts via the web

Robert's Cop Shop and Law Links
http://www.geocities.com/HotSprings/5298/
> Links to many police-related sites

SafetyCops.com
http://www.safetycops.com/
> Provides information on safety and crime prevention

Security on Campus
http://campussafety.org/
> Provides information on campus safety

Thin Blue Line
http://www.thinblueline.com/
> A collection of memorials and tributes to police officers

International Law Enforcement

Access to Justice Network
http://www.acjnet.org/
> A Canadian site focusing on law enforcement and justice

Canadian Police College
http://www.cpc.gc.ca/main/
> Courses, publications, and activities at Canada's central police training facility

Criminal Intelligence Service Canada

http://www.cisc.gc.ca/descipeng.htm

> Facilitates the joint effort of Canadian law enforcement agencies in their battle against the spread of organized crime

New Zealand Emergency Website

http://welcome.to/kiwiemergency

> Brief histories of police, fire, and emergency medical services in New Zealand with lots of photos of accidents and fires

NSW Police Service Online

http://www.police.nsw.gov.au/main/default.cfm

> Australian Police

Parking Fines Made Easy

http://www.biziworks.com.au/parkingfinesmadeeasy/

> Comprehensive information about parking regulations in Australia (apparently, parking fines are a big deal in Australia)

Police of India

http://www.policeofindia.com/

> An extensive site about policing in India

Police Shift-Work Guide

http://web.ukonline.co.uk/bjlogie/

> Information about the adverse effects of shiftwork among police in the UK

Polizeitrainer in Deutschland

http://www.polizeitrainer.de/

> News conferences and links for German law enforcement personnel (page is in German)

Royal Canadian Mounted Police

http://www.rcmp-grc.gc.ca/index_e.htm

> Canada's national police agency

U.K. Emergency Vehicles

http://ukemergency.8m.com/

> Photos and details of police and other emergency service vehicles in England

Investigative Resources

555-1212.com
http://555-1212.com/
>   Business, address, phone number, and area code searches, as well as reverse searches

Crime Scene Investigation
http://www.crime-scene-investigator.net/
>   Resources and links for crime scene investigators and forensic photographers

Cult Solutions
http://www.cultsolutions.com/
>   Provides education and consultation to institutions and individuals

David Wilshire's Forensic Psychology and Psychiatry Links
http://www.ozemail.com.au/~dwillsh/
>   A list of links to other sites

Effective Search and Seizure
http://www.fsu.edu/~crimdo/fagan.html
>   A long essay on search and seizure law

Electronic Privacy Information Center
http://epic.org/
>   Privacy issues on the Internet

ExtremistGroups.com
http://www.extremistgroups.com/
>   Dedicated to educating law enforcement investigators to deal with extremist groups

High Tech Crime Consortium
http://www.hightechcrimecops.org/
>   Seeks to educate law enforcement personnel to combat high-tech crime

Information Warfare Glossary
http://www.informatik.umu.se/~rwhit/IWGlossary.html
>   Terminology encountered in information warfare literature

Investigative Resource Center
http://www.lainet.com/factfind/database.htm
> Searchable databases and links for investigative professionals

Investigator's World
http://www.investigatorsworld.com/
> The one-stop site for professional investigators and those who use their services

MapQuest
http://www.mapquest.com/
> Street-level maps and directions to and from any location

National White Collar Crime Center
http://www.iir.com/nwccc.htm
> Seeks to prevent economic and hi-tech crime

Polygraph Testing of FBI Applicants
http://www.nopolygraph.com/
> A counterview to advocates of polygraph use

Reverse Phone Directories
http://www.officer.com/research.htm
> An index to investigative sites from Officer.com, including direct-input search forms for phone number lookups

Southern Poverty Law Center
http://www.splcenter.org/
> Focuses on hate crimes and supremacist groups

Telephone Directories on the Web
http://www.teldir.com/eng/
> Indexes to phone directories in the U.S. and foreign countries

Webgator
http://www.webgator.org/
> Index to various investigative resources

Legal Research

Appeals Law
http://www.appealslaw.com/
> Basic information on appeals

FindLaw
http://www.findlaw.com/
> An excellent and free resource for researching statutory and case law

HALT - An Organization of Americans for Legal Reform
http://www.halt.org/
> Seeks to improve Americans' access to the legal system

Law Journals Online
http://dir.yahoo.com/Government/Law/Journals/
> A directory of some online editions of journals from law schools

National Archive of Criminal Justice Data
http://www.icpsr.umich.edu/NACJD/home.html
> Criminal justice statistics of all types

Nolo's Favorite Lawyer Jokes
http://www.nolo.com/humor/jokes/index.html
> A collection of humor about lawyers from the self-help legal publisher

The Oyez Project
http://oyez.nwu.edu/
> RealAudio sound files of selected oral arguments before the United States Supreme Court

Public Agenda Online
http://www.publicagenda.org/
> The inside source for public opinion and policy analysis

U.S. Court of Appeals, 1st Circuit
http://www.law.emory.edu/1circuit/
> Indexes to recent decisions

U.S. Court of Appeals, 2nd Circuit
http://csmail.law.pace.edu/lawlib/legal/us-legal/judiciary/second-circuit.html
> Indexes to recent decisions

U.S. Court of Appeals, 3rd Circuit
http://vls.law.vill.edu/locator/3/
> Indexes to recent decisions

U.S. Court of Appeals, 4th Circuit
http://www.law.emory.edu/4circuit/
> Indexes to recent decisions

U.S. Court of Appeals, 5th Circuit
http://www.law.utexas.edu/us5th/us5th.html
> Indexes to recent decisions

U.S. Court of Appeals, 6th Circuit
http://www.law.emory.edu/6circuit/
> Indexes to recent decisions

U.S. Court of Appeals, 7th Circuit
http://www.kentlaw.edu/7circuit/
> Indexes to recent decisions

U.S. Court of Appeals, 8th Circuit
http://www.ca8.uscourts.gov/index.html/
> Indexes to recent decisions

U.S. Court of Appeals, 9th Circuit
http://www.ce9.uscourts.gov/
> Indexes to recent decisions

U.S. Court of Appeals, 10th Circuit
http://www.kscourts.org/ca10/
> Indexes to recent decisions

U.S. Court of Appeals, 11th Circuit
http://www.ca11.uscourts.gov/opinions.htm
> Indexes to recent decisions

U.S. Court of Appeals, D.C. Circuit
http://www.ll.georgetown.edu/Fed-Ct/cadc.html
> Indexes to recent decisions

U.S. Supreme Court
http://www.supremecourtus.gov/
> The court's official site, which includes recent opinions and the
> ongoing docket

Publications

Law and Order Magazine
http://www.lawandordermag.com/
> A magazine that focuses on police management

Law Enforcement Product News
http://www.law-enforcement.com/head.html
> Offers a free subscription for law enforcement officers

OnPatrol
http://www.onpatrol.com/
> A quarterly law enforcement magazine

Reference

Bureau of Justice Statistics
http://www.ojp.usdoj.gov/bjs/
> If you need a number about criminal justice, it's probably here.

Constitution of the United States
http://www.law.cornell.edu/constitution/constitution.overview.html
> The complete text of the Constitution, indexed

Crime Statistics by State
http://www.disastercenter.com/crime/
> Crime index rates for every state

Law Enforcement Online
http://www.pima.edu/dps/police.htm
> The most complete listing of law enforcement agencies on the web

National Law Enforcement and Corrections Technology Center
http://www.nlectc.org/
> Research into technology in criminal justice

Organized Crime - A Crime Statistics Site
http://www.crime.org/
> All sorts of crime data

PoliceCenter.com Grants Information
http://www.policecenter.com/funding/index.shtml
> An overview of grant opportunities

Webopedia
http://www.pcwebopaedia.com/
> One of the most complete glossaries of computer terminology on the web. This site was used a lot in preparation of this book.

Statutes and Laws of the Fifty States

Alabama - Code of
http://www.legislature.state.al.us/CodeofAlabama/1975/coatoc.htm

Alaska - Statutes
http://www.legis.state.ak.us/cgi-bin/folioisa.dll/stattx99?

Arizona Revised Statutes
http://www.azleg.state.az.us/ars/ars.htm

Arkansas Code
http://www.arkleg.state.ar.us/newsdcode/
> lpext.dll?f=templates&fn=main-h.htm&2.0

California Codes
http://www.leginfo.ca.gov/

Colorado Revised Statutes
http://www.leg.state.co.us/inetcrs.nsf?OpenDatabase

Connecticut - General Statutes
http://www.cslnet.ctstateu.edu/statutes/

Delaware Code Unannotated
http://www.state.de.os/research/dor/code.htm

Florida Statutes and Constitution
http://www.leg.state.fl.us/citizen/documents/statutes/index.html

Georgia Code
http://www.ganet.org/services/ocode/ocgsearch.htm

Hawaii Revised Statutes
http://www.capitol.hawaii.gov/site1/docs/docs.asp?press1=docs

Idaho - Statutes of the State
http://www3.state.id.us/idstat/TOC/idstTOC.html

Illinois Compiled Statutes
http://www.legis.state.il.us/ilcs/chapterlist.html

Indiana Code
http://www.state.in.us/legislative/ic/code/

Iowa - Code of
http://www2.legis.state.ia.us/Code.html

Kansas Statutes
http://www.ink.org/public/legislative/statutes/statutes.cgi

Kentucky Revised Statutes
http://www.lrc.state.ky.us/statrev/frontpg.htm

Louisiana Code
http://www.legis.state.la.us/trsr/search.htm

Maine Revised Statutes
http://janus.state.me.us/legis/statutes/

Maryland - Code of
http://mlis.state.md.us/cgi-win/web_statutes.exe

Massachusetts - General Laws of
http://www.state.ma.us/legis/laws/mgl/index.htm

Michigan Compiled Laws
http://www.michiganlegislature.org/MCLs.asp

Minnesota Statutes
http://www.library.leg.state.mn.us/leg/statutes.htm

Mississippi Code
http://www.mscode.com/

Missouri Revised Statutes
http://www.moga.state.mo.us/homestat.htm

Montana Code
http://statedocs.msl.state.mt.us/

Nebraska Statutes
http://www.unicam.state.ne.us/laws/statutes.htm

Nevada Revised Statutes
http://www.leg.state.nv.us/law1.htm

New Hampshire Revised Statutes
http://sudoc.nhsl.lib.nh.us/rsa/

New Jersey Permanent Statutes
http://www.njleg.state.nj.us/html/statutes.htm

New Mexico Statutes
http://198.187.128.12//lpBin20/lpext.dll?f=
  templates&fn=contents.htm&2.0&GLOBAL=G_&ADV_
  QUERY=false&G_DOC_FRAME=doc&G_DOCUMENT_TEMPLATE=do
  cument-frame.htm

New York State Consolidated Laws
http://assembly.state.ny.us/cgi-bin/claws

North Carolina General Statutes
http://www.ncga.state.nc.us/Statutes/toc-1.html

North Dakota Revised Statutes
http://www.state.nd.us/lr/statutes/centurycode.html

Ohio Revised Code
http://209.115.100.52/revisedcode/

Oklahoma Statutes
http://oklegal.onenet.net/statutes.basic.html

Oregon Revised Statutes
http://www.leg.state.or.us/ors/

Pennsylvania Code
http://www.pacode.com/cgi-bin/pacode/secure/infosearch.pl

Rhode Island General Laws
http://www.rilin.state.ri.us/Statutes/Statutes.html

South Carolina Code of Laws
http://www.lpitr.state.sc.us/code/statmast.htm

South Dakota Codified Laws
http://legis.state.sd.us/statutes/index.cfm

Tennessee Code
http://198.187.128.12/tennessee/ipext.dll?f=templates&fn=main-h.htm&2.0

Texas Statutes
http://www.capitol.state.tx.us/statutes/statutes.html

Utah Code
http://www.le.state.ut.us/~code/code.htm

Vermont Statutes
http://www.leg.state.vt.us/statutes/statutes.htm

Virginia - Code of
http://leg1.state.va.us/cgi-bin/legp504.exe?000+cod+TOC

Washington - Revised Code of
http://www.leg.wa.gov/pub/rcw/

West Virginia Code
http://www.legis.state.wv.us/Code/toc1.html

Wisconsin Statutes
http://www.legis.state.wi.us/rsb/stats.html

Wyoming Statutes
http://legisweb.state.wy.us/titles/20titles/statutes.htm

Substance Abuse

Center for Education and Drug Abuse Research
http://cedar.pharmacy.pitt.edu/main.html

> From the University of Pittsburg and St. Francis Medical Center. References and an index to articles online.

DanceSafe
http://www.dancesafe.org/

> A company that will test suspect drugs before they are used, which is better than taking poison.

Stop Drugs

http://www.stopdrugs.org/

> Supported jointly by the California Department of Justice and the California Narcotics Officers Association

Training

Bureau of Justice Assistance Training Database

http://bjatraining.aspensys.com/

> Directory of ongoing training programs nationwide

California Law Enforcement on the WWW

http://www.clew.org/

> Index to California law enforcement agencies and reference sites

Traffic Institute and Center for Public Safety

http://www.northwestern.edu/nucps/

> Home of the Traffic Institute, one of the leaders in traffic safety research and training

Glossary

.wav	The standard format for storing sound files under Windows. .wav files are usually digital recordings transcribed from some other format.
.zip	A compressed file format (*.zip) that can be uncompressed or expanded with WinZip or other software. .zip files are created to send a number of files in a single package while consuming less bandwidth or to save on storage space. A zipped file is usually significantly smaller than the sum of its expanded parts. Zipped files may require a password to decompress the file.
active matrix	See *thin-film transistor (TFT)*.
ActiveX	A group of technologies developed by Microsoft and used widely in games and some web sites. ActiveX controls interact with the user's operating system and usually affect the way that sounds, animation, and other multimedia features are handled and perceived.
alias	An alternate user name or e-mail address that directs messages to an electronic mailbox with another primary name. Autoforwarding and alias methods make it possible for a single mailbox to have any number of e-mail addresses supplying it.
American Online (AOL)	The largest ISP in the world. America Online has spread its corporate dominance by buying up competitors such as CompuServe and has also purchased the massive media conglomerate Time Warner.

analog	Continuous, not divided into discrete intervals. Most information is either analog or digital. A conventional clock with hands is an analog variety, as the information it provides is continuous. A digital clock, with a numeric display, divides each displayed time unit into a distinct interval, with no "in between" information shown.
applet	A small application or program. Programs written in Java are frequently called applets because they are small enough to be downloaded as needed to perform specific tasks.
application service provider (ASP)	ASPs are companies that provide software applications that reside mainly on a server, to be downloaded to the user's thin-client computer as needed.
ARPANET	Advanced Research Projects Agency Network. The forerunner of what we now call the Internet.
article	In the context of a news group, a message commenting on the topic under discussion.
ASCII	American Standard Code for Information Interchange, usually pronounced "ask-key." ASCII assigns a number from 0 to 127 to keyboard characters. These numbers are converted to binary numbers, which is the basic language of computers. Commonly, English characters, such as letters, numbers, punctuation marks are referred to as ASCII characters, as opposed to non-ASCII characters, which usually appear as gibberish.
asymmetrical digital subscriber line (ADSL)	One of two subcategories of digital subscriber lines (DSL). Data going upstream (from the user's computer to the Internet) moves at a slower rate than data going downstream (from the Internet to the user). ADSL is generally less expensive and more common than symmetrical digital subscriber lines (SDSL).
attachment interface (ATA)	An interface for hard drives used in connection or interchangeably with IDE.

audio–video interleave (AVI)	A full-motion video file that is the standard for Microsoft Windows. Other video formats tend to use less disk space to contain similar amounts of information.
autoforwarding	A method where messages sent to one e-mail address are instantly sent to another address. Autoforwarding requires very little in terms of network resources, and a number of corporations and organizations provide this service to their members and customers. Thus, someone with an address like customer@americanexpress.com might actually be receiving mail at an AOL account and have no other connection with American Express.
backbone	In this context, the primary data lines that comprise the Internet. Backbone lines are usually T3 quality, capable of carrying 43 Mbits of data per second. A very high-demand Internet user, such as a large corporation or university, might have its own T3 connection to the Internet.
bandwidth	The amount of data that can be transmitted in a unit of time. Bandwidth is commonly expressed as kilobits (1000 bits) per second, or Kbps, or megabits (1,000,000 bits) per second, or Mbps.
banner ad	An advertisement, typically in a box or banner that stretches the width of the web page, that loads at the same time as the page and directs the viewer to another site when clicked on.
baseband	A transmission medium capable of carrying only one channel of information at a time.
binary	A number system that has just two digits, one and zero. Computers use binary numbers to represent all data by translating the information into binary numbers. For example, the decimal number 11 is 1011 in binary.

binary forum	A newsgroup that encourages participants to attach binary files to their posted messages. The binary files can be anything that is stored in a computer file: graphic images, software, documents, etc.
bit	A single one or zero in a binary number. It takes eight bits, or one byte, to make a single character, such as an *A* or a *3*.
Boolean logic	Named for the 19th-century mathematician George Boole. A way of expressing terms so that the result is either true or false. Boolean terms are linked by operators such as *AND* (+), *NOT* (-), and *OR* (/).
bounce	To be returned to its source. An e-mail message with an incorrect address or one sent to a server that is out of service at the time the message is received will bounce back to its sender with an error message indicating that the message is undeliverable.
broadband	A computer and entertainment industry term, usually referring to systems that have a bandwidth in excess of 128 Kbps. Also used to describe a transmission medium capable of carrying multiple channels of information at one time.
browser	Also *web browser*. A software application used to locate and display pages posted on the World Wide Web. The two most commonly used browsers are Netscape Navigator and Microsoft Internet Explorer.
BTW	By the way.
buffer	A storage area where data is placed temporarily until it can be handled. Print buffers store documents until the printer is ready to print them. Video and audio buffers store multimedia information for playback to ensure against interruption of the program if the data stream is momentarily halted.

bulletin board service (BBS)

A computer that stored messages and files to be retrieved by their users, who connected to it by regular telephone lines and modems. BBSes used to be plentiful, but they are rare today, having been supplanted by the more versatile and more accessible World Wide Web.

byte

Eight bits, in a configuration such as "10001000." A byte forms a single character, such as an *A* or a *3*.

cable modem

A device that allows communication via the Internet by way of the cable television system. Cable modem connections are fairly fast, but they suffer from some privacy issues and are not available in every location.

cache folder

A repository of files recently downloaded from the web, stored on the user's machine. Web pages from the same site frequently use the same files repeatedly, such as image files of logos. Keeping these in a cache folder allows the download time of each page to be reduced. The browser will look in the cache folder to see if a file already resides there and will display it instead of retrieving it from the server again. This size of the cache folder can be adjusted by the user to save disk space.

case sensitive

Where a lowercase letter is not equivalent to an uppercase letter and vice versa. In a case-sensitive text string, *ThisSample* would not be the same as *thissample*. Most e-mail addresses and web URLS are not case sensitive, although some passwords are.

cellular digital packet data (CDPD)

A technology where cellular telephone channels are used to send data in packets, or uniformly sized groups. This method is faster and more reliable than sending data in analog form over cellular modems.

central processing unit (CPU)

Usually, this denotes the primary electronic chip that runs a computer, but this term is also used to describe the big box that holds the computer's motherboard, drives, modem, and other components.

checksum
A method whereby a packet or other unit of information is attached to a code that is based on the number of bits in the message. The computer receiving this data performs a mathematical calculation to determine if the checksum value and the number of bits in the message agree. If they do not, then it can be assumed that the packet was garbled or damaged in transmission, and the receiving computer asks that the packet be resent.

click-through
Navigating to a web page by clicking on a banner. Many advertisers pay rates to the sites that display their banner ads based on the number of click-throughs from the web site where the banner ad is displayed.

client
Most commonly, the client is a program or other software that runs an application and draws information from a server. E-mail clients are used to compose, read, send, and file messages, but they connect with a mail server to do any of this. Commonly used e-mail clients are Outlook Express, Eudora, and Pegasus.

common gateway interface (CGI)
A specification for transferring information from a web page to a program running on the web server. CGI scripts are commonly used to access information stored in database files from web pages and for other varied tasks.

cookie
A small file placed on a user's computer when the user visits a web site. The file contains information about the user that allows the web site to send the user a customized response on a future visit. When the user revisits that web site or one that looks for the same cookie, the cookie identifies the user and sends the web server the information contained in the cookie, which generates the customized page.

cracker	A person who tries to "crack" or break into other computers, usually by means of an online connection. May crackers claim that they do this only for the intellectual challenge, but they often erase, copy, steal, or otherwise illegitimately access other people's data. Computer cracking is a common but very serious crime.
crosspost	The act of posting a newsgroup message or article in multiple newsgroups at the same time. Crossposting is frowned on and may be the cause of a flame directed at the person doing the crossposting.
dead link	Hyperlinked text or images on a web page that, when clicked, connect to a web page or other resource no longer available, resulting in a **Page not found** error.
digital	Divided into discrete intervals. Most information is either analog or digital. A conventional clock with hands is an analog variety, as the information it provides is continuous. A digital clock with a numeric display divides each displayed time unit into a distinct interval, with no "in between" information shown.
digital subscriber line (DSL)	DSL service carries relatively high-bandwidth (from 32 Kbps to 1 Mbps) data traffic over regular telephone lines. The same line can carry conventional telephone traffic without interference. DSL service is subdivded into two subcategories: ADSL, or asymmetrical DSL, and SDSL, or symmetrical DSL.
disk operating system (DOS)	Sometimes called MS-DOS for Microsoft disk operating system. Early versions of Windows ran "over" or "on top of" DOS, since DOS was the basic operating system. DOS capability will be removed from future versions of Windows, and it verges on being extinct.
dock	See *port replicator*.

domain	A group of computers and devices on a network that are administered as a group with similar rules and procedures and that share a portion of a common IP address.
domain name	A word or phrase that defines one or more IP addresses. Domain names are registered and owned on a first-come, first-served basis but usually correspond to the name of their owners, like Microsoft.com and timdees.com.
dot	Slang for the punctuation character known otherwise as a period. The URL for the web site at http://www.yahoo.com might be spoken as "yahoo dot com," and the newsgroup alt.2600 would be spoken as "alt dot twenty-six hundred."
dot pitch	The diagonal distance between the phosphor dots on a computer display. This is a fundamental measure of the quality of the display. Dot pitches for monitors on personal computers generally range from 0.15 mm to 0.30 mm.
downstream	Data traffic moving from the Internet to the user's computer.
dynamic hypertext markup language (DHTML)	A variant of HTML that allows the displayed page to change each time it is viewed, based on the viewer's geographic location, local time, or previous visits to the web site.
dynamic IP addressing	IP addresses are assigned to a user's computer on an as-needed basis from a pool of available addresses and are only valid for that online session. When the online connection is broken, the IP address again becomes available for assignment from the ISP's block of addresses.
electronic mail (e-mail)	Messages sent over a network between users of the network.

emoticon	A crude cartoon face composed of keyboard characters, used to communicate humor or some other emotional state. The cartoon usually has to be viewed at a 90-degree angle to visualize the face. For instance the combination 8-) forms a basic smiling face. They are also called "smileys."
extensible markup language (XML)	An extension of HTML that allows designers to develop their own "tags" to define the behavior of code on a displayed page.
fair access policy (FAP)	DirecPC monitors the demand that individual subscribers place on the DirecPC system and temporarily restricts the bandwidth of subscribers who are downloading information in quantities that substantially exceed the norm, drastically slowing the throughput to the user. This is to discourage heavy users from taking up all of the available bandwidth and overtaxing the system. When a DirecPC subscriber's bandwidth has been restricted in this manner, he is said to have been "FAPed."
file transfer protocol (ftp)	This is the process used to transfer computer files from one computer to another over the Internet. Using ftp usually requires some type of ftp software, of which there are many varieties in commercial and shareware versions.
firewall	A hardware- or software-based barrier to access of a computer's resources by unauthorized persons.
flame	An insulting or inflammatory e-mail or newsgroup message. Also used as a verb, e.g. "Sending that spam message caused him to flame me."
Flash	An animation technology owned by Macromedia, Inc. that allows web designers to insert high-quality animations into their web pages without having to download huge files. Flash animations require a plug-in that allows the Flash code to be recognized and run.

freeware	Software that is available to anyone who wants it, with no payment of any registration or royalty fee required. Internet Explorer and Outlook Express are examples of freeware, but this type of software is usually created by skilled users with no commercial ties to software companies.
frequently asked questions (FAQ)	An information file for online communities and services. Pronounced "fack."
<G>	Stands for *grin*, a method of indicating in a message that humor is intended.
graphic user interface (GUI)	A method whereby computer graphics, rather than keyboard commands, are used to interact with the computer. A GUI's interface usually consists of a pointing device with which the user can move the cursor to a graphic on the screen and execute a command by clicking a button on the device.
hacker	A person who is a very skilled computer user or programmer. To be regarded as "a good hack" is a high compliment in the computer field, although this term can also be applied to a well-written program or modification of a program. The term is often confused with "cracker," which is a person with similar skills who uses them for illegal purposes. A skilled cracker must also be a hacker, but many hackers do not invade other people's files.
handle	A screen name or alias used on e-mail, in a discussion forum, or in a chat room.
header	A unit of information that precedes a data object. In the context of Internet traffic, a header might contain information indicating where the data originated, where it is supposed to go, the date and time that the information unit was created, and keys to the coding or encryption method used to transmit the data, so that it can be properly formatted on arrival.

high performance addressing display (HPA)	A type of thin-format display used in laptops and some desktop machines. Known interchangeably as passive matrix displays, these are cheaper to manufacture than their active-matrix counterparts, but they are not as bright and fade rapidly when viewed at a 90-degree angle.
home page	The welcome or index page of a web site. The home page usually includes hyperlinks to other pages or resources associated with the topic of the home page.
hyperlink	An area in an HTML document that, when clicked on, either takes the viewer to another section of the document or to another document entirely or activates a process that plays a sound or causes some other event to commence.
hypertext markup language (HTML)	The code that is the basis for nearly all of the World Wide Web. The seminal version of HTML was developed in 1991 by Tim Berners-Lee, working at CERN in Switzerland.
hypertext transfer protocol (HTTP)	The procedure that allows web pages to be formatted, sent, and viewed across the Internet. Most begin with the letters http.
ICQ	A widely used instant messaging client application.
identity	In Outlook Express an identity is a profile of settings, preferences, account structures, and message files. A user can post messages under one identity, then switch identities and respond to his or her own postings, making it appear that there is an ongoing dialogue between two different people.
IMHO	In my humble opinion.
instant messaging (IM)	An application that allows users to communicate directly and in real time in a chat room-like mode.
integrated drive electronics (IDE)	An interface for hard disk drives. Also known as ATA, EIDE, ATA-2, Fast ATA, and Ultra ATA.

integrated services digital network (ISDN)	ISDN lines are provided by the local telephone company and consist of two B channels, each of which is capable of carrying 64 Kbps of data. ISDN subscribers can use one channel for data while conducting a normal telephone conversation on the other or combine the channels for a data rate of 128 Kbps.
Internet	A global network connecting millions of computers that exchange data, messages, images, and any other media that can be transmitted digitally.
Internet café	A business where customers have access to computers connected to the Internet, usually paid for by the hour, or included in the purchase price of a meal or beverage. Free internet cafés furnished by commercial vendors are common at trade shows, where participants can check their e-mail or browse WWW pages while they are away from their home offices.
Internet message access protocol (IMAP)	A system for retrieving e-mail messages similar to POP3, but with some additional features. Servers running IMAP can allow clients to search for keywords in their e-mail messages while the messages still reside on the server.
Internet relay chat (IRC)	Participants in IRC log onto any one of many chat servers and then join one of the channels on that server. Participants can see all of the communications typed in by others on the channel in real time and can respond or add their own comments as they desire.
Internet service provider (ISP)	These range from Mom-and-Pop businesses that provide Internet access to a few hundred customers in a community to giants like America Online and Earthlink, which have millions of customers.
IP address	An identifier for a computer or other device on a TCP/IP network. IP addresses are 32-bit strings of numbers, from zero to 255, grouped into four

	segments of three numbers each, and separated by periods. For instance the sequence "160.125.23.254" could be a valid IP address.
Java	A general purpose programming language that is used by many small applications and web sites to produce animations, interactive components, and other features, such as specialized calculators. Java scripts or applets run in an isolated environment called a virtual machine, so that they are independent of the operating system.
Javascript	A scripting language based on Java but developed independently. Javascript permits web designers to insert code that allows viewers of the web page to interact with the page and customize the information that they see.
Kbit	1024 bits of data. Not to be confused with KB, which is kilobytes. (8 bits = 1 byte).
Kbps	Kilobits (1000 bits) per second, a unit of measure of the speed of a modem or other networking interface medium.
killfile	Blocking the receipt of all messages from a person or entity. This word can be used both as a noun and a verb. If a user killfiles a correspondent, all messages from that correspondent to the user creating the killfile will be left on the server or immediately moved to a folder that is usually ignored.
latency	The delay between the moment that a command is sent to a device and the moment that the device is able to deliver the information or perform the task requested. Latency is essentially wasted time. With an Internet connection, latency is the delay between the time that information is requested from the web or some other server and the time that the requested information is delivered.

lightweight directory access protocol (LDAP)	Used for accessing information directories. LDAP is used by some e-mail clients and servers.
link rot	The process that occurs when a web page containing hyperlinks is not maintained or updated, and the sites to which it is linked disappear, resulting in a **Page not found** error.
local area network (LAN)	A LAN is an interlinked system of computers, usually all situated within a single building or even in a portion of a building.
LOL	Laughing out loud.
lurk	What a user does when he or she reads but does not participate in interactive activities on the Internet and does not allow the other users to be aware of his or her presence.
Mbit	1024 kilobits or 1048576 bits of data.
message thread	A series of electronically transmitted messages under a single subject line or topic. Threads are formed by responses to a first (root) message and the responses to those responses.
meta tag	A portion of HTML code that does not affect the way that the page is displayed. Meta tags contain keywords that describe what the page is about, the author's name, the software that was used to create the page, and other administrative information. Some search engines create their indexes partially or entirely on meta tag content.
Microsoft Network (MSN)	An ISP that is owned by the Microsoft Corporation.
mIRC	A software application that is one of the most widely used chat clients, allowing users to participate in conversations on the various Internet relay chat channels.

mobile data terminal (MDT)	A generic term for computer terminals that use a wireless connection to send and receive data, especially from law enforcement databases and communications centers.
motherboard	The main circuit board of a computer. The CPU, video and sound cards, power supply, and most other components attach to the motherboard.
Moving Pictures Expert Group (MPEG)	Pronounced "em-peg." Developers of one of the most widely used full-motion video and audio formats on the Internet, *.mpg files.
MP3	An abbreviation for MPEG audio layer 3, a file format frequently used to convert music recorded on audio compact disks to a form that can be played back on a computer or solid-state MP3 player. MP3 files are commonly traded among fans of one recording star or another, and the copyright infringement issues associated with this are a major issue of contention in the recording industry.
multipurpose Internet mail extensions (MIME)	A format that allows nontext content, such as binary files, to be formatted as text and sent as a part of a text message. MIME encoding is frequently used to send binary files via Usenet.
musical instrument digital interface (MIDI)	MIDI files have the file extension *.mid. MIDI files are a kind of script, not unlike sheet music, but for a sound card. MIDI files play music when executed but take up considerably less space than *.wav files, which are actual recordings. A MIDI file played back by a low-end sound card sounds like the musical ringer on a cellular phone, but the same file played back on a sophisticated sound card can sound like a small electronic orchestra.
nag screen	A method that shareware producers use to encourage registration of their software. The nag screen appears every time that the software is used, nagging

the user to register the program and pay a fee. Once the shareware has been registered and the appropriate code has been entered, the nag screen disappears.

National Criminal Information Center (NCIC)
: A database administered by the Federal Bureau of Investigation that indexes information on wanted persons, vehicles, and property, criminal histories, and other information for use by law enforcement agencies.

network computer
: A computer that gets most or all of its operating system and/or applications from a network server. The computer holds very little data locally, which increases security and makes it more difficult for users to change the way that the machine operates.

network interface card (NIC)
: A circuit board that resides inside a user's computer and acts as the interface between the computer and the network to which it is connected. They are relatively inexpensive, running between $10–$50 for the less costly models. NICs for laptop computers usually reside on a PCMCIA card that plugs into a slot on the side of the laptop.

news server
: A computer connected to the Internet that hosts newsgroups. There are some public servers, to which anyone can connect, and others require a subscription or other mechanism for access.

newsfeed
: The message traffic or content of one or more newsgroups. The volume of messages via Usenet precludes any one news server from carrying all newsgroups, but some news servers take the newsfeed from others, acting as a kind of relay station or intermediary.

newsgroup
: An online discussion forum where members or subscribers (the terms are synonymous, in this case) post messages or articles that can be viewed and responded to by other members of the newsgroup.

newsreader	Software that allows users to conveniently read and create newsgroup messages.
nonvolatile	Not subject to loss due to power failures. Information written to a disk drive or a nonvolatile memory chip remains there until it is deleted or replaced by other data.
notebook	A portable computer with a total carrying weight of six pounds or less.
operating system	The software foundation on any computer. A computer may have more than one operating system installed on it (although they usually do not), but in most cases, two of them cannot be running simultaneously. Common operating systems for personal computers include various versions of Windows (3.0, 3.1, 95, 98, 2000, NT), BeOS, Linux, DOS, and OS/2.
operators	Logical connectors that either include or exclude a term or determine how the term is to be considered. Common operators include *AND* (+), *NOT* (-), and *OR* (/).
packet	A portion of a message transmitted over a network designed to transmit and deliver packet data. Each packet contains the address of its intended destination and sequencing information that allows the recipient to reassemble the message packets in the appropriate order, so that the message is as intended.
passive matrix	See *high performance addressing display (HPA)*.
PC card	A computer interface that is commonly used to attach peripheral components to portable computers. PC cards are roughly the size of credit cards and about twice as thick. Their most popular applications are for network interface cards, modems, and data storage. Also called PCMCIA

(Personal Computer Memory Card International Association) cards.

Personal Computer Memory Card International Association (PCMCIA)	The PCMCIA developed the standards for credit card-sized cards that are used in many portable computers. See *PC card*.
pixel	A single point in a graphic image. Computer displays are composed of thousands or millions of pixels, each of which is assigned a color. As the number of pixels in the display increases, the image on the display is perceived as being more detailed and with greater resolution.
plain old telephone service (POTS)	What most people use to connect to the Internet via a modem and a dial-up ISP, as well as to make telephone and fax calls.
plug-in	A software application that interacts with the web browser and allows the execution of code written in proprietary formats, such as Java, Flash, and Shockwave.
point of presence (POP)	A "node" or telephone number where one can dial to access an Internet service provider. Economic use of a dial-up ISP account requires that the ISP have a point of presence that the user can access without incurring prohibitive long distance toll charges.
port replicator	A device that attaches to a portable computer and provides connections to other components such as a full-size keyboard, pointing device, printer, power supply, network, or external storage device, saving the time and trouble required to connect each one of these devices each time the machine is brought to the location. These are also called docks or docking stations.
portal	A web site that includes multiple features, such as search engines, news stories, links to chat rooms, and other services. Many portals started as search

engines and added these features to encourage users to return and view their pages more often so that more users would see the advertisements that are usually posted there.

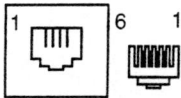

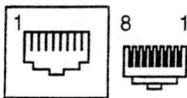

post office protocol version 3 (POP3)	Sometimes just called POP or POPMail, POP3 is an agreed-on industry format for retrieving electronic mail from a mail server.
queue	As a verb, "to line up." In computer terms, a queue is a file or list of items awaiting further action. Mail messages might wait in queue to be sent or read, and marking them with a special code (such as "High Importance") might bring them to the top of the queue.
QWERTY	The arrangement of keys on a typical typewriter or computer keyboard, named for the order of the first row of letter keys.
random access memory (RAM)	Solid state chips that contain memory modules, usually in increments of 32 megabytes (MB). Information contained in RAM can be accessed very quickly, as compared to information contained on a disk drive, but this information disappears when the computer is turned off or loses power and is considered volatile memory.
RJ-11	Registered jack-11. A telephone connection commonly used in home and office installations. The numbers in the illustrations refer to the pin or wire numbers on the male and female jacks.
RJ-45	Registered jack-45. A connection commonly used to hook computers to network via a NIC. RJ-45 jacks resemble RJ-11 telephone jacks, but they are slightly larger, as they carry eight wires to the RJ-11's six. The numbers in the illustrations refer to the pin or wire numbers on the male and female jacks.
ROTFLMAO	Rolling on the floor, laughing my ass off.

router
A switching device that connects two or more computers or local area networks (LANs). Routers are used in home and small office installations to share high-capacity Internet connections, such as those from television cable and DSL.

screen name
A user name or alias that may be the same as the user's e-mail address. A user with the screen name of Bubba may have an e-mail address of bubba@isp.com, or that name may be unrelated to his e-mail address. Some ISPs allow users to have multiple screen names.

script
A set of instructions that performs one or more tasks without any user interaction. Scripts are often used to execute a series of tasks quickly when performing these individually through user commands would require much more time.

search engine
A program that searches for terms called keywords and returns sites on the Internet where these terms or keywords may be found.

second-level domain
The portion of the domain name that occurs immediately before the top-level domain (e.g. *.com, *.org, *.net, etc.). In the example www.anytownpd.org, anytownpd is the second-level domain.

secure sockets layer (SSL)
A protocol where information sent from web pages using this technology is encrypted and is generally safe from interception before it reaches its final destination. SSL is commonly used on web pages that accept customers' credit card and delivery information for ordering merchandise. SSL-enabled pages have URLs that begin with https://, rather than http://.

server
A device (usually a computer) on a network that manages or shares resources with clients. A web server stores web pages that can be viewed using a browser, or web client, and a mail server stores

messages for pickup and sends messages composed by its clients to their destinations.

shareware

Software that is distributed over the Internet or on "bundled" CD-ROMs or floppy disks sold with computer books or other software. Most shareware is produced by private individuals or small-business people and is either free or distributed in a try-before-you-buy format. When software is distributed on a trial basis, the user is supposed to pay a fee to register the software after trying it for a designated period of time. Some shareware is time-limited, so it stops working after the trial period unless a registration code is entered. Other methods of encouraging registration are disabling certain features of the software or including a "nag screen," which will no longer display once the program is registered. Most shareware registration fees are less than $20.

Shockwave

An interactive animation technology owned by Macromedia, Inc. that provides web designers with the ability to insert animations, sounds, and other features into their web pages. Shockwave animations are often used for games, advertisements, and other small entertainment-type features on web sites. Viewers of "shocked" sites must have a plug-in for Shockwave, which is free from Macromedia.

sig, sigfile

A file similar to a signature block, which contains text that can be appended automatically to the end of e-mail or newsgroup messages sent by the owner of the sigfile.

simple mail transfer protocol (SMTP)

An agreed-on industry format for sending electronic mail messages between servers.

small computer systems interface (SCSI)

A hardware interface used by hard drives, scanners, and other computer components. SCSI interfaces are capable of handling large amounts of data at very high speeds, but they are relatively costly.

smiley

See *emoticon.*

spam

Unwanted or junk e-mail or postings to a Usenet newsgroup. Sending someone unwanted messages, such as advertisements or chain letters, is spamming and constitutes grounds per the TOS for some Internet service providers to cancel the sender's account.

spammer

A person or organization that sends out junk or unsolicited e-mail (spam), usually advertising a product or service.

spider

A program that searches for web pages and records the information contained in them in an index. A spider often "travels" by recording the information in pages hyperlinked to the ones that it is searching, so that its path, when diagrammed, much resembles a spider's web.

static IP addressing

IP addresses are assigned permanently to specific computers connected to the Internet, so that they never change. Static IP addresses are usually for web servers and other computers with a constant, always-on connection to the Internet, as is the case with mail and web servers and computers connected via T1, T3, or some DSL connections.

streaming

In this context, a method for processing audio and video information so that a user can see and hear a multimedia program before the entire file that contains the program has been downloaded. The user perceives the program as playing in real time, when in fact it is being sent in packets sufficiently far enough in advance that there is no interruption in the playback.

stripe pitch

Another way of expressing the distance between phosphors on a computer monitor. This measurement is essentially interchangeable with dot pitch.

symmetrical digital subscriber line (SDSL)	One of two subcategories of digital subscriber lines (DSL). The data carried by an SDSL line flow at equal rates both upstream and downstream. SDSL lines are generally more expensive and less common than their ADSL counterparts.
sysop	System operator or the person in charge of resources on a network. Sysops can grant or restrict privileges of users and generally have access to everything that a user stores or accesses on a network.
T1	An internet connection or "pipeline" with a great deal of bandwidth. T1 lines are dedicated (always-on) telephone connections capable of supporting transmission rates of 1.544 Mbits per second, which is over twenty-four separate channels, each of which supports 64 Kbits per second. T1 lines are usually leased by businesses that require high-speed, dedicated internet connections and cost between $500–$2000 per month to maintain. Some telephone companies allow the leasing of fractional T1 lines, where only a portion of the T1's capacity is available for a lower cost.
T3	A dedicated telephone connection to the Internet capable of carrying 672 individual channels at 64 Kbps each. The entire line has a capacity of 43 Mbps. These are often fiber-optic lines and tend to incur fees well into four figures per month of use.
tag	In HTML, a tag is an instruction telling the browser how to display text, graphics, or other elements on the web page. Tags can control the position, color, size, or other characteristic of the page's components. Tags are usually contained within brackets, e.g. <tag>
terminal adapter	An interface between a computer and a digital data line, such as an ISDN line. Terminal adapters work like modems, except that they do not have to translate analog signals into digital and back again

because the data on the ISDN line is already in digital form.

terms of service (TOS)   Most ISPs and some other computer-related service providers have terms of service, which are essentially contracts with the user. If the user violates the terms of service, then the service or account with the company can be cancelled. TOS is sometimes used as a verb, referring to those who have had their service or account cancelled for engaging in forbidden practices, e.g. "He got TOSed from America Online for sending spam e-mail from my account."

thick client   A computer where most applications and data are contained on the computer itself, and the computer is not reliant on a server or other outside resource to perform operations. The thick-client model is the one most commonly used for personal computers today. See *thin client*.

thin client   A computer or application where most of the data or application code resides on a server connected to the computer, meaning very little data and/or software is installed on that computer. Thin-client machines are relatively inexpensive to produce, as they do not require much processing power or storage resources, but they are not very useful when not connected to a server that holds their applications and data. See *thick client*.

thin-film transistor (TFT)   Also known as active matrix displays. Used in laptop computers and some flat panel displays for desktop computers. These are very bright and can be seen over a wide viewing angle but are difficult to manufacture and are thus very expensive.

third-level domain   A domain whose name appears before the standard or second-level domain. A third-level domain for www.anytownpd.org might be www.patrol. anytownpd.org, the patrol portion being the third-level domain.

thread	In forums or newsgroups, a group of messages under a single discussion topic.
thread creep	In newsgroup or forum discussions, the topic often drifts to issues other than the original one. Frequently, no one bothers to change the subject title or begin a new message thread with a new subject, and latecomers to the discussion who expect to see one topic under discussion find something very different. This drifting away from the original or nominal subject is called thread creep.
throughput	The amount of data transferred from one location to another in a unit of time.
top-level domain	The last characters in a web or e-mail address, which follow the period or the dot farthest to the right and denote the type of organization that sponsors or owns the domain. Some examples are .com (commercial), .net (network organizations), and .gov (units of the federal government).
transmission control protocol/Internet protocol (TCP/IP)	The protocols or conventions used over the Internet for hosts or servers to communicate with one another. Most networks, even those independent of the Internet, support TCP/IP.
troll	A person who posts inflammatory newsgroup messages in an effort to anger other users.
uniform resource locator (URL)	The address of a web page. URLs generally begin with http, which stands for *hypertext transfer protocol*.
universal system bus (USB)	An external method of connecting devices to the computer that supports data transfer rates of up to 12 million bits per second. Most newer computers come equipped with at least one or two USB ports, and most peripherals are available in USB configurations.

Glossary   267

upstream — Data traffic moving from the user's computer to the Internet.

Usenet — A bulletin board-like messaging system consisting of thousands of newsgroups discussing an extremely wide and diverse range of topics.

V.32bis — A modem protocol that allows a maximum transmission speed of 14,400 bps or 14.4 Kbps.

V.34 — A modem protocol that allows a maximum transmission speed of 36,600 bps or 36.6 Kbps.

V.90 — A modem protocol that allows a maximum transmission speed of 56,000 bps or 56 Kbps.

virtual machine (VM) — A self-contained operating environment that behaves as if it were a separate computer but runs on the same computer as other applications. Programs running on VMs have the advantage of not being able to affect or harm the host computer, but they cannot interact with that computer's operating system, so some features and resources are denied to it.

voice-over-Internet protocol (VoIP) — A method for making regular telephone calls via the Internet.

volatile — Retained only as long as there is power to the medium that holds it. Random access memory is said to be volatile, because anything stored there is lost as soon as power is turned off or the memory registers are filled with some other data.

warez — Illegally copied or otherwise bootlegged software, often offered for trade or sale over the Internet.

web host — An organization that owns or has access to a web server on which web pages and web sites are posted.

web page — A single HTML document that comprises all or part of a web site.

web server	A computer that hosts or contains a web site that users can access via the Internet. Web servers require a continuous connection to the Internet, so that people trying to get access to the server can do so at any time without getting an error or **Page not found** message.
web site	A collection of web pages, graphic images, sound files, documents, and other resources, all of which branch directly or indirectly from a home page. Most web sites are composed primarily in HTML, although other languages and technologies may be used, as well.
webcast	Use of the Internet to broadcast information, particularly streaming audio and video.
World Wide Web (WWW)	A system of web servers that contain documents formatted in a computer language called HTML. These HTML documents are often called web pages. With the use of a software application called a browser, the web pages can be viewed, and the viewer can immediately go to other pages linked to these via hyperlinks.
XML	See *extensible markup language.*
YMMV	Your mileage may vary.
Zip disk	A computer storage medium developed and marketed by Iomega Corporation. Zip disks are slightly larger than 3.5-inch floppy disks, but hold either 100 MB or 250 MB of data, many times more than a floppy disk can store. They require a special Zip drive that comes installed in some machines or can be attached as an external drive.

Index

link rot, 150–51
local area network (LAN), 49
locked padlock icon, 151
LS-120, 20
lurking, 10

M

mail
lists, 167–68
servers, 65
megabytes (MB), 16
megahertz (MHz), 15
memory, 16–17
message
boards, 38–39
rules, in Outlook Express, 86–87
threads, 114, 126–27
trees, 125–26
messages
creating newsgroup, 129
deleting newsgroup, 131
responding to newsgroup, 129–33
meta tags, 164
Microsoft
lawsuit against, 147
Virtual Machine, 177–78
Windows, 27
Microsoft Network (MSN), 37–38
Microsoft Outlook, 98, *see also*
Outlook Express
MIME (multipurpose Internet mail
extensions) coding, 135–37
mIRC, 195
mobile data terminals (MDTs), 57
modems, 24–26
monitoring
of e-mail, 106, 110
via the Internet, 193
monitors, 20–22, 23
choosing, 20–21, 22
flat panel, 22
types of, 21–22
Monty Python's Flying Circus, 89
motherboard, 18

mouse, 26, 27, 28–29, *see also* pointing
devices
pads, 29
MP3 files, 48–49, 190–91
multimedia files, downloading,
189–90

N

nag screens, 206
Napster, 190–91
National Center for Supercomputing
Applications, 7
National Institute of Standards and
Technology, 111
National Science Foundation, 6
nationwide ISPs, 40–41
Navigator, 147
Bookmarks, 168
NCIC (National Crime Information
Center), 56–57
NetMeeting, 192–93, 199
Netscape, 147
Messenger, 98
network, 2–3
computers, 179, *see also*
thin-client machines
configuration, 49–50
network interface card (NIC), 41–42, 44
networking, by Internet, 9–10
news servers, 115, 118–19
archives, 129
choosing, 122
public, 116
newsfeed, 116
newsgroups, 61
accessing via the World Wide Web,
116
articles, 114
binary, 129, 133–39
choosing, 139–40
choosing an e-mail address, 120–21
communicating in, 141
creating messages, 129
deleting messages, 131

POP3 (*cont'd*)
   server, 65
pornography, in binary files, 133
port replicator, 34–35
portable computers, *see* laptops
portals, 162
post office protocol, 96, *see also* POP3
POTS, 44, 51
predators, 95, 97, 196–97
printers, 30–32
printing press, 1, 7
privacy
   invasion of, 179
   on the Internet, 171–83
   protecting your, 182–83
processors, 14–16
   classes of, 15
proprietary data networks, 54
prospect lists, 173
protocols, 25–26

R

radio, on the Internet, 191–92
random access memory (RAM), 16
readme.txt file, 62
RealAudio, 191
RealPlayer, 191
RealVideo, 191
rebates, 40
refresh rate, 21, 23
refresh/reload, 180
research, on the Internet, 10–11
resolution, of monitors, 21
retrieving e-mail, 65–66
RJ-11 jack, 41–42
RJ-45 jack, 41–42
roundtables, *see* forums
router, 47, 48
running files, from the web, 160–62

S

Safetynet, 5, 9–10, 38

satellite
   dish connection, 51
   Internet systems, 51
satellite-based connections, 50–52
saving files, from the web, 161
scanning, 202–03
screen
   cursor, 27
   names, 120, 197
   size, of monitors, 21
search engines, 162
   as portals, 167
   customized pages, 167
   income sources of, 163–64
   methods of generating indexes, 164–65
   registering on, 167
secure sockets layer (SSL) encryption, 172
secured web pages, 151
security, 171–83
   setting options, 175–77
   software, 47
   of web-based e-mail accounts, 95
sending messages, in e-mail, 100
shareware, 11, 206–08
Shockwave, 146
shopping, using the Internet for, 12
signature
   block, 112–13
   files, 142
   line, 100, 131
SIMMs (single inline memory modules), 16
small computer systems interface (SCSI), 18
smiley, 100, 197
SMTP server, 62, 64–65
sound
   cards, 22–23
   transmission, 190–91
spam, 89, 95, 120–21
spammers, 89, 95, 120–21
speakers, 23
spider, 164
spindle speed, 17
StarBand, 52